AF505844

Islam, Women, and Violence in Kashmir: Between India and Pakistan
   by Nyla Ali Khan

Gender Epistemologies and Eurasian Borderlands
   by Madina Tlostanova

Gender Epistemologies and Eurasian Borderlands

Madina Tlostanova

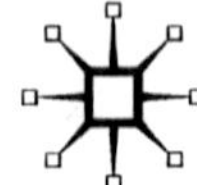

GENDER EPISTEMOLOGIES AND EURASIAN BORDERLANDS
Copyright © Madina Tlostanova, 2010.

First published in 2010 by
PALGRAVE MACMILLAN®
in the United States—a division of St. Martin's Press LLC,
175 Fifth Avenue, New York, NY 10010.

Where this book is distributed in the UK, Europe and the rest of the world,
this is by Palgrave Macmillan, a division of Macmillan Publishers Limited,
registered in England, company number 785998, of Houndmills,
Basingstoke, Hampshire RG21 6XS.

Palgrave Macmillan is the global academic imprint of the above companies
and has companies and representatives throughout the world.

Palgrave® and Macmillan® are registered trademarks in the United States,
the United Kingdom, Europe and other countries.

ISBN: 978–0–230–10842–4

Library of Congress Cataloging-in-Publication Data

Tlostanova, M. V. (Madina Vladimirovna)
     Gender epistemologies and Eurasian borderlands / Madina Tlostanova.
         p. cm.—(Comparative feminist studies)
     ISBN 978–0–230–10842–4 (hardback)
        1. Feminism—Asia, Central. 2. Women—Identity—Asia, Central.
      3. Postcolonialism—Asia, Central. I. Title.

HQ1735.22.T56 2010
305.420958—dc22   2010013774

A catalogue record of the book is available from the British Library.

Design by Newgen Imaging Systems (P) Ltd., Chennai, India.

First edition: October 2010

10 9 8 7 6 5 4 3 2 1

Printed in the United States of America.

Contents

Illustrations

Series Editor's Foreword

As I write this foreword it is two weeks (mid-June 2010) since the violence in Kyrgyzstan that displaced 400,000 people, with 100,000 refugees fleeing to Uzbekistan. Uzbekistan has now closed the border to refugees, and it is clear that this is a major humanitarian catastrophe. Even official figures put the death toll to at least 2,000. Central Asia is front and center in the public eye, and news pundits and scholars are debating the reasons for this particular "ethnic cleansing." Perhaps some of the colonial/imperial genealogies and analyses of gender, race, and empire brilliantly crafted by Madina Tlostonova in *Gender Epistemologies and Eurasian Borderlands* can help make sense of this current Central Asian crisis. Tlostonova's analysis provides a deeply decolonial feminist lens on the complex history of imperialism, and gendered racial formations in the Caucasus and Central Asia—the so called second world. Tlostanova sets up a dialogue between "gendered intellectuals in the ex–third world and in the West and the former and present colonies of Russia/USSR," and in doing so maps a legacy of orientalist, colonial violence as well as provocative, new sites of resistance and liberation. Without the kind of critical subversive gendered history of Central Asia provided in this book, the current "crisis in Kyrgyzstan" will continue to be spoken of in the reductive terms we see in the media—ethnic cleansing writ large.

Less than a year ago, The *New York Times* (August 23, 2009) declared "the oppression of women worldwide" to be the "human rights cause of out time," claiming that women's liberation would "solve many of the world's problems!" Some years ago, then UN Secretary-General Kofi Anan had announced that the status of women in was the key indicator of the "development" of a nation. These pronouncements supposedly recognize the global crises in women's lives, but they also reflect a history of women's struggles and feminist movements around the globe. The Comparative Feminist Studies (CFS) series is designed to foreground writing, organizing, and reflection on feminist trajectories across the historical and cultural borders of nation-states. It takes up fundamental analytic and political issues involved in the cross-cultural production of knowledge about women and feminism, examining the politics of scholarship and knowledge in relation to feminist organizing and social justice movements. Drawing on feminist thinking in a number of fields, the CFS series targets innovative, comparative feminist scholarship, pedagogical and curricular strategies, and community organizing and political education. It explores a comparative feminist praxis that addresses some of the most urgent questions facing progressive critical thinkers and activists today. Madina Tlostanova's *Gendered Epistemologies and Eurasian Borderlands* takes on some of these very challenges, mapping a little-known history of women's struggles in the Caucasus and Central Asia, drawing specifically on the secondary colonial difference and ideas of Eurocentrism, Racism, and colonial masculinity and femininity mobilized in the Russian colonies. This is a groundbreaking text, both in terms of the subaltern histories it excavates, and in terms of its contributions to the larger field of comparative, postcolonial, transnational feminist studies.

Over the past many decades, feminists across the globe have been variously successful at addressing fundamental issues of oppression and liberation. In our search for gender justice in the early twenty-first century however, we inherit a number of the challenges our mothers and grandmothers faced. But there are also new challenges to face as we attempt to make sense of a world indelibly marked by the failure of postcolonial (and advanced) capitalist and communist nation-states to provide for the social, economic, spiritual, and psychic needs of the majority of the world's population. In the year 2010, globalization has come to represent the interests of corporations and the free market rather than self-determination and freedom from political, cultural, and economic domination for all the world's peoples. The project of U.S. empire-building, alongside the dominance of corporate capitalism kills, disenfranchises, and impoverishes women everywhere. Militarization, environmental degradation, heterosexist state practices, religious fundamentalisms, sustained migrations of peoples across the borders of nations and geopolitical regions, environmental crises, and the exploitation of women's labor by capital all pose profound challenges for feminists at this time. Recovering and remembering insurgent histories, and seeking new understandings of political subjectivities and citizenship has never been so important, at a time marked by social amnesia, global consumer culture, and the worldwide mobilization of fascist notions of "national security."

These are some of the very challenges the CFS series is designed to address. The series takes as its fundamental premise the need for feminist engagement with global as well as local ideological, historical, economic, and political processes, and the urgency of transnational dialogue in building an ethical culture capable of withstanding and transforming the commodified and exploitative practices of global governance structures, culture and economics. Individual volumes in the CFS series provide systemic and challenging interventions into the (still) largely Euro-Western feminist studies knowledge base, while simultaneously highlighting the work that can and needs to be done to envision and enact cross-cultural, multiracial feminist solidarity.

Tlostanova's wide-ranging, generative analysis moves elegantly between the feminist epistemology of third world/U.S. women of color theorists, Latin American theorists of the coloniality of power and Mesoamerican cosmologies, and gendered and racialized colonial/imperial narratives of the Eurasian borderlands, to craft a very specific notion of "decolonial feminism" in the context of the multiple and layered genealogies of imperial rivalries (Russia, Western powers, and Ottoman Sultanate), religious practices (Christianity, Islam, Sufism, Buddhism, and indigenous cosmologies), and racialized gender formations. The book thus moves from a theoretical discussion of the grounds for a decolonial feminism to a historical genealogy of gender discourses and ideology in relation to race, religion, and the body in Caucasus and Central Asia. This complex genealogy is one of the most important contributions of the text—it shows the changing and shifting patterns of processes of imperial rule—othering, demonization, exoticization, eroticization, etc. in the particular context of subaltern empires and their colonies. The analysis also points to the distortion of narratives of Western modernity in Russia/Soviet Union and "their projection onto the orientalized colonies of Caucasus and Central Asia." A dialogue between Mesoamerican and Eurasian indigenous gender epistemologies illustrates what Tlostanova callls "trans-epistemic border thinking and being." Finally, the books concludes with a discussion on the prospects of a decolonial gender discourse, gender epistemologies in the Eurasian borderlands, and the possibilities for solidarity on a global scale.

I am delighted to introduce this complex and provocative text—I believe it is ground breaking at many levels and embodies the spirit of the CFS series. Scholars in multiple fields will be drawn to the analysis Tlostanova provides—and perhaps some of us will rethink the analytical categories we routinely use.

CHANDRA TALPADE MOHANTY
Series Editor,
Comparative Feminist Studies
Ithaca, NY

Acknowledgments

I would like to warmly thank Chandra Mohanty for including this book in the CFS series as several of its previous volumes made a significant impact on me and affected the gestation of this work. I would like to particularly mention *Dialogue and Difference: Feminisms Challenge Globalization* (2005) which impelled me to enter the dialogue.

I wish to thank Maria Lugones for her fascinating work on the coloniality of gender and for a lively, productive, and rewarding dialogue on Coloniality and Gender in November 2007 at John Hope Franklin Center at Duke University.

I would like to strongly acknowledge the importance of Sylvia Marcos's works and stance for me both in points of her undoing the established methodologies and her insightful analysis of Mesoamerican cosmology.

Thanks also to an anonymous reviewer of the earlier draft of this book for extremely useful and constructive suggestions and comments indispensable in shaping of the final version.

I wish to thank Svetlana Shakirova for letting me interview her by e-mail and for our numerous conversations on Central Asian gender studies.

Special thanks go to a Kyrgyz NGO activist and healer Lira Karagulova and a Northern Caucasus healer Fatima Zhakomikhova. Without their interviews this book would be incomplete.

Introduction

A few years ago I happened to attend the Social Forum of Americas and was astonished by one talk which triggered me to eventually write this book. An elderly woman with radiant dark eyes climbed onto the stage. Her voice was calm and confident, yet she finished every other phrase with a soft questioning note as if looking for the audience's response. The woman spoke of very simple things: her village, her neighbors, her five children and many grandchildren, of the fact that soon it would be harvest time and she needed to be back when it starts because her husband died long ago and she must cope herself, even if the children help her, that she promised to baby-sit her grandchildren and this is one more reason why she needed to go back soon, that the land where they live has fed them for many centuries and people need to treat it with care and love, that water should not be sold for money because every person has the right to water, that her daughter had recently gotten a Ph.D. and was now working as a professor in a real university. She spoke of the heart that is wiser than the mind and she said this not because she read Antoine de Saint-Exupery. She told us how difficult it was when her husband died and the children were still small and she had to starve, to do hard work. She mentioned how they almost managed to take her small piece of land away to build a highway, but she fought and she stayed on her land and she was able to give education to her children and teach them to help each other and think of their sisters and brothers first and not of themselves. Her speech would circle and come back to its beginning, each time rotating more and more images, thoughts, people, yet always retaining some basic thread, very clear even if not always verbalized.

"We want to live and not to survive—she said—just live well, so that children are happy and go to school and grown-ups are confident in their future. Then her people would get their dignity back, the dignity they have been systematically robbed off." She spoke and I thought that no one would ever be able to take her dignity away. She would always keep it. This woman did not think that she was doing networking and she did not belong to any NGO sponsored by Western or local grants. Her village simply collected money to send her to the Social Forum because they knew that she would have something to say and she would find proper words to do it. The audience was listening to her with bated breath and a few seconds passed before we started applauding when she finished, as we were still enchanted with the rhythm of her deceivingly simple speech.

She reminded me of my grandmother who had also five children and had to support them alone because her husband was killed in World War II. But my grandmother born in the very beginning of the twentieth century could never possibly come to a Social Forum, not to mention the fact that there have never been any social forums in our part of the world and common women could never attend them to begin with. Had she had such an opportunity I am sure she could have spoken no worse than the Amerindian delegate. In any case they would have found a lot to discuss. I think she reminded me of my grandmother because both of them had dignity and a wise heart as well as an extraordinary sense of responsibility toward their loved ones. This is probably why when the relatives offered my grandmother to divide her orphaned children between several families she said: no, if we die of hunger, we will die together!

Yet the Amerindian delegate had something else that my grandmother lacked—the support of the community with its constantly reproduced system of values and the sense of unity with this community and with the land that remembers many generations of ancestors. My grandmother had to become a migrant in spite of herself, long before anyone started talking about globalization, she was forced to change her identity in order to survive. In her case it was not a happy juggling of one's "selves" but a forced necessity. Moreover, she sought to grow back into some soil, to reterritorialize in a once alien environment. It is too bad that I will never find out how she felt about it.

My mother and later I were also marked by this unhomeleness and uprootedness, each in her own time and context. Yet there was something that my grandmother passed on to her children and my mother passed on to me. This was not an ethnic-cultural tradition or some cosmology in any completed way. It was a specific ethos centered around dignity, a firm realization that we are not victims or beggars, even if we are poor or discriminated against, that it is more important not to look for material success in life but rather for the reason for your arrival into this world, and to fulfill your life task in such a way as not to hurt anyone around you and, if possible, to be good to them.

Today, when I am writing this, there is an old picture of my grandmother in front of me. It was taken some time in the mid-1920s. I feel her invisible presence, her calm look, full of dignity, in spite of everything, though she knew what despair was about. I remember that she liked very much the old Santiago from Hemingway's *The Old Man and the Sea* and she said: "He is like me, he always thinks non-stop. He keeps coming back to his past, remembers various people and events." She did not say it, but I think she liked Santiago because he never gave up, no matter what and in spite of everything.

My grandmother was born in the South Urals town of Troitsk. The basic caravan roots connecting Asia and Europe used to go through Troitsk until the late nineteenth century. Having lost her parents rather early (either for political reasons or due to infamous famine), she escaped together with her sister and brother to Tashkent. It was the bloody Civil War years when many representatives of Troitsk Tatar Diaspora would leave for Central Asia. Mostly they were merchants, but also people involved in education (both Muslim and Secular) and mass media. They were fleeing from the beginning repressions hoping to hide in Turkistan. This was a migration along the vast spaces of the collapsing Russian empire from one colonial locale with a completely erased history, to another. From an imperial military fort Troitsk turned into a prosperous merchant town, but history went around it when in the early twentieth century a railway connecting Europe and Asia was built bypassing Troitsk. Their destination city of Tashkent was also an artificial space distorted by imperial power, a space which was to become a Soviet colonial capital. The geographic contour of this journey reproduced the collapsing and doomed trading, cultural and economic links between Central Asia and the Urals which from then on had to be built according to the Russian/Soviet plans.

Later my mother went through a similar journey negotiating the imperial and colonial topi. My generation story is already a globalization narrative of seemingly erased boundaries which turn out to be more impenetrable, than in the Cold War years, even if we can study abroad or travel a lot. Home has become very early a virtual concept for us and any links with it are extremely complicated. We are dispersed around the world and the past for us often shrinks into a thin pack of discolored photographs, a couple of old objects and a few memories and oral histories. Yet we strive to retain it—that transient illusive sense of community and continuity based on the urge to keep one's dignity, honesty, and decency, to never be a victim or a beggar, and to remember that each of us has her own task in life which she must discover for herself, understand and fulfill. In our family women have always remained the carriers of this element. I wrote this book for my grandmother and mother who managed to become what they were and are, and always remain faithful to themselves, their kin, and their purpose in life, in spite of all the cataclysms that the twentieth century had in stock for them.

This is not a book about feminism and not even about gender in the generally accepted sense of the word. Rather through the prism and at the crossing of gender, ethnic-racial, and religious relations I attempt to look at the ways of decolonizing thinking and knowledge. By decolonizing I mean freeing them from the established paradigm and intellectual grounds, human taxonomies, and communication models, imposed by Western modernity and based on the dichotomy of the same and the other, subject and object, thus leading to othering and exclusion. In this sense the book is an example of decolonial feminism as a part of the emerging decolonial humanities. I start and depart from Maria Lugones's concepts formulated within the frame of the colonial difference and the local histories of the ex-colonies of the capitalist empires of modernity. I attempt to widen the geography and the conceptual apparatus offered by Lugones, focusing on the Russian/Soviet empire and its former and present non-European, mostly Muslim colonies (Caucasus and Central Asia). This leads to the emergence of specific concepts and problems that are not to be found in the relations of the ex-first and ex-third world, including gender discourses, roles, and identities regarded in the context of modernity and its darker colonial side, and within the frame of emancipating thinking, knowledge, and being, expressed in different forms in transcultural gender epistemologies and subjectivities.

This problematic has been for a long time in the focus of women of color and third world feminism and since recently, Muslim feminism, but it is practically lacking in Russia and in the majority of post-Soviet countries. Gender discourses of the ex-socialist world and its colonial spaces, are marked by a strong influence of Western feminism or/and area studies, both directly and through Russian intellectual mediation. Gender studies in Russia have remained a closed, pseudo-elite, and intellectually secondary endeavor with little influence on civil society. My book has nothing to do with this trajectory going from Western feminism to Russia as its weak distorted copy. Rather I am interested in gender because it is an indispensable and crucial part of border subjectivity, which, as I argue, demonstrates a number of specific features in Eurasia, yet can be put in a fruitful dialogue with other borderlands and border dwellers of the world.

I will not attempt to describe a certain locale and subjectivity of its inhabitants either using the detached Western anthropological means or simply applying the categories of decolonial feminism to my analysis.

Instead I will try to ground myself in the logic, cosmology, and epistemology of Eurasian borderlands and their inevitable clash and correlation with modernity. Consequently, the analyzed material will generate new categories and concepts for its adequate interpretation, creating a possibility for a future dialogue between a number of gender discourses in Eurasian borderlands, and third world feminism, Diasporic women of color feminism, and decolonial feminism. If we stop applying universalist feminist categories to every space, women identities of the "enigmatic" Caucasus and Central Asia may become the source of other concepts, epistemologies, and ways of survival and reexistence. This refers to the idea of subaltern empire, external imperial difference, secondary colonial difference, self-orientalizing, and self-racializing in multiply colonized spaces, to distortion of racial discourses and the emergence of secondary racism, Eurocentrism, and Orientalism, to the complicated and contradictory nature of colonial masculinity and femininity, to colonial gender tricksterism and several other concepts addressed in the book.

With this book I am trying to start a dialogue between the decolonial gendered intellectuals in the ex-third world and in the West and the former and present colonies of Russia/USSR. It may turn out to be productive in the future in the global process of emancipating thinking and knowledge, building coalitions and alternative visions, global networks and political society movements, where the voices of the multiply colonized and racialized gendered others of Eurasian borderlands would be finally heard.

I am a trans-diasporic scholar with mixed ethnic belonging (Circassian, Tatar, Uzbek). I was born in Moscow and I have lived in this city for the past twenty-five years, but I remain an internal other in Russia. This positioning gives me a certain access to the nuances of gendered subjectivities of the (post)colonial locales because in many ways it is my subjectivity as well. My "inappropriate" gender, appearance, and last name are often interpreted as threatening signs even in the relatively successful professional academic area still marked by intellectual racism. At the same time, I do not claim to represent other (post)colonial and post-socialist women, or speak on their behalf. Finding intersections in our experience and sensibilities, I would like to recreate a flexible and changing decolonial gender discourse which would answer our logic and our specific conditions yet would be able to correlate with other decolonial gendered voices of the world. In order to do this it is necessary to take a border pluritopic position negotiating between modernity in various forms and its internal and external others.

In part I, I dwell on theoretical grounds of decolonial feminism and offer a short genealogy of its origins, links, and differences with third world and women of color feminism and the decolonial option. Here the focus is on the necessity of elaborating a critical methodological basis that would take into account the existing parallels between various echoing concepts and epistemic grounds of gender discourses and would find an interdisciplinary language for expressing the oppositional gendered thinking and agency, within the frame of the imagined transvalue and transcultural pluriversal locus.

Part II presents a historical genealogy of gender discourses, identities, and stereotypes in relation to race, ethnicity, religion, and body in Caucasus and Central Asia. Specific attention is paid to how the well known features of the colonial gendered other and the historically changeable principles of demonization and exotization alter in the subaltern empires and their colonies. This part also focuses on the distortion of the discourses of Western modernity in Russia/Soviet Union and their projection onto the orientalized colonies of Caucasus and Central Asia. I specifically dwell on the ways of constructing the colonial gendered trickster identity, and close this part with an analysis of a testimony of such a trickster.

Part III opens with a chapter on Sylvia Marcos's book on gender aspects of Nahuatl cosmology that I put in dialogue with some Eurasian indigenous gender discourses. Then comes an interview with a Caucasus healer and a conversation with a Central Asian gender activist demonstrating different sides of trans-epistemic border thinking and being.

The book closes with a reflection on the problems and future prospects in the development of decolonial gender discourse, thinking and agency in Eurasian borderlands, on the ways of emancipation of thinking from the myths and delusions of modernity, on the necessity of coalitions and dialogues with other others on a global scale in order to throw a bridge from the past to the present and the future, where finally out of resistance there would emerge reexistence, an other world, in which many worlds would coexist.

Part I

From Third World Feminism to Decolonial Gender Epistemologies

Chapter One

Between Third World/Women of Color Feminism and Decolonial Feminism

For a number of decades third world feminism has emphasized the correlation, intersection, and interaction of race, class, gender, religion, national discourses, and modernity, which has weakened the Western feminist monopoly of the absolute and universal knowledge of women as such, as well as the ways they should take to achieve equality regarded as an ultimate goal.

Women of color and third world feminists did not see it as their main task at first to offer something radically new and different from Western knowledge in methodological sense. Their position was surely contesting, yet they inclined to the use of the already existing and well established approaches or to their mixture. It could be Marxism, Postcolonial Studies, Ethnic Anthropology, and so on. Such works are certainly important both in informative sense and as examples of local criticism of different aspects of gender problematic formulated within the Western system of knowledge.

Yet, such approaches are often based on open or hidden Eurocentric grounds, even if externally they are directed toward a debunking of Eurocentrism, Orientalism, and racism. Behind them there inevitably comes a trace of locality of particular theories, which are often used as if they were universal. It can refer to Anglophone and Francophone experience seen through the theoretical lens of postcolonial studies; it can be a postmodernism or neo-Marxist approach slightly seasoned by orientalist exotics, and invariably hiding its darker Eurocentric side. In appealing to the readymade methodologies or readymade disciplines created in the West, in order to understand the non-Western subject there is always a danger of objectification, an often unconscious strive to present the world from some imagined objective position—from the epistemology of the zero point in which the Western subject regards the rest of the world as an object of its study.

As third world and women of color feminism came to realize this important defect, which had been for centuries aimed against the racialized and gendered others of Western modernity, that is, those very people that the non-Western feminists write about and on behalf of whom they often speak, there originated an internal division inside the non-Western feminism. The rejection of the all encompassing Eurocentric universalist theory led in many cases to a fear of any meta-theory as such. Hence the proliferation of mini-discourses, compartmentalizing particular concrete problems of otherness, be it race or sexual orientation, nation or class, always stressing the concrete empirical experience of a particular limited group of others.

Paradoxically, third world feminists were themselves partly responsible for reproducing what they were opposed to: once again a familiar power hierarchy was rebuilt. According to it the West had the privilege of formulating high theory while the rest had to apply it or limit themselves by just a description of their group and personal experience which would be later properly analyzed by the Western colleagues. As Jacqui M. Alexander and Chandra Talpade Mohanty point out in the introduction to their seminal *Feminist Genealogies, Colonial Legacies, Democratic Futures*, women of color research is constantly appropriated by the Western high brow gender studies, particularly of the postmodernist sort: "Token inclusion of our texts without re-conceptualizing the whole white, middle-class, gendered knowledge base effectively absorbs and silences us. This says, in effect, that our theories are plausible and carry explanatory weight only in relation to our specific experiences, but that they have no use value in relation to the rest of the world" (Alexander, Mohanty 1997, xvii).

However, a number of women of color feminists took a different way—instead of proliferation of mini-discourses they chose coming to a more fundamental problematic of formulating theory which would grow beyond the experience of a concrete group of others, and would lead to trans-epistemic and transvalue dialogues. Here they faced one more impediment—women of color feminism has largely remained a marginal exotic variant of feminism while feminism as such has been seen as an exclusively Western discourse. Many discoveries and formulations of third world feminism remained unknown to the wider academic audience, and continued to be seen as local descriptive studies confined to their immediate experience. Hence, women of color feminism remained an outsider among other feminisms. More globally oriented alter-modern theories[1] also have seldom taken it into account, because they regarded it as a particular gender case, even if women of color and third world feminism have been responsible for the formulation of fundamental questions going far beyond gender and into the spheres of imperial-colonial relations and the critique of modernity.

A typically Western deafness in relation to the other, a narrow disciplinarity denying any dialogue, and exotization and appropriation were accompanied by an internal problem of non-Western feminism: its representatives questioned the concepts and notions of Western feminism without destabilizing, at least consciously, the more general frames and cognitive constructs, a part of which Western feminism has always been. A shrewd criticism of Western feminism inevitably led non-Western feminists to a wider problematic, questioning the intellectual Eurocentrism and Western disciplinarity as such. But these discoveries have not been noticed by the scholarly community for a long time, while women of color continued to be excluded from any serious theoretical and critical constructs. The situation has started to change in the past several years when women of color feminism lost their frequent previous expectations of the automatic unification based on their subaltern status, and started looking for more serious grounds for building global coalitions. The necessity of formulating a new pluri-versal (as opposed to uni-versal) theory which would help to establish a dialogue and volatile connections between gender discourses of various locales, has come forward and a few women of color feminists attempted to satisfy the need for meta-theory and offer an all encompassing interpretation of subjectivity and ethos of the decolonial gendered other which would not slide into the familiar Western disciplines and theories and at the same time, would not be limited by mere empiricism.[2]

A crucial achievement of third world feminism is criticizing the category of women as such and the Western universalist claims linked to it, as well as a strive to regard women's experience, feminist and gender studies within the frame of particular social, economic, cultural, and political contexts, especially in the presence of power asymmetries of the North and the South. Any phenomenon then first is regarded in its particular context and the more complex and subtle the picture drawn by the researcher would be in the end, the farther from flat stereotype the result would be. Gender activism of the global South takes into account that each of the postcolonial societies has its own unique configuration connected with its cultural traditions, religion, social norms, and strata, the ways of adapting the Western modernity and building of national discourses and, later, entering globalization.

In this respect third world feminism is contradictory by definition, always questioning and self-questioning. It balances on the verge of similarity of experiences and their difference. It attempts to take an intermediary border position between Western universalism, Western anti-universalism of a postmodern kind and the local universalism of a pro-Western or traditionalist orientation. Tactically it is a very difficult position. But in most successful cases it leads to important insights. So it would be unwise to reject the umbrella term of third world feminism as it carries a possibility of solidarity, not homogenous but necessarily pluriversal. Previously the tag of "third world feminism" was often imposed by Western "sisters," for whom it was convenient to pile all non-Western women together as silent, backward, and suppressed, while the logic, the ways, and the forms of this suppression were not really of any interest to the West. Third world women were simply needed as an antithesis to the normative image of the White middle class woman. That is why it is important that feminists of the South problematize the category of woman itself. Women as a group category are not homogenous and it is precisely within the third world feminism that the previously universal umbrella terms such as "women's problems," "women's question" or "women rights and freedoms" began to be questioned, and the scholars started to pay attention to how the same events and phenomena differently influence the lives and experiences of women who differ in class, race, religion, culture or language.

The second point connected with third world feminism is rethinking of agency, directly linked with the participation of gender activists in the political and social movements, and with their ethical positioning. White feminists have always stressed this problematic, yet they tended to interpret these questions in a one-sided way, seldom touching upon colonialism and neocolonialism, race, ethnicity and religion, or much less their complex interaction. Agency presupposes an understanding by women themselves of particular conditions of their marginalization, oppression, and subordination. The very ability of the third world women to do that had to be proven and brought to the notice of White feminists, who were preoccupied with the projects of emancipation and enlightenment of the unhappy women of the global South without ever thinking that they are possibly infringing upon the ability of these women to conscious agency. In other words, White feminism as well as other European post-enlightenment liberatory discourses suffered a missionary syndrome, without stopping to think of a possible subjectivity and agency of the other. That is why within the non-Western feminism there emerged the idea of working *together* with third world women, not to study them as objects, but to form a team with them and to create an atmosphere of mutual learning and teaching instead of preaching. Only this would help put together feminist theory and practice in the non-Western spaces and melt the ice of misunderstanding.

It is important to realize that third world feminism has its own genealogy and should not be simply written into the history of Western feminism. An in-between position in this respect belongs to Kumari Jayawardena's classical book *Feminism and Nationalism in the Third World* (1986). On the one hand, she claims that Asian feminism was not borrowed from the West but developed independently. On the other hand, discussing the forms, conditions, contexts, and reasons for women's suppression, she stays within the frame of Western evolutionist social sciences and feminist values, marked by Orientalism and progressivism. Jayawardena is not interested in Asian women's subjectivities or indigenous cosmologies, as she works in the mode of Marxist anticolonialism. Colonial modernities are interpreted based on the mythic opposition of modernity and tradition, on developmentalist paradigm and stagist approach which is manifested in her implicit belief that third world feminism is stuck at some earlier national stage, already unimportant for the West, and therefore is limited.[3]

A similar position is taken by an Egyptian gender activist and writer Nawal el Saadawi who remains epistemically within the Western logic of dividing and explaining the world, yet is also sensitive to the issues of neocolonialism and neo-Orientalism. She manages to express her contesting position both in relation to the West and to the state gender politics of Arabic countries. This gives her a special negotiating border stance which allows at times to overcome the binarity of her Marxist interpretations. El Saadawi and Jayawrdena were also among the first who addressed the problem of essentialized identity and questioned the privilege of intellectual asymmetry, in accordance with which only the West is allowed to ask others about their identity and use it as an effective instrument against the people who are subjects of postcolonial othering (Saadawi 1998, 117). Jayawardena's and Saadawi's position signalized the beginning of the shift in third world feminism in the direction of radical questioning the Western theoretical assumptions. This shift culminated in the works of the next generation of women of color and third world feminists who stand in the beginning of decolonial thinking and agency.

1.1. Chandra Talpade Mohanty and M. Jacqui Alexander: Women of Color Feminism as an Independent Approach

Chandra Talpade Mohanty is one of the preeminent women of color feminists in the United States and worldwide, whose ethical positioning and a theoretical stance, take this area of gender studies onto a level of an independent approach, not a derivative from the West. As early as in her 1984 article "Under Western Eyes: Feminist Scholarship and Colonial Discourses" she questioned the validity of the construct "third world women," regarding it as a product of Western feminism imposing itself as normative and collapsing all other women into a convenient homogenous discursive construct of "women of color." Mohanty has been steadily interested in the differences between the non-Western women and the diversity of their experiences of subordination. She constantly stresses the local, historically and culturally contextual nature of these experiences, and at the same time, tries to find a basis for the dialogue and solidarity of the women of the global South. The scholar shrewdly criticizes the inability of Western feminism to adequately interpret third world gender movements. She demonstrates how the Western consciousness constructs the homogenous object of "third world woman" which then can be studied in the frame of the well known methodologies of interpreting the other, or ignored. Mohanty points out that for Western feminists it is tempting to present colonialism as a real material practice which presupposes political, economic, and social systems of direct dominance, while she herself stresses a discursive colonialism or, in other words, a scholarly discourse which reproduces the power asymmetries and naturalizes them in people's minds. Mohanty draws the attention to the necessity of nourishing a critical approach to our own academic practices, stressing that the majority of Western feminist works on third world women remain convinced in their own superiority, based on ethnocentric universalism and inadequate interpretation of the influence of Western knowledge on the "third world" (Mohanty 1984, 335).

Understanding the West (consciously or not) as the norm and the only subject, and the third world as an artificially homogenized other or object, Western feminists deny the possibility of discursive subjectivity in third world women, and refuse to regard them existentially as active agents. Such discursive categorization, in Mohanty's idea, is grounded in liberal humanism. In the context of Western scholarly dominance, the analytical problem turns into political. That is why an important part of Mohanty's criticism is the analysis of approaches and methods used by Western scholars to theorize the women of color experience.

Mohanty stresses that the discursive construct of "women" is ahistorical and decontextualized. Women are defined primarily by their status as objects in the way they are effected by various systems and institutions. In the frame of Western feminism it is acceptable to regard third world women as victims, forever dependent and catching up with Western subjects in the process of political changes. Gender is often taken out of the system of social relations and given a special independent status. Women identities are seen as constituted before they are placed in social situations and institutions instead of regarding the creation of meaningful identities through interacting with these institutions. Gender then begins to be interpreted as a source of suppression instead of regarding suppression as a generator of particular forms of gender. For Mohanty the non-Western women do share a specific group status, but its meaning lies not in their common history as objects but in their common history of political and other forms of resistance.

She also points out that Western feminism uses problematic arguments to prove the common universal status of objects shared by all non-European women. One of the typical arguments is the arithmetic model within which the decontextualized emergence of particular phenomena divested of any symbolic interpretation, is used as a sufficient ground for generalizations (Mohanty 1984, 347). Religion, reproduction, and family are used ahistorically and decontextually. Western feminism operates uncritically with such deeply Western binary oppositions as man-woman, nature-culture, to misinterpret other locales. As a result typically Western oppositions are regarded as a basis for representations as such, distorting reality and human relations. Consequently, there emerges a specific kind of struggle and subjectivity, which does not allow for the non-Western women's agency to develop to the full. In the interpretation of Western feminists third world women can have needs and problems but they can hardly make a conscious choice or express their freedom of will (Mohanty 1984, 344).

Parallel to African American feminism Mohanty offers an alternative theoretical model based on constructing the category of women in the frame of several political contexts which often exist simultaneously and are overlaid onto each other (Mohanty 1984, 345). Such an analysis is politically focused and highly contextual, it takes into account the links between women and groups of women, without falling into any false generalizations, as well as both differences and similarities of women's experience.

Mohanty's numerous essays as well as the well known collection *Feminist Genealogies, Colonial Legacies, Democratic Futures* (1997), co-edited with M. Jacqui Alexander, have influenced the successive development of third world and women of color feminism. Particularly important were the two moments—shifting the attention to contemporary problems connected with globalization, and continuing efforts to deconstruct the grounds of Western feminism and come up with a different methodology of understanding the non-European gendered other.

A few of Mohanty's and Alexander's conceptual discoveries demonstrate crossings and differences with decolonial option. This refers among other things to the complex subjectivity of the authors themselves who fall out of the simple logic of Western feminism and ethnic-racial studies. According to their ironic comment, being "colored immigrants," in the eyes of their colleagues from Women's studies departments in the United States, they were "neither of 'right' color, gender, nor nationality in terms of the self-definition of the U.S. academy…In Women's Studies context the color of their gender mattered…Their experience could be recognized and acknowledged only to the extent that they resembled those of African American women" (Alexander and Mohanty 1997, xiv). In the United States they had to become women of color and face the politics of racial fragmentation, while they were not allowed to speak about the experience of some other racism or discrimination. The problems of race, class, nation, and nationalism were invariably dismissed by Western feminists as unimportant for today's stage of feminist movement. From this limitation there came Mohanty's and Alexander's urge to recreate other feminist genealogies and communities, not confined within the narrow experience of Women's Studies departments of Western universities.

Mohanty and Alexander accurately stress the link between the power positions occupied by White women at the Women's studies departments, the subject of their theorizing (gender) and those analytical instruments which they use. The scholars are against the appropriation of the works of women of color within the frame of postmodernist feminist theory which reproduces the general logic of silence and invisibility. Alexander and Mohanty pointed out the unfavorable influence of some postmodernist ideas on third world and women of color feminism. This refers to militant anti-essentialism frequently leading to epistemic dead-ends, determined by the links between place, identity, and the constructs of knowledge. However, it is impossible to understand the specific processes of dominance and suppression without applying at least some idea of identity bounded with local histories and experiences. Yet this is precisely what postmodernism rejects based on its standard accusations in essentialism and primoridalism. The scholars persuasively argue that problematizing the analytical applicability of the concepts of race, gender, class, and sexuality, postmodernism makes these concepts unusable in research. However if we dissolve the category of race it becomes impossible to speak about racism which has not been dissolved. Mohanty and Alexander accentuate the complexity and variability of racial discourses instead of simply dismissing them as essentialist. They stress the necessity of analytical and political definition of racialization which places them on the level of conceptual polemics with Western feminism signalizing an important shift in women of color and third world feminism. The scholars claim that it is crucial to pay attention to what racialized and gendered bodies are produced at the juncture of transnational and postcolonial. They are shaped outside the hegemonic heterosexual model which defines the dominant Western understanding of identity. In order to do it one needs special transformative practices that would coincide in a particular way with feminist decolonization (Alexander and Mohanty 1997, xvii–xviii).

Mohanty and Alexander repeatedly use the term "decolonization" which in some ways echoes the way decolonization is understood in decolonial option. However they mean mostly a political decolonization and the sphere of law. Decolonization in their interpretation constantly crosses the problems of citizenship and the national as well as individual rights and choices. While epistemic questions and processes of knowledge-production that are in the center of attention of decolonial option remain in the shadow. In this sense it is interesting to look at their criticism of international feminism as a Western product which sees difference as pluralism and claims to create an inclusive paradigm of global sisterhood, yet is based on maintaining the center and periphery, erasing of race, and replacing it with nation. In opposition to international feminism with its transhistorical and decontextual understanding of patriarchy and heterosexualism Mohanty and Alexander offer to regard women in similar contexts but in different geographic locales, without trying to see them as a homogenous group. They take into account the asymmetry between various groups instead of coding all Western women as the norm and all the rest as a homogenous deviation (Alexander and Mohanty 1997, xix). Similarly to decolonial option third world feminism always regards capitalism hand in hand with racism in economic, political, and ideological oppression. Mohanty and Alexander see capitalism as a set of practices and processes mediated by simultaneous functioning of gender, sexual, and racial hierarchies. Capitalism merges with the state, particularly, the postcolonial state which does not only maintain the heterosexual patriarchy as a basis for its definitions of citizenship, but is also unable to offer people anything attractive in the material, emotional, or psychological sense, thus making them turn elsewhere for comfort (Alexander and Mohanty 1997, xxix–xxx).

Yet Mohanty and Alexander, in contrast with decolonial option, are more clearly marked with socialist principles. This becomes obvious in their definition of feminist democracy opposed to Western liberal democracy going hand in hand with capitalism. Feminist democracy is connected with decolonization and is an anti-colonial and anti-capitalist vision of feminist practice. It takes into account dehumanizing and objectifying effects of colonization and the necessity of building anti-colonial relations taking into account the social-economic, ideological, cultural, and psychological hierarchies and their influence on the disenfranchised in the frame of transformative organizational practices (Alexander and Mohanty 1997, xxxvi). This would allow to build a new model of agency where third world women and women of color in the West would stop seeing themselves as victims and start feeling as free and responsible agents and creators of their own lives. Such an activity must be grounded in the practice of seeing oneself as a part of feminist collectives and has nothing to do with liberal pluralist individual self. Therefore for Mohanty and Alexander decolonization is the central concept of feminist democracy. It presupposes a merging of theory and practice, a powerful pedagogical dimension and a reflection beyond the paradigm of colonialism and colonization. Finally, they stress the transnational dimension of feminist democracy, which means a necessity of theorizing transborder participatory democratic forms escaping the Western surveillance. Instead of international feminism with its idea of global sisterhood the scholars offer transnational feminism (Alexander and Mohanty 1997, xli). However, transnational feminism remains vulnerable in front of neoliberal global capitalism and is in danger of being appropriated within the Western feminist frame thus weakening its potential role as a common field of agency and coalitions of non-Western gendered others.

Feminist democracy for Alexander and Mohanty is first of all an anti-capitalist democracy, focusing around the project of decolonization (Alexander and Mohanty 1997, xxvii). They mention repeatedly that they oppose their socialist principles to capitalism and recolonization, even realizing the difficulty of their implementation in the conditions of flexible and adjustable capitalism. Here lies their difference with decolonial option which sees socialism as one of the variants of Western modernity's rhetoric of salvation and liberation against the will. Alexander and Mohanty do not reject the rhetoric of modernity altogether, remaining within its logic though clearly inclining to its socialist pole. Transformation of consciousness and rethinking of identity are for them the necessary aspects of democracy, seen as a decolonizing practice, while socialism acts as a part of feminist democracy with decolonization at its center. In the feminist model of democracy material success and consumerism are replaced with the goal of decolonizing of one's "self" and redefining citizenship on the cross-roads of national and regional borders. Mohanty and Alexander maintain that feminism must be global and anticolonial, as well as based on socialist principles.

I do not intend to delegitimize socialism, yet I would like to stress that in the present conditions keeping the pluriversality of contesting projects is an important task. In the past two decades there has emerged a number of other-than-socialist and wider, other-than-modernity models of radical gender resistance in the world. They would not fit the idea of transnational feminism if it were based on socialist principles. Besides, uncontested socialism may scare away millions of women in the world whose local histories were marked by various forms of socialist fundamentalism, such as Eastern European and CIS countries. Yet, Mohanty and Alexander's ideal of transborder participatory democracy remains extremely viable even if it requires, in my view, a deeper epistemic radicalization and delinking from the rhetoric of modernity, including a rupture with an outdated opposition of socialism and capitalism.

1.2. Chela Sandoval: A Double Translation of Women of Color Feminism and Western Philosophy

Chela Sandoval also stands on the verge between women of color feminism and decolonial feminism, but she comes to this position from a different angle—trying to engage in a dialogue with Western postmodernism and feminism in a quest for an overarching global and essentially inclusive critical perspective. Her *Methodology of the Oppressed* (2000) remains one of the most important works in women of color feminism and can be regarded as a transit to decolonial stance. Sandoval is equally familiar with Western philosophy of the second half of the twentieth century and the non-Western epistemologies, social and cultural theories. Her book is a consistent attempt at a double translation (Mignolo and Schiwy 2003) of the non-Western gender theory into the language of postmodernism and of postmodernist theories into the language of third world gender discourses. At the crossing of these vectors there emerges a multiple and changing meaning of the methodology of the oppressed. Sandoval's position does not come to a comparison of two "othernesses" based on Western philosophy and culture as a reference point. The double translation in Sandoval's case is grounded in a different logic similar to that of the Zapatistas theoretical revolution (Mignolo 2002a, 248).

Sandoval rejects the asymmetrical translation of all othernesses into the language of Western epistemology. In her ethical and epistemic position she is close to third world gender activism. The difference is the higher degree of conceptualizing and self-reflection and a successful use of the Western instrument of comparison with different goals: she turns it inside out and makes women of color feminism a new reference point subsuming Western high theory. Sandoval's style of argumentation coincides with the comparative idea of looking for parallels in the development of human thought. Such a commonality or a connector for her is the methodology of the oppressed. She finds it in various places—from women of color feminism to French deconstruction.[4]

Sandoval sees the methodology of the oppressed as consisting of five skills: semiotic, deconstruction, meta-ideologizing, democratic, and differential. She argues for the complex use of these methods as an apparatus necessary for the launching of the global decolonization of consciousness. For her it is primarily an apparatus of "love, understood as a technology for social transformations" and as a form of hermeneutics (Sandoval 2000, 2). The gist of oppositional consciousness and methodology of the oppressed lies in the sphere of differential. This hermeneutics of love overcomes the disciplinary decadence (Gordon 2006) or, in Sandoval's own words, the academic apartheid. It also easily defeats the usual order of perception as it expresses the "prophetic vision" (Barthes 1977), simultaneously stressing the vanished grammatical middle voice theorized by Derrida who stated that the Western philosophy has "commenced by distributing the activity of the middle voice of the verb...into the active and passive voice of being—and then it has itself been constituted in this repression" (Sandoval 2000, 149).

In Sandoval's opinion, women of color feminism is able to save from academic apartheid of narrow specializing because it has a tendency to build political and intellectual coalitions. Speaking of every academic sphere's claim to create the only true theory, the scholar stresses that the existing disciplinary divisions point at the firm link between knowledge and power, because the logic they reproduce is conceptually a product of colonial geographic, gender, sexual, and economic power relations (Sandoval 2000, 71). Women of color feminism destabilizes the binarity of scholarly terms and oppositions and offers a third term as a basis for conceptualizing—neither a man, nor a woman but an other gender. This third term generates a political differential consciousness which is open to individuals with access to a specific psychological state of the inhabitants of the global public sphere and creators of new coalition of oppositional consciousness.

In her treatment of hermeneutics of love Sandoval is close to María Lugones's essay "Playfulness, 'World'-Travelling, and Loving Perception" (Lugones 2003). Lugones regards love as a basis for a successful intercultural and interpersonal communication, marked by ludic nature. However her playing is different from Western agonistics, as loving playfulness is connected with a special attitude. It carries us through the activity and turns it into a play. It has no rules, though it is certainly intentional, while its playfulness is marked by uncertainty and openness to surprise: "We are not self-important, we are not fixed in particular constructions of ourselves, which is part of saying that we are open to self-construction. We may not have rules, and when we do have them, there are no rules that are to us sacred. We are not worried about competence. We are not wedded to a particular way of doing things. While playful, we have not abandoned ourselves to, nor are we stuck in, any particular 'world.' We are there creatively. We are not passive" (Lugones 2003, 95–96). Lugones links her concept of love with the idea of traveling to other people's worlds and knowing them, when she claims that "by this traveling we can understand what it is to be them and what it is to be ourselves in their eyes. Only when we have traveled to each other's "worlds" are we fully subjects to each other" (Lugones 2003, 97).

Even if it is radical, Sandoval's position is also integrative in the long run. It is aimed at the quest for understanding and stresses that the majority of Western twentieth-century philosophers (from R. Barth to F. Jameson, H. White, D. Haraway, J. Derrida, J. Butler, and M. Foucault) were shaped by oppositional consciousness and contributed to the methodology of the oppressed, however inadvertently. As R. Tapia correctly points out, Sandoval "declares that the critical sensibilities of all oppressed communities have formed both the constitutive outside and the invisible inside of much of twentieth-century Western thought" (Tapia 2001, 736).

For Sandoval, the ideal manifestation of hermeneutics of love is critical theory elaborated by women of color with a focus on tactical subjectivity. Therefore her book is built as a quest for connections and parallels between postmodernism and decolonial methodology of the oppressed. Yet the structure and the goals of her book are not so simple: presenting third world and women of color feminism of the 1970s as a paradigmatic example of the methodology of the oppressed, Sandoval is also aware of its faults. And while continuing this tradition she also attempts to take it beyond women of color feminism onto a global decolonial level.

Sandoval deconstructs the generally accepted genealogy of Western feminist movements demonstrating how hegemonic feminism legitimizes particular models of culture, consciousness, and practices, belittling oppositional gender activism. She attempts to build a different genealogy of the oppositional forms of gendered consciousness where the oppositional element is more important than gender. This links her with the latest forms of decolonial feminism as I will show below.

Particularly important is the way Sandoval conceptualizes trickster problematic (Sandoval 2000, 60) which is crucial for the women of Eurasian borderlands. Differential mode of consciousness depends on the ability to read concrete situations of power and choose ideological positions that is most adequate for the opposition to power configurations. The individual practicing such a mode needs to perform, in Lugones's idea, a nomadic journey between the worlds of meaning. Differential consciousness as trickster's mind inclines to particular principles of mobility and to metamorphosis and tranformationism. In Sandoval's definition of the trickster the oppositional agent practicing subjectivity as masquerade does not do it exclusively for the survival's sake anymore. There is a pronounced ethical principle here at work, a "set of principled conversions that requires (guided) movements, a directed but also a diasporic migration in both consciousness and politics, performed to ensure that ethical commitment to egalitarian social relations be enacted in the everyday, political sphere of culture" (Sandoval 2000, 62).

According to Sandoval, hegemonic Western feminism in the 1970s discovered for itself the differential tactics of non-Western contesting movements and subsequently interiorized and transcoded it. As a result there emerged a possibility of a dialogue on the very understanding of the differential. She gives examples of Haraway's manifestos and manuals of situated subjectivity, Teresa de Lauretis's eccentric discourse, questioning the boundaries of feminism as such and Judith Butler's idea of performativity.

Particularly important for Sandoval's theory is Donna Haraway's definition of a revolutionary form of human being (Haraway 1991) in the amalgam of technology and biology, the machine and the human, the dominant society and the oppositional social movements, the men and the women, the first and the third world. Cyborg feminism is more capable than previous hegemonic feminisms to attune itself to the specific historical and political positions of otherness without losing the crucial goal of looking for connections and for producing global protest movements and their agents.

Sandoval demonstrates Haraway's appropriation of certain third world feminist concepts such as radical mestizaje and the metaphor of trickster (coyote). She claims that Haraway's Cyborg machine produces a methodology congruent to the differential critique of third world feminism. She allows to combine traditional feminism with oppositional theories of indigenous people, with critical mestizaje and with methodology of the oppressed. In Sandoval's interpretation Cyborg looks for similarity in difference, thus expressing a complex form of love in the postmodern world where love is seen as an alliance and a manifestation of tenderness across the borders of difference.

Sandoval touches upon the problem of the continuing underestimation of women of color discourses which she calls a demographic understanding, preventing from considering the theoretical approach, sensibility, and specific forms of consciousness of the non-White women. In this respect Sandoval agrees with Haraway's idea that instead of trying to join the gendered femininity, it is necessary to acquire an insurgent identity of the female social subject. It means that the focus of women studies should be shifted to the efforts to understand how power circulates through, across, between, and beyond the binary division into male and female (Sandoval 2000, 171).

Sandoval's methodology of the oppressed is a set of processes, technologies, and procedures which work for decolonizing the imagination. Starting from the 1970s such a methodology has been gradually growing within the frame of women of color feminism in the United States, in post-structuralism, in postcolonial studies, in queer-theory, in global studies, etc. She points out various concepts that can be regarded as defining the theory and method of oppositional consciousness. Among them she mentions hybridity, nomadology, marginalization, Mestiza's consciousness, situated knowledges, strategic essentialism, difference, and schizo-discourse. This indicates "the existence of what can be understood as a cross-disciplinary and contemporary vocabulary, lexicon, and grammar for thinking about oppositional consciousness and social movements under globalizing postmodern cultural conditions. Oddly, however, the similar conceptual undergirding that unifies these terminologies has not become intellectual ground in the academy for recognizing new forms of theory and method capable of advancing interdisciplinary study" (Sandoval 2000, 69). This diagnosis is still correct today, but Sandoval does not touch upon its deeper reasons which lie in the colonization of knowledge that I will turn to in the next chapter.

In the epilogue, Sandoval claims that the differential resides in such a space where meaning escapes from any finalized definition or fixation in order to penetrate the shifting contours of power. This migrant improvisational subjectivity of the differential is hard to define and is never loyal to dominant ideologies. Its intellectual curiosity "demands an explosion of meaning" or "meaning's convergence and solidification" for the "sake of survival or of political change towards equality" (Sandoval 2000, 180). The differential is subjunctive as it joins together the possible with what is. This form of political subjectivity is always ready for anything to happen. It depends on the conditions of the dominant power and, at the same time, is able to question and challenge them. Differential consciousness then is a transconsciousness which emerges in a "register permitting the networks themselves to be appropriated as ideological weaponry" (Sandoval 2000, 181).

Sandoval argues that the differential allows for the emergence of a new type of coalitional consciousness and a new citizen beyond men and women divide. Differential consciousness, methodology of the oppressed, and oppositional differential social movements are parts of the global emancipatory alliance of difference which moves in the direction of more egalitarian social relations and economy. Yet she seems to regard the women of color theorists as a privileged identity and vision unavailable to anyone else. This makes her position a bit vulnerable for accusations in essentialism and totalization. Still her book is in itself an example of unfinished and open methodology of the oppressed in the way it negotiates the contradictory identities and produces an array of interconnected transformations. The way she understands women of color denies a "demographic" stable interpretation and emphasizes on theoretical and methodological strategies and fluid flexibility of difference instead. Sandoval's own position is not equal to women of color discourse as she transcends the limits of consciousness-in-opposition theories enriching them, according to R. Tapia, with a truly comparative, transdisciplinary mode of action—a hermeneutics of love (Tapia 2001, 742).

Chapter Two

Decolonial Feminism and the Decolonial Turn

2.1. The Decolonial Turn

One of the recently emerged approaches in the humanities and social sciences that attempts to act in the role of a connector between various experiences of otherness, determined by the imperial-colonial dimension of modernity, is the decolonial turn or decolonial option. There are several points formulated by decolonial humanists which I attempt to dialogue with here. First of all, it is a fundamental rethinking of modernity from its underside (Dussel 1996). According to Enrique Dussel, modernity as a European phenomenon is "constituted in a dialectical relation with a non-European alterity that is its ultimate content. Modernity appears when Europe affirms itself as the 'center' of a World History that it inaugurates: the 'periphery' that surrounds this center is consequently part of its self-definition…(Dussel 1995, 65) Modernity includes a rational 'concept' of emancipation that we affirm and subsume. But, at the same time, it develops an irrational myth, a justification for genocidal violence. The postmodernists criticize modern reason as a reason of terror; we criticize modern reason because of the irrational myth that it conceals" (Mignolo 2007, 454).

Decolonial thinking aspires to be a trans-modern intellectual project in the sense of other-than-modern, surmounting modernity. According to A. Escobar, "this group suggests that an other thought, an other knowledge (and another world, in the spirit of Porto Alegre's World Social Forum) are indeed possible" (Escobar 2007, 179). The limited interpretation of the word "decolonial" in a strictly political sense is immediately questioned and taken to epistemic level.

Modernity/coloniality group was influenced by many theoretical conceptions of both Western and non-Western origin (from critical European and American theory to South Asian and South American subaltern studies, from Chicana feminism to African philosophy and modified world-system analysis). Yet decolonial option is consciously built as an *other* paradigm falling out of the linear history of paradigms, epistemes, and grand narratives of modernity and focusing instead on borders of epistemic systems and on shifting toward the non-European ways of thinking. Decolonial thinkers do not limit themselves by Western Europe or North America alone. They are open to many other locales and see them not as mere sources of culture or passive recipients of the Western challenges of modernity, but as sources of knowledges and generators of other epistemes, often rejected or ignored by the West.

The key concept of decolonial option is coloniality of power or the colonial matrix of power. The term was coined by Anibal Quijano who claimed that in the sixteenth century together with the formation of the Atlantic commercial circuit and the so called 'discovery' of the Americas that led to the genocide of the indigenous people and the African slave trade organized by the Western Christian states of Europe, there emerged a global structure of power which can be called coloniality of power. This structure was created by two fundamental axis. One of them was the system of dominating people's subjectivity and establishing authority through the concept of race as the main criterion of the social and cultural classification of the planet. The other was the labor control and exploitation system, based on capitalism and market. Coloniality of power manifests itself through the formation of race (racism), the control of labor (capitalism), the control of subjectivity (including gender), and the control of knowledge production (or a Western monopoly of knowledge) (Quijano 2000).

Epistemically, decolonial thinking starts from the position of the critical Amerindian and African intellectuals in the sixteenth through eighteenth centuries later revived in the nineteenth and twentieth centuries among the thinkers of European descent in the South America and the Caribbean. Decolonial thinking shifts away from the Western historical narratives—Christian, Liberal, or Marxist—and turns instead to the colonial matrix of power. Decolonial option starts with the idea that modernity is impossible without its irrational colonial-imperial side generating coloniality of power, of thinking, and of being. Neither is it possible without the capitalist world system. And the rhetoric of modernity has always concealed underneath the logic of coloniality. Coloniality is an effective weapon of modernity which justifies any actions, including war with the purpose of destroying or overcoming of barbarity and traditionalism. Then coloniality is the hidden weapon of the civilizing and develomentalist missions of modernity (Mignolo and Tlostanova 2009).

Structurally, decolonial thinking works on two levels: the analysis of the colonial matrix of power and its historical transformations and working out the desirable scenarios for the future. They lead to the necessity of the decolonial option, a philosophic projection of the future, arguing with neoliberal and developmentalist options leading to the death of humanity. Decolonial thinking rejects the most fundamental claim of modernity—its belief in abstract universals. Therefore it questions Christian, Liberal, and Marxist conceptions of life and society, arguing for the world of pluriversal coexistence instead of universal dominance, imposed by force or cunning of the ruling minority (Tlostanova 2008).

Political and epistemic positioning at the border allows the decolonial option to deconstruct Eurocentrism as a form of knowledge linked with modernity/coloniality and to question the myth of modernity built on the idea of progress and development at any price. Decolonization thus becomes an intellectual and existential and not just a political or social process. Coloniality of being and of knowledge goes hand in hand with the rhetoric of salvation which has marked modernity throughout. The rhetoric of modernity and the logic of coloniality act as two sides of the same coin.[1] It is an efficient tactic of modernity serving the interests of Western imperial-colonial expansion. Attempting to escape from the grip of the totalizing logic of modernity the decolonial option demonstrates that modernity is not something natural, imminent, and unavoidable as the Euro-Atlantic civilization is trying to claim. In its meta-narratives it efficiently acts as a means of indoctrinating the minds on a global level, generating an enchantment with modernity, in W. Mignolo's term (Mignolo 2002b).

One of the typical delusions imposed by Western modernity onto the rest of the world lies in its philosophy of history. It is a specific spatial-temporal matrix, based on the invention of modernity and tradition as its dark other, on juxtaposing the new and the old, on turning geography into chronology, in W. Mignolo's formulation (Mignolo 2000), or even, on colonization of space by time. The decolonial option fundamentally rethinks this spatial-temporal matrix, within which the edited history of humanity is built on the familiar myth of linear, successive, homogenous historical development, on vector genealogies of culture, knowledge, and art. This logic of modernity based on the invention of tradition as modernity's evil other, stitches through many scholarly discourses today. There emerges a self-contained and self-generating ideal for the humanities, associated exclusively with modernity as a specific space for the embodiment of prescribed ideals. Tradition has been equally an invention from the start, a similarly constructed arbitrary notion.

It was needed to counterbalance modernity and localize it in Western Europe. This was linked with the claims of the European system of knowledge production to make sense of everything and everybody it encounters. In the first modernity[2] it was expressed in a theological drive, while in second modernity it was expressed in the quasi-scientific inclination to classifications, taxonomies, evolutionary schemes, and typological parallels. In the basis of this comparative drive there lied a universalist quest for the common origin of all human beings.

The problem was what sort of human being was chosen to represent the humanity. It was a recognizable White Christian Modern male as opposed to the traditional savage of the "wrong" religion, sexual orientation, color of skin, or any other combination. The Renaissance conception of man and mankind has remained the main instrument in disavowing the non-Christian and non-European knowledges until now. It emerged through and in the clashes between European Christians and their difference—Muslims, Jews, Amerindians, Africans, Asians. Such an understanding of the human being was necessary for giving the Europeans their desired privilege of the presumably objective rationality, while legitimating of the human taxonomy created by Europeans was epistemological rather than ontological.

Classification of humankind needs a system of knowledge which would justify and reproduce the human hierarchies. Classification is not in the object itself, but in the knowing subject and in the system of knowledge in which she/he operates. The European imperial subject by way of people, institutions, and disciplines have been colonizing knowledge and being by appropriating the content of knowledge or by denouncing someone else's knowledge as illegitimate. In the basis of classification of certain groups of people as not quite rational, "raw," underdeveloped, or sexually deviant, there lies nothing else but colonization of being, that is the way the modern/colonial system of knowledge production has created, sustained, and reproduced racism and patriarchal order. These internal impulses and key factors of the Eurocentric system of knowledge production, based on the colonial and imperial epistemic differences, have been expressed in all modern disciplines grounded in the study of the other as a deviation from the same, on taking it to the common denominator of sameness, or on radicalizing its difference.

On the basis of this dominant system of knowledge there stands the hubris of the zero point, in terms of Santiago Castro-Gómez: "The coexistence of diverse ways of producing and transmitting knowledge is eliminated because now all forms of human knowledge are ordered on an epistemological scale from the traditional to the modern, from barbarism to civilization, from the community to the individual, from the orient to the occident" (Castro-Gómez 2007, 433). The scholarly thought then is positioned as the only legitimate form of knowledge production, while Europe acquires an epistemic privilege over all other cultures. The hubris of the zero point is the place of the observer and the locus of enunciation that in Christian Theology was taken by God and in Secular Philosophy—by Reason. The zero point is the limit in which there is an observer that cannot be observed (Mignolo and Tlostanova 2011a). Practicing zero point epistemology legitimates European languages and thought systems simultaneously disqualifying all others.

Decolonization of thinking and knowledge is directly linked with rethinking of the social sciences and humanities. It radicalizes and questions the well known Western endeavors in this area, from Diltey to Habermas, Foucault, and Wallerstein. However decolonial option is not interested in improving modernity. It offers a radical shift in the geography and biography of reason, from technological education and corporate university to rehabilitation of humanities, operating in the sphere of understanding, and to stressing the critical and not just positive knowledge, connected with ethical and political imperatives, with critical, ethical, and political responsibility of the scholars and academics for the production, distribution, transformation, and application of knowledge.

In the past few years the decolonial option turned more in the direction of ontology, existential philosophy, ethics, and aesthetics. The conceptual frame of coloniality has been complicated, while previously less stressed problematic of coloniality of being, of gender, and of knowledge has come forward. One of the most interesting scholars in this respect is Nelson Maldonado-Torres who defines coloniality of being in the following way: "Coloniality is different from colonialism…It refers to the set of long-standing patterns of power that emerged as a result of colonialism but continue to exist long after colonialism and colonial administrations as such are gone, surviving in culture, labor, intersubjective relations, knowledge productions, books, cultural patterns and other aspects of modern existence. In a way, as modern subjects we breath coloniality all the time and everyday" (Maldonado-Torres 2007, 243).

A no less important concept for the decolonial option is pluritopic hermeneutics defined by Walter Mignolo and connected with the double critique of modernity from the position of coloniality (Mignolo 1995, 12–13). Pluritopic hermeneutics is an antipode of zero point epistemology. It questions the position and the homogeneity of the understanding subject. It moves toward interactive knowledge and understanding, reflecting the very process of construction of the space under cognition with its social and human interests in histories. The pluritopic approach is not interested in cultural relativism or multiculturalism. It is opposed to Western monotopic hermeneutics where the space of enunciation is always inside the Western tradition, artificially constructed from Ancient Greece to postmodern Europe, within the frame of modernity's myth invented by the monotopic act of understanding and imposed onto the multilinguistic and multicultural spaces.

If in monotopic hermeneutics an object was studied by various disciplines with the help of their respective instruments, in pluritopic hermeneutics various knowledges come into a dialogue on what is knowledge as such and what kind of knowledge is necessary to make the world a better place for everyone. Instead of the object in the Western understanding there emerge problems discussed from various positions. Pluritopic hermeneutics corresponds to transcultural model within the frame of which the former zero point epistemology is being overcome. Transcultural model creates a rupture with previous disciplines and a transdisciplinarity in the sense of overcoming the disciplines and including along with academic or university knowledge those forms of knowledge which were discredited in the monotopic hermeneutics (such as aboriginal cosmologies, social movements knowledge, etc.). Pluritopic hermeneutics seeks a way out of the limiting categories imposed by Western epistemology and a specific attention to gender, ethnic-racial, sexual and other previously marginalized aspects of knowledge production. It makes a shift in the geography and biography of reason (Gordon 2006, 107–131) placing at the center of knowledge production, not development and progress achieved at the expense of human lives, but a concept of the never healing "colonial wound" between the first and the third worlds, formulated by Gloria Anzaldúa (Mignolo and Tlostanova 2007).

Decolonial turn is different from both postmodernity and postcoloniality, as it radically questions the essence, logic, and methodology of the existing system of knowledge and disciplinary spheres. It attempts a conceptual denaturalization, a qualitative shift not a quantitative one, as it sometimes happens in those variants of postcolonial studies which rely exclusively on Western postmodernist concepts, seldom questioning the disciplinary matrix established in modernity. The majority of postcolonial studies start from the version of modern colonial history with the British empire (or sometimes France) at its center.

This is one of the limitations of postcolonial discourse from the point of view of decolonial option.[3] Not that this genealogy and local history is irrelevant, on the contrary. Problems start when there are attempts at making a universal traveling theory out of postcolonial studies, applying their contextually bound insights to completely different locales. A relatively new material is studied in postcolonial studies by (ex)representatives of the third world, and by means of postmodernist analytical tools, or with a minimal variation/deviation. What remains untouched is the fundamental logic of modernity and its disciplines and the Western monopoly of knowledge. Even the most elaborate and original examples of postcolonial theorizing tend to interpret the other through the concepts of the same and seldom the other way round, and in this fundamental sense they remain loyal to and inadvertently reproduce the coloniality of knowledge. One can hybridize J. Lacan with an Indian colonial history and subjectivity and create rich and polysemantic concepts in the vein of Homi Bhabha, but this is not what the decolonial option is after. We attempt to start not from Lacan but from Gloria Anzaldúa or from the Zapatistas, from Caucasus cosmology or from Sufism. Postcolonial studies would not formulate their task like this because they remain "studies," that is, they are confined within the frame of the modern division into subject (who is studying) and object (which is studied) and often take research to application of Western high theory to local material.

Postmodernism is at variance with decolonial option on a different level. Both approaches are conceptually radical, striving to work out a new categorical apparatus, new mechanisms and logic of meaning production and dismantling modernity and its major discourses. Yet decolonial option is radical in a different way, from the position of alterity. It is not trying to deconstruct modernity from within and for the sake of its repairing, and it is not provincially fixed on Western experience as the only point of reference (even if negatively interpreted). The grammar of decoloniality is a new border critical theory which goes beyond the European critical theory still formulated within the European ego-politics of knowledge. In its radicalism and critique it exceeds Frankfurt school, postmodernism, and poststructuralism, replacing the concept of "free market" with the concept of "free life" (Mignolo 2007, 485).

Decolonial option consciously attempts to get rid of its own possible epistemic provincialism as it opens to more and more locales and contesting epistemic stances along with the original South American basis. Decolonial program of agency and struggle does not come with readymade answers. The answers are born while and after the questions are being asked and as a result of a critical dialogue with the multiplicity of oppressed subjects. More and more European scholars turn to decolonial option both in the so called peripheral Europe (Romania, Belarus, Slovenia) and in the capitalist ex-empires of modernity (Germany, Spain, Holland, Great Britain). This emerging dialogue allows the decolonial option to go beyond the Americas with their paradigmatic idea of race, in the direction of intersecting ethnicity, class, and religion.[4]

Decolonial option is performed through border thinking and knowledge which emerge as a reaction to violence of imperial/territorial epistemology and the rhetoric of salvation. Instead of reproducing abstract universals it turns to border episteme which thinks from the position of suppressed knowledges (such as folklore, traditional cosmology, religion, nonrational knowledges). Border thinking is the epistemology of the exteriority that is of the outside created from the inside (Mignolo and Tlostanova 2006, 206). Practicing it means going beyond the categories imposed by Western epistemology. But it is not a simple change of one (Western) epistemology to another or others. All the models continue to exist and remain viable as sources and targets of criticism. This echoes the Zapatistas principle of the world where many different worlds would coexist on a nonhierarchical basis.

Critical border thinking leads to decolonial shift and a dismantling of previous managerial epistemology of the zero point. Decolonial thinking is based on epistemic borders between European imperial categories and the languages and models which were discarded by modern imperial epistemology. Border thinking is a response to the colonial and imperial differences, which were assigned by the dominant discourses to all other people classified as inferior and epistemically disregarded. Border thinking is not about studying borders and those who cross them, it is about being the border and thinking from the border, remaking the geographic frontiers, the imperial-colonial subjectivities, and territorial epistemologies. To paraphrase W. E. B. Dubois, the problem of the twenty-first century will be not merely the color line, but also the "epistemic line" (Bogues 2003), or the color of reason. "At the moment when the epistemic line is interrogated from the perspective of the color, gender or sexuality, there emerges the border thinking—*in* the crack and *as* an epistemic shift" (Mignolo and Tlostanova 2006, 214).

Another important concept for decolonial option is epistemic delinking, leading to decolonial epistemic shift and bringing forward other principles of knowledge and understanding, an other economy, an other politics and an other ethics. Delinking subverts the universalist claims of Europeans as a particular combination of ethnic groups localized in a particular place in the planet where capitalism was shaped as a result of colonialism. Delinking potentially leads to pluriversality as a universal project and is an act of epistemic disobedience (Mignolo 2007). Without it decolonization of thinking and of being would be impossible and we would be left within the frame of internal opposition to Eurocentric ideas of modernity. So the decolonial shift means to learn to unlearn what we were taught before, to delink from the thinking programs which were imposed on us by culture, education, and environment marked by imperial reason (Mignolo and Tlostanova 2011b).

Instead of studying and analyzing the existing (post)colonialist phenomena and processes and keeping the boundary between the studied object and the studying subject, the decolonial approach regards the analysis of a particular social phenomenon, idea, or a work of art as merely an initial preparatory step in trying to answer the questions, hidden by the rhetoric of modernity. Decolonial approach refuses to ground itself in the canonized difference between understanding and explanation. After the preliminary step there comes the formulating of decolonial arguments that "leads any investigation through the scholar, intellectual or researcher, into the world, rather than keeping him or her within the discipline. The problems that concern the decolonial option are problems that have been set up by the modern/colonial matrix of power, with its rhetoric of salvation hiding the colonial logic of control, domination and suppression. That is why the analytic of coloniality is a necessary condition for the future decolonial arguments" (Mignolo and Tlostanova 2009).

Decolonial thinking is necessarily a decolonial behavior as well, a specific ethos of decoloniality. What is meant here is not an abstract declarative ethics of giving rights back to the wretched of the Earth but more importantly, a link of the ethical moment with the self-positioning of decolonial humanists. By self-positioning I mean not an ego-logical contemplation of one's own navel, but a critical assessment of oneself as a scholar, an activist, and a human being. Instead of the public intellectual, there emerges a scholar as a true activist, who is not studying the contesting movements from outside but becomes their integral part instead. A crucial role here is played by the subjectivity of the scholars themselves, but again, not taken outside of their local history, not interpreted as merely their individual intellectual genealogy. What decolonial humanists should be after is a dynamic interpenetration of serious activism and scholarly activity, stressing the painful question of the researcher's and activist's ethical stance, her/his scholarly, existential, and political positioning that inevitably leaks into research but is seldom acknowledged. They/we should be thinking and living according to the very principles they/we define. This is a difficult yet necessary task for any radical rethinking of the humanities and social sciences.

A. Escobar points out that economics, ecology, and gender should receive more attention in decolonial thinking in the future (Escobar 2007, 192). In fact, these spheres are already being put in the focus of decolonial research today. The most interesting contributions in gender area have been made by María Lugones, Sylvia Marcos, Nelson Maldonado-Torres, Freya Schiwy, and several others.[5] Yet gender requires more attention and nuancing within the frame of decolonial humanities which can also help reframe the accepted hierarchy of disciplines and build bridges between them, such as the bridge with third world feminism which contributed a lot to the dynamic and multi-logic analysis of the intersections of gender, race, class, and religion. Bringing together the insights of third world feminism and the decolonial thinking would allow to introduce back into analysis the forgotten spaces, people, and concepts erased from contemporary humanities and social sciences. Along with the critique of Western modernity, decolonial option opens up in the direction of a more profound engagement with other religious, cosmological, and cultural traditions, such as Islam or Buddhism. Western modernity historically imposed itself onto the world in the forms of Christianity, Liberalism, or Socialism. But this is only part of the story. And it is not enough to simply add new voices and perspectives to the global dialogue. It is crucial to reconstruct a genealogy of internal hierarchies within these other spaces and focus on their particular power relations and their logic of coloniality clashing against that of the dominant Western modernity.

Thus, in peripheral Eurasia, Islam originally acted in a similar unattractive role to that of Catholicism in the New World. But both in South America and in Central Asia the indigenous peoples elaborated specific strategies of domesticating the imposed religions (be it Catholicism or Islam), through keeping the external shell and changing the meaning, and incorporating these religions into the larger universe of indigenous cosmologies. This was one of the early examples of the shift in the geography and biography of reason that decolonial option is after. The Amerindian religious duality, the peculiar symbiosis of Muslim and indigenous beliefs in Caucasus and Central Asia and even the Russian "double faith" that existed for several centuries after its official Christianization, are all examples of this decolonial sentiment that was later recast in secular political terms and can be recast today once again in rethinking of humanities and social sciences from the perspective of these locales.

Decolonial option is an open and unfinished intellectual modality which allows to enrich it with more and more other local knowledges without endangering its basis. In its center there stands a genuine interest in other others which is lacking in many intellectual endeavors today. One of the crucial ways for the future enfolding of the decolonial option lies in the gradual shift from criticism and negation, that have been in the center so far, to affirmation of something different, to a careful elaboration of the grounds for a non-racist and non-patriarchal future. It is a way from resistance to reexistence, to use a Colombian artist and activist Adolfo Alban's term (Alban Achinte 2006). Without having access to decision-making, which is the case of most academics, it is a difficult task, if we do not alter the previous forms of engagement and shift to spiritual, aesthetic, nonrational, and virtual practices instead, attempting to slowly modify consciousness instead of power structures. Changing the terms and not just the content of the conversation (Mignolo 2007), we should also change the tactics of criticizing modernity moving this struggle outside the system of values, coordinates, rules, and conditions that modernity created for itself, and in which it feels comfortable.

One has to be particularly careful with these new decolonial humanities as the conceptual apparatus of the previously existing disciplines is fundamentally biased through the rhetoric of modernity with its ability to appropriate any concepts of alternative thinking. This is what has happened with transcultural humanities which quickly lost their contesting edge and turned into a cliché. A decolonial reading of culture would stress its obvious birth marks of coloniality of being and of power, a hidden synonymy between race and culture and an inferior interpretation of culture in relation to knowledge or philosophy. So instead of transcultural humanities it may be more apt to discuss trans-epistemic and transvalue humanities and subjectivities. That way we stress the radical shift from a mere addition of cultural features for the sake of their description within the frame of Western humanities to the interpretation of other cosmologies in their own terms and preferably, by representatives of these locales, who were not first turned into the intellectual slaves of modernity.

Demarcation from modernity in the epistemic sense is necessarily connected with the change in conceptual apparatus as each concept carries an array of various associations and is not objective or innocent. It is important to continue decolonizing the concepts in the humanities and social sciences. Otherwise semantically false similarities, as in case of race or the meanings of the word "colonial," may endanger the very decolonial option by dissolving it in the well known theories and approaches already digested by modernity. When we start thinking of the meanings behind the terms "transcultural humanities" and "trans-epistemic humanities" we venture into the sphere of elaborating the language and discourse necessary for the new human sciences rethinking the humanities globally.

A decolonial denaturalizing of generally accepted concepts is best performed in multiply colonized spaces with a developed trickster subjectivity, such as the Caribbean region. For the "heart of Europe" shifting the geography and biography of knowledge is a more difficult task as a European scholar risks to slide into postmodernism or occupy an area studies seemingly disinterested observer's standpoint. Even more complicated is the configuration of the world of imperial difference, that is, the difference between first class (Britain, France, Germany) and second class (Russia, the Ottoman Sultanate) empires of modernity. In the presence of imperial difference the projection of modernity was indirect and mediated by the secondary empires which created their own distorted and redoubling versions of modernity, history, genealogy of human sciences, etc.[6]

A crucial aspect of decolonization of humanities is getting away from strict disciplinarity in the direction of transdisciplinarity. It means establishing a dialogue between the disciplinarily marked investigations from different areas which leads to the birth of new forms of research. Within the decolonial option there is a clear tendency toward the un-disciplining of social sciences (Walsh et al. 2002) and building theories without disciplines or beyond disciplines (Castro-Gómez and Mendieta 1998). This process is connected with venturing into the areas that traditionally have not been taken seriously by modern sciences, thus making philosophy or sociology equal to various marginalized forms of knowledge.

There seem to be the three basic spaces and the three main types of agents of the political change connected with decolonial option. The first is the subaltern social actors and movements, for example, the Confederation of Indigenous Nationalities of Ecuador (CONAIE), or the Zapatistas. The second is the intellectual activists in the mixed spaces—from NGOs to the state. The third is the universities and, to a lesser extent, the museums as the new topi of contestation and diversality (Glissant 1998).

2.2. Western and Decolonial Feminism: Leitmotivs of Difference

Humanities and social sciences as we know them, including Western feminism, were shaped in accordance with the spatial-temporal matrix of modernity based on the invention of tradition as modernity's dark other. Western feminism built its main argumentation of gender egalitarianism and the struggle with the patriarchal order on the basis of the invention of secular modernity as a questionable ideal of emancipation and on marking of all other models as traditional (interpreted negatively), particularly if they were linked with non-Christian cultures. Western feminist claims are formulated exclusively in terms of Western modernity and modernization, whereas the negative features (humiliation, violence, economic dependency, lack of access to education, etc.) are associated with traditionalist society which is presented by default as always and everywhere patriarchal. Yet as a number of scholars from all over the world have demonstrated recently (Oyěwùmi 1997, Marcos 2005, Lugones 2007) the patriarchal nature of traditional society is a Western myth, such features were often generated by colonization and modernization together with the invented concept of tradition.[7]

Building of feminist genealogies is often marked by the same enchantment with modernity. For example, a generally accepted division of feminism into three waves was naturalized in the minds of many Western scholars of gender, even if in reality it was a contextual product of Western-centric and evolutionary ideology of modernity, and one more particularity claiming a universal status. Julia Kristeva offered a more nuanced yet absolutely confined to her own problematically European experience, monologic division into three stages of feminism, in her 1979 essay "Women's Time." In a universalist way she replaces the human with pan-European and (provincially) cosmopolitan because feminist movement for her remains an exclusively European movement. This is connected with Kristeva's continuing enchantment with the myth of modernity and her theorizing from a zero epistemic point (Kristeva 1981).

Another falsely universal idea of Western feminism questioned in decolonial gender discourse is the idea of egalitarianism in politics, economics, society, and even psychology. This idea is not viable in communitarian or mixed societies, where the ideal of equality is either nonexistent or coded negatively. Sylvia Marcos gives an example of the Zapatistas women (Marcos 2005), who instead of gender egalitarianism appeal to parity. Hence comes the motto of marching together—men and women. In Mesoamerican cosmology there is no concept of egalitarianism as the universe consists of elements which are balanced with each other as nonexclusive differences. The indigenous cosmic and moral equilibrium is based on a complex wholism, full of tension, which does not separate the sphere of individual's private life and his good and evil acts, from the sphere of community as a whole, the land in all its multiple overtones, and the universe. There emerges a constantly changeable and flexible balance, a state of "extreme dynamic tension and not a pragmatic compromise between the opposites" (Marcos 2006, 25). For Zapatistas equality means stagnation and death as they think that no two beings can be totally equal. That is why they are against a radical Western feminist position of excluding men from alliances and struggles. Similar attitudes are to be found in a number of works written by Chinese feminists (Wu 2005, Li Xiaojiang 1993), not persuaded by the Western idea of sisterhood or in the position of women from non-European Russian/ Soviet ex-colonies, who take an intermediary stance between individualism and communitarianism, and reluctantly accept the separatist notion of exclusion of all men.[8]

One of the important differences between women of color and decolonial feminism on the one hand and Western feminists on the other is that the former lack, at least to a similar extent, a typical Western discourse on fragmentation of identity, both individual and group. Women of color often deliberately aim at creating a world in which men would be included on certain terms for the tactical union in the mutual struggle with coloniality of power. This is why the colonized women seldom endorse the modern Western individualistic types of feminism. There is a lack of understanding between these feminist extremes. Thus, Zapatistas women take a double stance— they defend their specific agenda as women and also take an active part in all Zapatismo political actions. They want to be seen as equal, yet different within the pluritopic nation, occupying the position of collective subjectivity and nonexclusive duality of men and women. Their task is to build a world where they can practice their right to difference because all people are equal. They perform a mutual multidirectional transculturation of Marxism and Feminism through Amerindian cosmology and philosophy and back.

Western feminist wars against sexism in language make perfect sense in the majority of Western European languages, yet they would not always work in other locales. A graphic example is Oyěwùmi's analysis of how Yoruba culture is misinterpreted through Western gender categories (Oyěwùmi 1997). She discusses the concepts of *obinrin* and *okunrin,* mistranslated as "woman" and "man," arguing that in Yoruba language they are not opposed to each other through a binary opposition and are not hierarchical. The word *obinrin* does not come etymologically from the word *okunrin,* as it happens in English. The common suffix "rin" means belonging to humankind. While the first parts of these words simply stand for anatomical differences. There is no initial notion here that the human norm is a man, and a woman is a deviation from this norm. Both belong to *aniyan* (humankind). The difference between *okunrin* and *obinrin* lies in the sphere of reproduction and not gender or social status (Oyĕwùmi 1997, 33–34). In Yoruba language even pronouns have no gender. Yet they strictly observe the age difference and hierarchy in social contacts and kinship terms. This linguistic system has started to change in the direction of genderization due to the Western influence.

The sexist power of Russian would be different and more blurred, less dimorphic than English, compare for example man-woman, where the root concept is man, while a human being is identical to man, and a Russian less binary *muzhchina* (man)-*zhenschina* (woman)-*chelovek* (human being)). A more pronounced discrepancy would emerge in case of Turkic or Caucasus languages: the Turkic *odam* (human being), *ayel* (woman), *erkak* (man); the Adyghean *tsyf* (human being), *bzylfyg* (woman), *kale* (young man), *pshashe* (young woman). This does not mean that there is no sexism or seeing women as others of men (although such variants also exist) in these cases, it just means that the principles of linguistic gender identification work differently and need to be contextually investigated in their own terms and not in terms of universalized Western linguistic sexism.

As Marcos points out in her analysis of Zapatista women, one of the key elements of Mesoamerican cosmology is a close interconnection of all beings in the world. Hence comes a specific understanding of human community and a lack of necessity in individualism or individuation. The world is indivisible and inseparable from human beings; it exists in and through the human beings. In Toholabal language there is an intersubjective correlation between the first and third person, a structure with no direct or indirect objects. This is totally different from European languages with their subjective correlation. As a result, when someone speaks in Toholabal she or he does not represent herself or himself as in Western languages, but becomes involved in intersubjective relationship with other people, nature, cosmos instead. And all of these potential actors are intrinsically present in any utterance.

As María Lugones points out, when terms such as *koshskalaka,* *chachawarmi, vato, obinrin, uman,* are translated into the language of Western gender and its dichotomous heterosexist racial hierarchies, it manifests coloniality of gender by means of colonial translation (Lugones 2008). In Amerindian languages instead of binary logic there is a logic of mutually supplementing (and not mutually exclusive) oppositions. This does not allow to mechanically render the concepts of this language by a simple binary opposition of man/versus woman.

It is also necessary to deconstruct the internalized Western feminist idea of the visual (masculine) nature of any culture, which in fact is most typical of the Western European "gaze," but not of many other locales with different or mixed predominant communication channels—sound, tactile, etc. As Oyěwùmi argues, in the Western perception of the world, body and gender are regarded predominantly as a visual difference, while in Yoruba even the Western concept "world vision" would be impossible and we would have to speak of the "world-sensing" or "world-smelling" or "world-hearing" instead (Oyěwùmi 1997, 2–3). Because of the tonal structure of Yoruba language, hearing is more important than vision. Besides, the world is perceived as a whole and not divided into physical, spiritual, moral, or the world of ideas. Whereas in the West even the metaphor of cognition and perception is always linked with the visual sphere and with insight. This is connected with the male gaze and leads to objectification of those who are looked at. The combination of intonation and phonetic features of Turkic languages with a specific influence of Muslim culture in these regions overlaid onto the previous rich sensual traditions definitely shifts the role of the visual in comparison with Western culture. Radical feminism regards the oppression of women as the most fundamental form of oppression which stitches through all other spheres (racial, cultural, economic, class interactions) and hence becomes the main field of revolutionary social changes. It was in the frame of radical feminism that the first discussions on difference between biological sex and gender and the established gender roles that both men and women needed to get rid of emerged. However, radical feminism tended to impose onto the rest of the world the social, economic, and political principles that have been shaped in and by European culture in the past five hundred years and favoring gender neglected all other spheres of human life. Within third world and decolonial feminism it becomes clear that the prescribed and culturally determined gender roles that Western feminists so much want to get rid of turn out to be different in different locales (while gender roles themselves are far from being a major division in many societies) and need to be understood before being destroyed.

2.3. Race/Body/Gender and Global Coloniality

The idea that gender and body are closely linked with social class and racial discourses and sexuality has become commonplace today. Race is manifested in the clearest form through body imagery and particularly through gendered bodies. In decolonial option this problematic is conceptualized through coloniality of being, the geo-politics and the body-politics of knowledge, and, since recently, the coloniality of gender. The body-politics refers to the individual and collective biographical grounds of understanding and thinking, while the geo-politics means the local historical grounds of knowledge (Mignolo and Tlostanova 2006, 210). The hegemonic philosophy and knowledge principles in the West are theological (in the first modernity) and ego-logical (in secular modernity), which is clearly seen in Descartes' principle "I think therefore I am." Foucault (Foucault 1998) analyzes one of the aspects of the ego-politics, when he speaks of the state which produces knowledge for the control of bodies, naming it a "bio-politics." Theo- and ego-politics of knowledge determine the norm and the deviation, so that the nonrational and nonscientific forms of knowledge, formulated outside the main avenue of modernity, are excluded. Therefore the geo-politics and body-politics of knowledge are in constant argument with the state bio-politics and emerge precisely as forms of contestation and delinking from racist epistemology (Mignolo and Tlostanova 2009). They analectically, in E. Dussel's formulation (Dussel 1985, 158–159), or anti-dialectically, signify the geographic and body-graphic grounds of knowledge and cognition in history, memory, and languages of people who found themselves, often against their will, at the cross-roads of imperial and colonial differences and experiences and who were refused in their belonging to modernity, and hence, to humanity.

According to N. Maldonado-Torres, a barbarian acquired new connotations in modernity—he/she became a racialized other and this racializaiton was marked by a radical doubt in the humanity of the other. Consequently, the legitimating of colonization project was based on the doubt or skepticism which helped the European ego in its self-assertion. The Manichean misanthropic skepticism was skeptical not about the existence of the world or the normative logic. This was a doubt in the human nature of slaves and subjugated people. Maldonado-Torres speculates that Descartes' idea of the rupture between consciousness and matter, mind and body, human and nature is "built upon an anthropological colonial difference between the *ego conquistador* and the *ego conquistado*. The very relationship between colonizer and colonized provided a new model to understand the relationship between the soul or mind and the body; and likewise, modern articulations of the mind/body are used as models to conceive the colonizer/colonized relation, as well as the relation between men and women, particularly, the woman of color" (Maldonado-Torres 2007, 245–246).

Maldonado-Torres reformulates the Cartesian "Cogito, ergo sum" into a more complex statement, referring to the darker side of modernity: "I think (others do not think, or do not think properly), therefore I am (others are not, lack being, should not exist or are dispensable)" (Maldonado-Torres 2007, 252). The racialized and gendered others are examples of such invisible people, who do not exist. It is their humanity that is being questioned and negated. Thus, coloniality of being, naturalized in the situations of war, racism, slavery, violates the meaning of "human alterity to the point where the alterego becomes a sub-alter" (Maldonado-Torres 2007, 257) and begins to signify liminality in relation to the idea of being as such, leading to ontological colonial difference.

The colonial imaginary from the start was permeated with gender dimension which helped in the establishing of European masculinity. The White man imagined himself in opposition to the colonized males who were presented as feminine or simply a part of nonrational nature, while nature itself was firmly linked with metaphors of femininity. Within the colonial imaginary gender was used as a metaphor and a way of control which was clearly expressed in the female presentation of territories—the virgin land waiting to be inseminated by the male colonizing auctor. Gender dimension was an important part of the European cartographic imaginary and topological creativity because the "discovered" lands symbolically acquired a feminine nature while the parallel between the physical possession of a woman and the possession of the new lands became visualized (Pratt 1992, Rabasa 1993).

The idea of war, contest, and genocide brings out one more aspect of coloniality, which is firmly linked with gender. It is the concept of the "just war." When the conquerors decided to take part in the just war against the Indians they already formed a specific attitude to the people they were going to colonize which did not correlate with

European ethical standards at home. Soon the situation in the Americas was transferred onto the rest of the world and became typical of modernity as such. Coloniality can be seen as a radicalization and naturalization of the non-ethics of war. It included practices of eradication of certain groups in the process of colonization and liberated the colonizer from any moral responsibility for his actions (Maldonado-Torres 2008).

Within the just war, gender relations also acquired specific forms. Even today sexual violence against women in war time or in ethnic and religious conflicts is regarded as legitimate. Such violence itself acquires an additional symbolic taste of insulting the national, ethnic, or religious pride, while the woman is completely divested of her humanity in the eyes of both the rapist and the defender of this pride. In many colonized cultures the metaphor of sexual violence intensified patriarchal relations if they already existed or enforced them where they did not exist. Within such relations women were seen as objects and their insult was regarded as an infringement upon the man's honor. Such a practice confirmed the normative nature of heterosexual relations and led to the imposition of male dominance in decolonization processes later.

The use of sexual violence as a strategy of conquest and maintaining of racial hierarchy powerfully demonstrates the links between colonialism, gender, and religious discourses. Sexual violence as a strategy of colonization of the Americas is one of the best documented and persuasive examples (Goldstein 2001, Smith 2005, Amina Mama 2001). It is used as an instrument of racial terror aimed against the aboriginal people and, later, the African slaves. Legitimating violence acts as an effective way of sustaining colonialism. The White man's violence against the non-White woman is not merely sexual as it is racially marked. Their female nature makes these women vulnerable in the face of racist dominance, while the color of skin becomes a justification of their deprivation of any legitimate defense.

Maldonado-Torres firmly links race and gender in his reflections on coloniality of being: "Hellish existence in the colonial world carries with it both the racial and the gendered aspects of the naturalization of the non-ethics of war…While in war there is murder and rape, in the hell of the colonial world murder and rape become day to day occurrences and menaces. 'Killability' and 'rapeability' are inscribed into the images of the colonial bodies…In its most familiar and typical forms the Black man represents the act of rape—'raping'—while the Black woman is seen as the most legitimate victim of rape—'being raped' " (Maldonado-Torres 2007, 255).

Extreme manifestations of coloniality of being come to genocide, but war here does not just mean murder. It also refers to a particular interpretation of sexuality, femininity, and rape. Coloniality is a system in which the racialized others are constantly under the pressure of sadistic and deadly European gaze. The main targets of this violence are women. Yet racialized men are regarded through sexual violence as well, due to their feminization. As a result they are seen by the *ego conquiro* as fundamentally penetrable. As Maldonado-Torres claims, racialization here works through gender and sexual relations, while *ego conquiro* is expressed as a phallic ego. Conquest then can be regarded as rape and exploitation of women justified by the ethics of war (Maldonado-Torres 2007, 248).

This logic acquired its finalized forms in the nineteenth century due to the emergence of scientific racism. Violence in relation to the conquered people came to be seen as the norm even after the "just war" against them was over. Just a color of skin or a non-belonging to European culture became enough for a justification of the continuing slavery, oppression and violence, including the sexual violence. Race and gender in modernity then are the results of the naturalization of the ethics of war. Violence is firmly linked with the racial factor, as if violence were the gist of the non-White person, who automatically becomes a dispensable life. A non-White body (both male and female) comes to be signified by an excessive cruelty and eroticism, justifying the desire of the dark other—both sexual (the desire to possess) and destructive (the desire to kill). Hence there emerges a phenomenological signification of the non-White bodies with violence and eroticism.

Now let us imagine schematically a gender colonial hierarchy in Western modernity marking with arrows (power vectors) the relations between European men and women and the colonized of both sexes. We will see that the largest number of arrows will be pointed in the direction of the colonized women who experience discrimination on the part of all the remaining three groups, yet have no opportunity to project power onto anyone else. The second type of relations is presented by the colonized males and European women. They are linked because, on the one hand, they experience the influence of a more powerful oppressing agent—the Western male, and, on the other hand, they are themselves agents of discrimination in relation to other groups. In the case of the colonized men it is a still weaker group of the colonized women, and in the case of Western women it is both the colonized men and women. European men in this hierarchy are exclusively the agents of power, who are not effected by anyone else's oppressing force. Consequently, the resistance to these power vectors also takes place differently in various groups. Obviously, the most complicated case is the colonized women, as here the oppression is multilayered and the resistance takes intersectional forms.

These really existing power relations were hidden and distorted by the rhetoric of modernity by means of projecting its own strategies of violence onto the victims of this violence. As a result we find a totally different hierarchy, which was successfully sold to the world through various myths. The colonized man was accused of violence or desire of violence against the White woman, as well as against his own woman who was presumably in need of salvation from his barbarity. The colonized woman was accused of sexual dissoluteness and voracity, closeness to animal nature, inclination to filth, etc. She was seen as not merely a seductress of the White man, but also a threat to the happiness and well being of the decent White woman. All that legitimized violence against the colonized women. The real power relations were replaced in this discourse with the constructs of demonization, exoticism, racism, sexism, and Eurocentrism.

A number of race theorists come close to the discussion of the paradox of colonial masculinity and femininity. The definition of the darker side of femininity and masculinity is done according to the rule of contraries and denies itself preventing the colonial subject from creating any positive identity. The colonized male lacks real authority and power and is constantly feminized. At the same time the non-White males are regarded as a threat for the realm of the same and any hint at their possible agency or will as well as any presence of the phallic element is immediately exaggerated in the Western ego's hysterical fear.[9]

The non-White woman is also a victim of misanthropic skepticism and the paradox of the colonial femininity: she is seen as sexually available from the start and exposed to the raping gaze of the White man. Her stereotypical features include the heightened sexuality, which in secular modernity acquired an additional pseudoscientific explanation, based on direct correlation between sexuality and the presumably low evolutionary status. The main function of the Black woman in colonial society, as seen by Europeans, consists in satisfying the sexual appetites and in reproduction. She is said to desire to be raped and hence deserves such an attitude as well as the consequent sufferings and further sexual harassments. At the same time, the defense of the White woman by the Western heterosexual society can hardly be regarded as real caring about her remaining an expression of the male rights of property, and maintaining of male honor and control. But in case of the Black woman, honor cannot be outraged or defended, because she is denied honor as such. In the eyes of the dominant culture men and women marked by ontological colonial difference, deserve to be punished as potential if not real actors and victims of violence. The artificial division into gender and sex, biology and culture, inherent in Western tradition, becomes particularly graphic. The White European woman has been always regarded as a normative manifestation of femininity in social and cultural senses, while the colonized women have not been simply below the Western ladies. They have never belonged to the sphere of gender remaining entirely in the realm of biological sex.

It is important to take into account the intersectionality model as described by K. Crenshaw. Although she concentrated mainly on African-American women's experience, her reflections are applicable to other multiply colonized women and have been recently revisited by the emerging decolonial feminism. Crenshaw insists that feminist theory and antiracial policy often remain blind to specific problems of non-White women connected with the intersection and merging in their every day experience of racial, gender, class, and sexual discrimination. This happens because these discourses are one-directional and one-dimensional, unable to accept the idea that discrimination of the non-White women does not come to just a simple sum of all of her discriminations on gender and racial terms, but is in itself a separate and complex kind of discrimination. The boundaries of sex discrimination are based by default on the experiences of White women, while the limits of race discrimination are defined against the experience of Black men. All the nuances of Black women discrimination which do not fit the narrow frames of these definitions are ignored by law, the society, and the scholars. They are crammed into the "but for" logic according to which there can be only one legitimate factor of discrimination, differentiating the individual from the norm and preventing from keeping the status quo in society. Besides, race and gender become important only if they are openly used to discriminate the victims, whereas the privileging interpretation of White skin or male sex is never regarded or even noticed as such (Crenshaw 1989, 151).

2.4. The Modern/Colonial Gender System and the Coloniality of Gender

The main decolonial gender theorist María Lugones attempts to connect women of color feminism with coloniality of power and comes to the idea of the modern/colonial gender system which permeates all human taxonomies with its dichotomous logic. She points out that coloniality of power as it was formulated by A. Quijano remains blind to the multiplicity and complexity of gender problematic in the colonial world. This is linked with his specific interpretation of gender—biological, strictly heterosexual, and patriarchal. Quijano claims that the struggle for the control of sexual access and its resources and products defines the sphere of gender and can be interpreted within the frame of coloniality and modernity. Lugones attempts to go further and regard the intersection of race, class, gender, and sexuality, to better understand the indifference of racialized males to the systematic violence against the non-European women. She states that none of the liberatory movements on a local or global level today can afford to ignore this question and stresses the problem of the lacking dialogue between scholars researching different spheres of discrimination. It is not merely a result of narrow specialization. The modern/colonial gender system is quite effective in subordinating of non-European people in all spheres of life, including the dissociation of possible links and solidarity in gender and other areas (Lugones 2007, 188–189).

Following the principle of intersectionality, Lugones offers a mixed analysis of the categories of race, class, gender, and sexuality, which allows including more people who otherwise remain excluded because they stand at the crossings of various aspects of discrimination. For Quijano gender remains a biological concept based on the norms of dimorphism, heterosexuality, and patriarchal division of power, in contrast with race which in his opinion should not be biologized. Lugones wants to stop biologizing gender as well, drawing attention to the constructedness of this concept. According to her, decoloniality is not possible without decolonization of gender and none of the aspects of decoloniality—from language and being to knowledge and nature—could ever be exhaustively interpreted without the gender dimension.

It would be incorrect to regard the modern colonial gender system as merely a circulation of power, organizing the private sphere, the access to sexuality and the control of sexuality and demography. This would lead to biologization of gender and neglecting of its epistemic, cognitive side, of knowledge instead of nature. Lugones points out that the colonial modernity brought a heterosexual dimorphous interpretation of gender and a hierarchical dichotomy of man/versus woman which became a sign of belonging to humanity (Lugones 2007, 190). Within the modern/colonial gender system only representatives of the Western world were strictly divided into gender categories. The racialized people and groups were not always defined through sexual dimorphism. The majority of non-Europeans turned into subhumans, based among other factors, on their lack of gender. From then on, only a civilized Western person could have the right to be called a man or a woman.

Naturalizing of sexual differences is yet another product of the modern use of science for the purpose of othering. Gender differentiation was introduced where it had not existed before. It created additional possibilities for discrimination, exploitation, and objectifying. The civilizing mission became a euphemism for the violence of the bodies populating the colonial difference. This violence could take the form of exploitation, fertility control, rape, or terror. It justified any measures applied to make the real women and men out of the colonial subhumans. And this metamorphosis in modernity's eyes had to do not with identity but with nature itself. Such a civilizing transformation, which was meant within the rhetoric of modernity to change the nature of the barbarian, completely justified the colonization of memory, of self-interpretation, of interpersonal relations, of seeing the world and the human, the cosmos and the earth. The modern/colonial gender system has had its sunny and darker side. The sunny side was not particularly rosy as the condition of the White women remained that of discrimination. As Lugones demonstrates, taking gender to the private sphere and limiting it by the control of sex and its resources and products is a cognitive result of modernity which understands race as signified by gender and gender as signified by race in one way for Europeans, and in a different way for the non-White/colonized people. In this sense race is no more mythic than gender. Both concepts are highly fictitious.

In twentieth-century Western feminism the links between class, gender, and heterosexuality as racialized concepts have not been openly discussed or even stated until recently. Feminists concentrated on the struggle against seeing women as physically and mentally weak, sexually passive and doomed to stay within the private sphere. No one stopped to think that these were just the characteristics of White middle class women and that biological sex could not unite all women. Those excluded from the universal women's history (which was in fact a European and American narrative and genealogy) were not merely below the Western ladies. They were interpreted as animals in the sense of their non-belonging to gender, the females lacking femininity (Lugones 2007, 202–203). The racialized gendered others were then turned from animals to various versions of "women," depending on what was needed for the Western capitalist modernity for the justification of the sexual and other use of these ex-animals. Even if they became the bad copies/caricatures of the White ladies in colonial societies, they could never reach the status of the White lady or her privilege.

Lugones argues that sexual violence and gender stereotyping have been written into the economic context of modernity/coloniality in such a way that they have mutually served as each other's cause and effect. This system defines the models of behavior of men and women as such, though in reality it is particular men and women that are implied. For the White middle class women it becomes necessary to observe sexual purity and passivity. Her mission lies in the reproduction of her class, the imperial and racial position of the White males. Yet this woman has been consistently excluded from the sphere of decision making or knowledge production. Heterosexualism permeates the racialized patriarchal control over the production, including the production of knowledge and the collective authority. For the White women this system is cruel in hidden forms while for non-White women it becomes openly violent reducing them to the status of animals, forcing them to work until they drop dead and making them to have sexual relations with the colonizers (Lugones 2007, 206).

In her later works Lugones continues conceptualizing gender problematic through the prism of modernity/coloniality and introduces the category of coloniality of gender (Lugones 2008). This brings us back to her earlier[10] article on traveling along other peoples' worlds with a loving perception (Lugones 2003). For Lugones the transformative mobility of Diaspora presupposes an oppositional element and only seems to be assimilative. She concentrates on the meaning of resistance seeing it as a complex process which begins with subjectification and results in active subjectivity. The scholar asks a question: how to understand the resister, the resisting and what is being resisted? The answer for her lies in coalitional opposition to coloniality of gender from the stance of colonial difference. This is the gist of decolonial feminism, its historical and bodily basis. By basis Lugones means not an abstract theoretical concept, but "the peopled ground on which one stands, that runs through one as an active subject" (Lugones 2008). Such an understanding of decolonial feminism is close to the position expressed by M. Jacqui Alexander in *Pedagogies of Crossing* (Alexander 2005). It is connected with the grass-roots level of women's movements and with colonial difference, linked with the historical and bodily conditions of intersubjectivity.

Lugones stresses how the typical modern concept of conquering the nature and transferring exploitation from the (European) man to nature has been reinterpreted through coloniality of gender. She draws the attention to the link between the shaping of the modern instrumental notion of nature, standing in the center of capitalist imaginary, and the essentially colonial invention of the modern concept of gender. This link generated an aesthetics and ethics of macabre which has marked the history of humanity since then. Its integral part has been dehumanization, constitutive of coloniality of being.

Gender is regarded by Lugones as a colonial concept not just because it was imposed onto the colonized spaces erasing the previous harmony of cosmologies functioning beyond the modern dichotomous logic. It is also crucial that coloniality of gender generated a specific counteraction, a virus of resistance on the part and in terms of colonial difference. Such oppositional subjectivity is reproduced again and again on the basis of half-erased history and is opposed to zombification of the colonized and their continuing forced assimilation to the man/woman dichotomy. Lugones wants to stress and maintain—and not take to a homogenous sameness—the multiplicity of readings of resistant subjectivity. It is important to take gender into account in the understanding of resistance and its sources, instead of reading gender categories into the texture that shapes the self in its relation to opposition. Then a different logic which organizes the social-in-resistance would open. If we see the social from the point of view of those cosmologies that constitute it, instead of starting from their gender reading, if we refuse to mechanically read gender into the social, we would be able to see the organization of the social in terms, demonstrating a deep conceptual incongruence in the process of imposing gender constructs onto our selves.

Lugones believes that it is necessary to regard the opposition to coloniality of gender concretely, always from inside, not on a personal or individual level, but on coalitional one, from the environment of those who reside in the cracks of the colonial difference where we, as scholars, are not necessarily insiders. Here she echoes her earlier concept of traveling in other people's worlds with love. In this case it means that we refuse to do the objectifying scholarly analysis and turn to an understanding of active subjectivity in our efforts to look for the fractured locus in resistance to coloniality of gender, at a coalitional starting point.

The scholar stresses that concrete selves react to coloniality differently. But their reaction and resistance reject the logic of the capital, and refuse to follow it. The fragmentary locus of movement allows maintaining creative ways of thinking and agency which are "antithetical to the logic of capital." This basis is constantly changing and moving, incarnating a weaving of various possibilities "from the fractured locus that constitutes a creative peopled recreation." Lugones believes that adaptation, rejection, adoption, ignoring, integrating are never just modes in isolation of resistance. They are always performed by an active and complex subject, complex because of its existence in the fractured locus of colonial difference. The fragmentary locus generates multiplicity and contradictoriness of both the coloniality of gender and the resisting responses from the subaltern selves. Without this multiplicity the picture would be simplified and distorted and the coloniality of gender would be seen as an accomplishment. At the other extreme there stands a frozen vision of oneself in relation to the precolonial sense of the social. For Lugones as a decolonial feminist it is important to constantly retain the sense of tension between dehumanization and "paralysis of coloniality of being" on the one hand, and the "creative activity of being," on the other (Lugones 2008).

Lugones argues that a persuasive affirming position does not lie in rethinking the relations with the oppressor from the position of the oppressed. Rather it lies in the development of the logic of difference and multiplicity as well as in creating coalitions in these points of difference. Multiplicity must be maintained at the point of reduction and not erased through hybridity which only masks the colonial difference. In this respect Lugones echoes the idea of opacity as articulated by E. Glissant (Glissant 1997, 190). Hybridity is localized in the complex work of the myriads of logics which are never synthesized, but rather transcend the boundaries and limitations. The logics of many colonial differences meet at the logic of oppression. For Lugones resistance from the space of fragmented loci is creative in its coalitional nature. This decolonial coalitional resistance creates an oppositional consciousness of social erotics, coming from differences and making our existence creative. This leads in the end to the negation of dichotomous logic. Differences are not regarded as dichotomies. But in opposition to this logic there stands the logic of power which always strives to take the multiplicity to unity (Lugones 2008).[11]

2.5. Decolonial Feminism and Islam

It may seem that decolonial feminism has an exclusively South American origin. In what follows I will try to show that many key elements of decolonial thinking and activism are to be found, among other places, in Muslim gender discourses. I refer to them also because in the next part I will focus on the Muslim ex- and present colonies of Russia whose women's identities intersect with other Muslim women's selves. Muslim gender activism and theorizing today make it at once similar and different from other non-Western feminist discourses. For example, Muslim gender activists share a frequent third world women's refusal to be called feminists, as they seldom practice radical separatism and a single minded fixation on gender. In Muslim case feminism often becomes an especially negatively marked product of the Western imperialist discourse. Again, similarly to a number of other non-Western gender theorists, Muslim women often accentuate coalitions, where multiple identities, including the religious ones, can coexist. They do not want to leave the system that in many ways marginalizes them. They prefer to fight with it from within.

According to Miriam Cooke (2000), a large number of Muslim women assert their identity as feminists yet they are marked by an interest in Islamic epistemology. Theorizing Muslim women's identity Cooke resorts to a multiple identity model also discussed by many Muslims (Cooke 2000, Ahmed 1992, Badran 1995). She interprets it positively, as a radical act of subversion and liberation. She also stresses that the combination of often conflicting religious, gender, political, and personal elements of Muslim women's identity allows them to build no less conflicting coalitions to protest against globalization, local nationalism, Islamism and patriarchal order. When contemporary Muslim women question Muslim epistemology they do it not as a radical rejection of Islam but as a way of its improvement.

Muslim women criticizing some aspects of Islamic history and hermeneutics struggle for the right to be equal citizens of a just society along with men. They can be called feminists yet in this case the concept of feminism describes merely an intention to look for justice and full citizenship for Muslim women. As L. Ahmed points out, men excluded women not just from the production of history and hermeneutics but also from religion. Hence the two Islams—one for men and the other for women. Women interpret Islam as a wide ethos and a way to understand and reflect on the meaning of human life. The official male Islam on the contrary seldom pays attention to what is important for women—justice, peace, compassion, humanity, kindness, truth, and so on (Ahmed 1992).

Muslim women's protest against the male hegemony in the production of Muslim knowledge is not new. But today this protest is contextualized in a specific local and global situation of neoliberal globalization and its aftermath and in the conditions of the opposition of the West and Islam. Muslim feminists need additional efforts to legitimize their contesting views and bring them back into the intellectual discourse. From the Muslim feminists' point of view women must have an equal access to the interpretation of Quran and other religious texts. In order to enter the public discourse and argue effectively, these women have to be simultaneously local in their commitments and global, a part of the Muslim community at large. They try to combine within themselves the values of Islam and transnational self-positioning.

Cooke argues for the specific features of Muslim identity which make it easier for Muslims to enter the transnational globalized world. Being at odds with a number of Western theorists Cooke sees Islam as a religion which supplies its practitioners with a symbolic capital for constructing transnational identities, unavailable for many new nations. Instead of the purity of blood here the purity of the Muslim nation is at work. As many new borders are being constantly drawn some Muslim communities may turn out to be politically divided between different states. Yet in a cultural and symbolic sense they remain connected with other inhabitants of the region because they have a common transnational imaginary which in this case is religious. Feeling at home in border zones which help their physical and cultural survival, they resemble migrants and refugees. However, Muslims have been accustomed to migration and deterritorialization for a long time. For them a flexible identity balancing between Diaspora and the national locality is not new. As R. Euben persuasively demonstrated (Euben 2006), cosmopolitanism and traveling were already a crucial part of Muslim identities much before modernity or globalization. Islam itself accentuates the real and symbolic journey and allows positioning oneself in the local and global sense, in the past and in the present.

Women can take part in this particular Muslim identity which is situated differently from the Western models as it allows them to be transnational and national at once, to stay historically contextualized, yet outside history. Their critique is multitargeted and based on strategic alliances, which also help to balance religious, local, class, ethnic, and national dimensions. Their contesting discourse is more immune to the Western or local co-optation and commercialization.

Muslim feminists effectively balance their collective and individual identities by intersecting and interacting with many different selves. Resorting to skillful strategic essentialism, they offer one of the most effective models of double or multiple critique. They juggle their selves on various levels of oppression—from transnational capital to unjust gender relations, from colonial legacy to objectification of women and their role of passive cultural emblems in Islamism. Rejecting simple victimization as a convenient yet epistemically miserable position, a growing number of Muslim feminists practice a very self-conscious multiple critique which allows them to deconstruct various institutions, systems and people who contribute to complex oppression (including a self-criticism at times).

One of the important differences between contemporary Muslim feminism and other variants of decolonial and third world gender discourses is that Muslim women are not necessarily involved in post-colonial struggle and dynamics. The racial and sexual elements of othering in their case turned out to be less pronounced than in case of African and Amerindian women. Due to the radical difference with the women's condition in slaveholding colonial societies and due to a transnational character of their religious and political commitments Muslim feminists are capable of going beyond multiple consciousness in the direction of multiple critique and building new forms of protest aimed against multiple marginalizing (Cooke 2000).

The term "Islamic feminist" is contradictory in itself. Yet this contradictoriness is used creatively by its practitioners. They form coalitions with certain attractive groups within Islam, yet they can also be in opposition to the patriarchal deviations from the "original" Islamic justice and equity. These women use the same weapons and strategies that have been used for a long time by men in anti-colonial struggle: they try to make the patriarchal order responsible for the ethical discourse which its own actions contradict. Multiple critique allows Muslim feminists to have an effective dialogue with several often conflicting audiences at once. Rejecting objectification of women and performing a knowledge decolonizing process Muslim gender discourse de-centers the previous teleology of modernity and questions the simplicity of the opposition of dynamic modernity/versus essentialist tradition.

A South African Muslim gender activist Sa'diyya Shaikh describes herself as one of the "progressive Muslims." The term is clearly derivative from the Western discourse. Yet the positioning of progressive Muslims can be defined as a double critique from the border between the Western discourse and the Islamic community and Muslim values. As a result both positions are criticized and destabilized. Discussing Muslim feminism we cannot avoid the dichotomy of Western modernity and its dark other—in this case, Islam. The self-consciousness of the modern Muslim thought (as well as African, Caribbean, or South American) has to go through a rejection, a dialogue, or an assimilation of Western modernity and Western philosophy. The thinkers of the Muslim world have been long reflecting on the problem of tradition and modernity trying to envision a possible future built on the elements of both Western modernity and Islam. This is a result of the intellectual asymmetry of modernity. Starting from the mid-nineteenth century the Muslim thought has been marked by a double awareness of its own deficiency both in relation to the great past (the Golden Age of Arabic philosophy) and in relation to Western modernity. Various ways out of this situation have inclined either to the idea of catching up with modernity or maintaining authenticity and homogenous stable identity.

Similarly, Muslim gender discourse cannot avoid taking a particular side in the opposition "Western modernity/versus Islamic tradition," or paying attention to the imperial-colonial configurations. Shaikh reflects that "current debates on feminism, gender, and women's rights in Islam are ideologically charged, since they are embedded in a history of larger civilizational polemics between the Islamic world and the West. Gender discourses in contemporary Islam are prefigured by a history of a political conflict between Islam and Christianity, the European colonial encounters in different parts of the Muslim world, and the nationalist responses by colonized peoples. The processes of globalization, in tandem with neo-colonial configurations of power, currently pervade not only the concrete economic and socio-political spheres of most parts of the world but also the areas of knowledge production" (Shaikh 2003, 148).

Shaikh draws the attention to the way gender categories are politicized in contemporary opposition of the West and Islam. She comments that both sides tend to stereotype and demonize each other. The West continues to practice xenophobia and Orientalism, presenting Islam as a cruel, medieval, and misogynist religion. In many Muslim countries gender questions have acquired a symbolic dimension going far beyond the problematic of injustice in relation to women and into the spheres of cultural, political, and national loyalty. This is a result of the besieged camp mentality that has been shaped in several Muslim countries today. It is a manifestation of a negative reaction to constant criticism and Western misinterpretations of Islam. As a result the Muslim other starts behaving at times precisely the way the Western islamophobe describes, becomes intolerant, and turns the Western weapon against the West accusing it of greediness, immoralism, and cruelty. Shaikh attempts to step out of this vicious circle and stop using the West/Islam dichotomy, she wants to problematize and destabilize both concepts, paying attention to the multiplicity of ethical models formulated in the West and in Islam and attempting to maintain a difficult position of being culturally Western but religiously Muslim. Gender sphere is particularly sensitive to these changes.

A tendency to generate mutual negative stereotypes in the West and in the Muslim world is expressed in feminism as well. For many Western feminists Islam remains a sexist religion. A Muslim scholar Azza Karam comments on the negative interpretation of Western feminism by some Muslims: "The term "feminism"…in postcolonial Arab Muslim societies is tainted, impure and heavily impregnated with stereotypes. Some of these stereotypes are that feminism basically stands for the enmity between men and women, as well as the call for immorality in the form of sexual promiscuity for women…some religious personalities…have associated feminism with colonialist strategies to undermine the indigenous social and religious culture" (Karam 1998, 5–6). Such a stereotyping of Western feminism leads to an excessive romantization of Islamic legacy by those Muslim scholars who interpret it as singularly empowering for women. This is also dangerous, as it does not allow the Muslim women to seriously and critically analyze the real cases of injustice and violation of women's rights.

Muslims defending the patriarchal law often see gender activists as agents of Western colonialism. These accusations are accepted because the memory of Western imperial missionary feminism is still alive. The civilizing mission in these spaces was targeted, among other things, at the liberation of the downtrodden local women. The persisting double standards divided the women of metropolis, where the patriarchal order worked against the interests of European women, from those of the colonies, where the colonizers could use the arguments of Western feminism in order to advance colonialism. The double standards remained intact even after the collapse of the colonial system and the emergence of the first feminist organizations. Since then Western feminism has become much more sensitive to the non-Western women's problems, to their right to be different and have their own discourse. Yet, according to Shaikh, Muslim women remain the least understandable or included into the global feminist process. They continue to be the opaque and dangerous others of Western feminists: "Such Western discourses on Muslim women are predicated on unquestioned cultural and social assumptions that do not allow for the engagement of specific Muslim societies in their own terms" (Shaikh 2003, 151). In other words, together with other non-Western women, Muslim women experience a dictate of Western gender normativity. Muslim women are also additionally ostracized as a result of today's negative attitude toward Islam.

Shaikh's second important point is her critique of the homogenous interpretation of all women as victims within the frame of Western feminist discourse. Under such an approach we ignore the specific material conditions and ideological frames generating the disempowering contexts of concrete groups of women. Instead of that, particular horrifying showcases are used to prove the generalized opinion of women's weakness as a group. The structure of social relations and the main social processes are simply ignored. Further on Shaikh demonstrates how the demonizing of Islam and the victimization of Muslim women are expressed in the Western misinterpretation of hijab. She distinguishes between the cases when hijab is used indeed as an instrument of oppression and control, and other meanings which the West prefers to ignore. The scholar demonstrates the multivalent meaning of hijab in various Muslim societies showing that it is contextually determined and far from having a fixed religious meaning. Modern working Muslim women often consciously choose hijab in order to assert their specific identity which combines the Muslim self with a number of values associated with career, education, professional self-realization erroneously seen in the West as exclusively Western. Within the changeable Muslim society hijab can carry a feminist and anti-capitalist meaning as well. Then the veiled women argue that hijab helps them to reject the patriarchal prioritization of women's sexual attractiveness. Besides, hijab provides resistance to Western consumerism and commodifcation of women. As Shaikh demonstrates, hijab really can liberate women allowing them to occupy the public spaces which would otherwise be problematic for them. In this case it acts as a catalyst of gender mobility and a neutralizer of public space (Shaikh 2003, 153), which is seen as patriarchal, though differently in the Muslim world and in the West. These overtones of hijab are often ignored by Western feminists who see hijab as an emblem of Muslim gender oppression. As a result a possibility of a dialogue with other aspects of religious tradition which could lead to emancipation of women is lost. Muslim women continue to be objectified as victims and their voices and ways of resistance and reexistence continue to be ignored.

Shaikh tries to find common points with third world feminism as similar in its spirit to Muslim gender activism. Both reject the homogenous unifying categories often used by Western feminists ("women of color," "third world women," "Muslim women," etc.). Both stress the multiplicity of the forms of othering and oppression at the crossing of various spheres of discrimination (race, religion, ethnicity, gender, class, sexual orientation, etc.) which have to be taken into account in any adequate analysis.

Shaikh attempts to define Muslim feminism. She argues for keeping the term even if some activists are against being called feminists. This would help place their practice into the global political context. It would also allow creating an appropriate vocabulary for the accumulation of ideas linked with critical consciousness in gender politics. At the same time the use of the term "feminism" is dangerous as it can lead to marginalization of local histories of non-Western women's resistance to patriarchal order. Muslim feminists have to always negotiate between a critique of sexism in the interpretation of Islam and patriarchal element in their own religious communities, and a critique of neocolonialist feminist discourse on Islam. Muslim women are capable of opposing both narratives and moving beyond their critique.

Here comes an interesting argument between Shaikh and Cooke who calls such an adaptation of various positions a "multiple critique." Cooke derives this concept from two sources—a double critique as formulated by a Tunisian writer and philosopher A. Khatibi (Khatibi 1990), and multiple consciousness as theorized by an African American sociologist D. King (King 1988). Khatibi describes the ways for the postcolonial subjects to develop their oppositional discourses targeted against both the local and the global enemies. He focuses on the ambiguity and the possibilities of its dialectic mobilizing. If we add gender to his double critique we can imagine a certain third position beyond binarity. Such a critique opens toward multiplicity and resolves the problem of mutual exclusion. Its sphere can easily contain religious fanatics and heretics, homophobes and women with other histories. King describes the multiple dangers for African American women who became invisible in contemporary oppositional politics and seen as mere victims even if they challenged various oppressing and excluding systems. Cooke argues that Muslim women in Arabic countries, in contrast with African slaves, were separated from those spaces which came to be occupied by Western colonizers, that these women were systematically excluded from the collective memory in their only prescribed role of the outsiders of colonial history. In a way the European colonizers in the Muslim world were made to respect the public/private life divide. Here women remained impenetrable for all newcomers and particularly for European men. Something similar happened in the Russian colonization of Central Asia.[12]

Shaikh agrees with Cooke's concept of multiple critique as it allows to conceptualize the dynamic and multilayered subjectivities of Muslim women in various contexts and to take into account that the position of the speaking subject is necessarily effected by the audience in front of which he/she speaks. Yet Shaikh departs from Cooke's interpretation when she questions her idea that the term "Islamic feminism invites us to consider what it means to have a difficult double commitment, on the one hand, to a faith position, and on the other hand to women's rights both inside the home and outside" (Shaikh 2003, 155). For Shaikh the idea of difficult double commitment implicitly carries an unchallenged notion that Islam and women's rights belong to completely different spheres or worlds and that Muslim women bring these realms strategically together in an act of radical subversion and as a part of postcolonial women's juggling of space and power. In Shaikh's view this contradicts the self-definition of many Muslim feminists, who see their feminism as growing organically and naturally out of their commitment to faith. She claims that their contestation of gender equality is more than just a result of postcolonial struggle for power.

Many Muslim women today become critics of the notions of male normativity in Muslim societies, and as believers, offer an alternative way of interpreting Muslim gender relations. There is a radical view according to which feminist agenda is an integral part of Islam corresponding to the basic Quranic appeal for justice. Modern Muslim feminists are interested in how Islam came under the influence of particular social contexts. They argue that the patriarchal interpretations are a result of an exclusively male nature of institutional Islam. Others stress the contradiction between patriarchy and egalitarianism yet speak for the prevalence of egalitarianism in Muslim spiritual and ethical ideals (Mernissi 1987).

A number of scholars stress religious and spiritual grounds of gender discourses arguing that egalitarianism is already intrinsic in Quran and the problem is its patriarchal misinterpretation. For Muslim women theologists the aim of feminism is precisely the restoration of the true understanding of Quran and the necessary inclusion of women into this process. In the contemporary Muslim world there is a whole tradition of women theologists who are trying to remove the male biases in the interpretation of holy texts. This stance is to be found in an Egyptian gender historian L. Ahmed's book *Women and Gender in Islam* tracing the historical emergence of gender discourses in Muslim societies and the development of patriarchal and egalitarian relations in various Muslim cultures through the centuries (Ahmed 1992).

In contrast with Western postmodernist feminism, Muslim gender discourses are seldom marked by fragmentation of identities. Instead they concentrate on gathering the multiple selves together under the larger commitment to Muslim identity, which gives them a key existential leitmotif. Their understanding of Islam can be highly individualized because there is no monolithic idea of Muslim identity which would be free of social, political, or cultural factors. Yet, the basis of faith, the existential relations with God and the world, and the five pillars of Islam can be found in the grounds of practically all experiences and notions of Muslim feminists. Possibly it is connected with the fact that religious identity in itself presupposes a certain degree of free choice. We cannot choose our sex, color of skin, or class. But we can, according to M. Faruqi (Faruqi 2000), choose our religion, our spiritual and ethical values. That is why Muslim identity, however widely interpreted, turns out to be more powerful than anything else, for Muslim women. Far from being silent victims, Muslim women do a lot for rethinking feminism. Their efforts include a more accurate and unbiased (self)representation of various complex groups of women. Such an approach allows us to link feminism with formulating Muslim women's participation in gender issues. Besides, it allows starting a meaningful dialogue and a horizontal camaraderie between Muslim women and women of other religions and cultures.

2.6. Decolonial and Post-socialist: Chinese Gender Discourses

A Genealogy of Chinese women liberation movement is a subject of a separate study. Here I would only try to point out a number of its elements that are concordant with decolonial feminism and also parallel the post-Soviet Caucasus and Central Asian gender discourses. The beginning of gender activism in China is usually associated with 1919 when the new culture movement together with the massive influence of Western modernization brought about a dichotomy of nationalism and the imported Western values. Chinese feminism had to negotiate the anti-imperialist and anti-feudal tendencies. Wang Zheng pointed out that after 1919 Chinese feminism functioned as a struggle between the two variants of liberal humanism. The first was socially progressive and based on regarding women as human beings different yet equal to men. The second was a masculinist philosophy in which men meant educated, modern males from the first world. And it was them that the Chinese revolutionaries had to follow. While women who attempted to imitate this type of liberal humanism, were forced, if they wanted to get equal rights with men, to mimic and finally, to simply become neutralized, "castrated" males, republican revolutionaries, and political transvestites. Wang called this the Mulan subjectivity in remembrance of the legendary woman warrior who replaced her sick father at the battlefield. However these feminists hardly had any access to decision making (Wang 1999). Yan Haiping (Yan Haiping 2006) claims that the Darwinist biopolitical association of weakness with femininity came to China together with Europeization in the early twentieth century. Little by little a specific category of "ruozhe" (weakness) came forward. It is essentially intersectional as it goes beyond gender and into other spheres of discrimination. Many Chinese women intellectuals in the twentieth century would not agree to be called feminists, as feminism fails to address those problems that they found important in their lives—the anti-colonial struggle, the multiple forms of resistance to global inequity, etc. (Yan Haiping 2006, 4).

Between 1949 and the 1980s the women's question in China was regarded as an important aspect of building socialism. The socialist state proclaimed and legitimized gender equality in political and social spheres. However as in the Soviet Union this often came to slogans and formal gestures, seldom going in the psychological or epistemic direction. Maoism in a way institutionalized the Mulan subjectivity. However, equality was reached by taking both sexes to the common denominator of the ideal sexless socialist worker. This mainly came to economics and not to changing the patriarchal models of female sexuality.

With the victory of Maoism the mission of the women's liberation was officially fulfilled and after that it was not allowed to criticize the conditions of Chinese women. As in the USSR this caused a decline of Chinese feminism. The formal rights imposed from above, created a false impression of well being. As in the ex–Soviet Union with the coming of the market economy the state refused women even its symbolic support and they quickly became the most vulnerable stratum. The 1980s brought such discourses as the necessity of opening China to the world. They were marked by an interest in Western modernization and cultural cosmopolitanism. Socialism (as feudalism before) became the new enemy of the disavowed past. The rhetoric of enlightenment, progressivism, individualism, humanism penetrated the revamped gender studies in China. But similarity with Western feminist agenda soon gave way to disappointment. In the 1990s Chinese gender activists became skeptical about Western feminism with its reductionist tendencies. Chinese gender activists saw this as a manifestation of universalism, imperialism and neocolonial regime of knowledge preventing them from autonomous thinking. Disappointment in Western discourses touched many other intellectual movements, which quickly noticed the catastrophic signs of Western cultural dominance and global capitalism. In contemporary Chinese feminism there are many trends—from pro-Western, to Maoist and radical border positions—attempting to build an alternative way and genealogy of Chinese gender movement.

Let us concentrate on the radical border positions that echo other ex-third world and ex-second world contesting gender discourses. Many Chinese gender activists today refuse to be called feminists. Yenna Wu argues that Chinese women are not attracted by the Western feminist slogan of sisterhood. It is weaker in its effect than the Chinese slogan of "unity is strength," which did not exclude men (Wu, 2005, 42). She points out a lack of understanding between Chinese and Western feminists who "appear to have had a missionary zeal to convert other women to their type of feminism, and to apply their own values and standards universally. That is why they were "angry" with Wang Anyi for not being a feminist, rather than communicating with her, listening to her explanations, and trying to understand an alternative point of view" (Wu 2005, 30).

Chinese gender activists are skeptical about Western efforts to impose a universal women's goal of struggling for equality and emancipation and the well known slogan "personal is political." In China, as in post-Socialist societies, this would not be attractive because the whole social field in these places, including the private and everyday spheres, was so completely politicized that a natural reaction of women is precisely an apolitical or depoliticized stance. In contrast with Western post-industrial society with its shrinking social and political sphere, where an individual of any gender desires to come back to politics, even if in peculiar forms, in China or the post-Soviet space, it is more natural to encounter the opposite wish to forget about politics and go back to conventional femininity. This causes the Western feminists' lack of understanding of the post-socialist women's tendency to resexualization.

One of the most interesting representatives of Diasporic Chinese gender studies in the United States, Shu-mei Shih reflects on this lack of understanding between Western feminists and Chinese gender activists in her well known text "Towards an Ethics of Transnational Encounters, or "When" does a "Chinese" Woman Become a "Feminist?" (Shih 2005). American feminists in Shu-mei Shih's rendering see difference either as absolute and immediately dismiss it as too difficult to understand, or as something that can be taken to sameness. This happens within the well known progressivist universalist model according to which the second and third world women stand at some earlier stage already overcome by the West. Consequently a Western feminist can dismiss their ideas and take her usual position of maternalistic condescending sermons. An other woman is regarded as either too different or too similar or both. Shu-mei Shih calls this an asymmetric cosmopolitanism, which means that Western scholars never have to learn anything about other cultures to be considered intellectual cosmopolitans, whereas representatives of the second and third world must buy their right to speak in the global dialogue by means of mastering the Western theories, languages, and notions. What Shu-mei Shih actually speaks about is the coloniality of knowledge.

The scholar makes a decolonial nuancing of difference, when she says that the problem is not that Western feminists do not understand what is difference or similarity. The problem is that they have the power to assign difference or similarity to non-Western women without trying to really learn something about them or fake an interest in them. What is at work here is the logic of selective recognition of the non-Western other by means of two familiar modes—Orientalism and modernist ideology. Shu-mei Shih sees Orientalism as an alibi for the lack of interest in comprehending the non-Western other in his or her own terms, reducing him/her to absolute difference and erasing the very possibility or necessity of understanding. Modernist ideology sees history in linear terms as moving from primitive to developed, and regards the other as similar to the West, interpreting him/her as the West's own past (Shih 2005, 5).

Echoing el Saadawi, Shu-mei Shih shows that efforts to criticize Orientalism or progressivism often come to nothing because they are aimed at questioning the fundamental discourses of modernity. This demonstrates a lack of willingness in the West to really understand or know the other. She is convinced that it is precisely the ignorance and not the difference that is the reason for the lack of understanding. Today Western intellectuals are aware of the possible accusations in Orientalism. This is why they delegated the task of imposing discursive universalism to Diasporic scholars. Their criticism is formulated within the Western discursive frames and uses the established paradigms and well known parameters. An artificial impression that there is nothing beyond the Western discourse is thus restated again. And this allows the West to continue playing its role of the only producer of knowledge. What is the role of the other in this scenario? She/he is first assigned a primitive temporality and then imbued with the mimetic desire to become similar to Western subject and catch up with the West.

Shu-mei Shih offers a short genealogy of Chinese gender movement in the twentieth century in order to question the fundamental grounds of Western feminism based on the "enchantment with modernity." Deconstructing the Western aberration of development and backwardness the scholar demonstrates that in socialist China women indeed had more rights than in the West in many areas. Consequently the fundamental grounds of Western feminism did not make any sense in China. This allows us to question the temporal logic imposed by Western feminism as universal. Within this logic Chinese women must be backward in comparison with Europeans. When they find out that the opposite is correct Western feminists become openly jealous, perplexed, and irritated. They cannot bring themselves to combine the two images of Chinese women—as free and equal and as silent manifestations of the ancient Orient.

Deconstruction of Western myths of Chinese gender history has been in the focus of attention of Li Xiaojiang—the first representative of the revamped gender studies in China after the 1980s. Shu-mei Shih traces her evolution from an almost Western feminism to its almost complete rejection. The scholar debunked both the simplified Western myth of Chinese women as forerunners of women's liberation movements around the world, and the myth of the double oppression of tradition and the antidemocratic state, invented by Western feminists. This is how Chinese women turned from the forerunners of global women's liberation movement into the backward sisters living in an underdeveloped country. Li accuses Western feminism in its inability to get rid of the epistemic limitations of stagism, leading to decontextualizing of Chinese women experience and to proliferation of such myths (Li 1996, 88–89).

In the 1990s Li attempted a double critique of Chinese gender liberation myth which was shared by Western feminists and the Chinese socialist state. It only seemed that after a short socialist deviation China came back to the teleology of liberal modernity and capitalist development. The trajectory of Li Xiaojiang and other Chinese women activists in the 1980–1990s demonstrates something more complex. When Western feminists started to criticize Chinese women's recoil from their previous gains and their refeminization, a writer Wang Anyi and later other Chinese intellectuals stepped forward to explain that it was an important agenda for Chinese women to regain their gender identities as they were forcefully liberated from gender under

Mao. She regarded difference as a key to the understanding of women's identity and her empowerment. In accordance with Western progressivist logic such a position was interpreted as corresponding to an earlier essentialist Western stage. But classifying Chinese women as advanced or backward did not really say much (Shih 2005, 12). It was needed in order to displace the need to pay attention to really substantive complexities of existential experience and history of Chinese women. Instead of that, the Western scholars continue to analyze and study (even if critically) the Western-produced constructs of Chinese women, not trying to see or hear any real people behind them. Such constructs remain the eternal objects of study and one cannot have a dialogue with them because it would question the narcissistic Western position of the producer of ideas and truths. It is within this logic that the co-optation of the local intellectuals into the Western knowledge takes place. In Shu-mei Shih's words, Li refuses to be ethnicized within the limits of Western feminism which usually contains ethnic differences "by way of multiculturalism...Her refusal of the imposition of feminism can be chiefly interpreted as the rejection of its mode of incorporation and containment, which swings between the two extreme poles of treating the non-Western intellectual as the recalcitrant ethnicity (the embodiment of absolute difference and the other) or the assimilated ethnic minority (as is the case for diasporic feminists)" (Shih 2005, 19).

Shu-mei Shih argues that translatability and opaqueness in transnational dialogue depends not on the essential differences but on automatic reactions of assigning difference and similarity by means of value-codings of time, space, ethnicity, and gendered subjectivity. The opacity is often created by the Western subject's ignorance of the historical situation of the other and the continuing asymmetry of discursive constructs. On the other hand the fluidity and complexity of transnational encounters escapes the production of disciplinary knowledge. For example, the postcolonial theory grew based on the experience of post-capitalist ex-colonies and does not fully take into account the Chinese situation or the post-socialist discourse in general. Western feminists tend to apply the double standard policy when they change their roles depending on the direction in which they preach. As Shu-mei Shih ironically points out, their feminist agenda at home is totally different from their agenda in transcultural situations (Shih 2005, 20).

The ethics of transnational encounters that Shu-mei Shih calls for, is neither assimilationist nor conflictual. Instead of that she stresses the importance of the ethics of transpositional and transvalue relationality and regards it as the only possibility for a dialogue today. In the end she comes back to Li Xiaojiang's principles which answer relational ethics, overcoming both affectation and recognition. Li stresses that the future gender studies in China should be based on transposition of gender and on the inclusion of men's perspectives and points of view. She argues that it is necessary to bring all the problems back to their original contexts and calls for the analysis of the simultaneous losses and gains in all ideologies and paradigms, in order to make them more multidimensional and contradictory. This could help avoid the main deficiencies of Western feminism such as monistic narrowness of scholarly perspectives and the political narrowness which moralizes in order to critique any non-feminist stance (Li 2001). The main goal of dialogue, necessary for various groups of disadvantaged is defined by Li Xiaojiang as precisely maintaining the differences (Li 1998, 52) which would allow deriving the powerful points from each other in order to tamp down the weaknesses.

Part II

Coloniality of Gender in the World of the Secondary Colonial Difference (Caucasus and Central Asia)

Chapter Three

Race/Body/Gender and Coloniality in the Russian/Soviet Empire and Its Colonies

3.1. Secondary Orientalism in the Janus-Faced Empire

I am not going to give a detailed descriptive history of gender discourses in Caucasus and Central Asia or present a report of a field study done in these regions. There are already enough works written on this problematic and in such a genre both in the West, in Russia and in the (ex)colonies themselves. Instead of that I am going to look at the main historical and contemporary intersections of gender, race, religion, and body in these locales through the lens of decolonial thinking, and address the conditions for the possible women's dialogue in Eurasian borderlands with other gendered and racialized others in the world.

Scholars tend to regard Caucasus and Central Asia within the frame of Orientalist discourses because in the imperial-colonial configuration of the Russian Empire Caucasus and Central Asia as decidedly non-Western spaces indeed played the part of the mythic Orient.[1] Any kind of Orientalism is a manifestation of a wider phenomenon of coloniality of knowledge. Nineteenth-century Orientalism included regarding the East and its people as an object of study marked with an absolute and inescapable otherness with reference to the European subject. In decolonial terms this is a manifestation of the Occidentalist hubris of the zero point, an epistemology that was retained in Orientalism as it changed Christianity to civilizing discourses as a rationale for discrimination and othering. It also stood in the center of Orientalist comparative measuring instrument to classify humanity in relation to its closeness to the human ideal—the white Christian heterosexual middle-class European male, and to sanctified modernity as opposed to archaic tradition as its dark double. Racial taxonomies that came to replace the former religious taxonomies transformed the purity of blood into the color of skin and into ethnic characteristics as a basis of othering. Primitive people took the place of infidels. In Western Orientalism the Orient was regarded within the racial and ethnic, rather than religious taxonomies.

It is important to see from the start the distortions in the Russian variant of Orientalism and the forms of resistance it has generated, linked with the fact that Russia has been a secondary empire of modernity marked with external imperial difference while its colonies have been of a doubly or multiply colonized status which has led to a specific multiplication of colonial identities and interaction vectors. Therefore one cannot uncritically apply Saidian theory to the geo-politics and body-politics of the Russian/Soviet Empire and its colonies. Here instead of Western Orientalism one finds secondary Orientalism which is the direct result of secondary Eurocentrism—an old and incurable Russian disease. Both of them reflect and distort the Western originals in the Russian cultural and mental space. Orientalist constructs in this case turn out not only more complex but also built on the principle of double mirror reflections, on copying of Western Orientalism with a slight deviation and necessarily, with a carefully hidden, often unconscious sensibility that Russia itself is a form of a mystic and mythic Orient for the West. As a result, both mirrors—the one turned in the direction of the colonies and the one tuned by Europe in the direction of Russia—appear to be distorting mirrors that create a specific unstable sensibility of Russian intellectuals, writers, and artists. It can be defined as balancing between the role of an object and that of the subject in the epistemic and existential sense.

For the quasi-Western subaltern Russian Empire it is the secondary Eurocentrism and the imperial (and not just the colonial) difference with the more successful capitalist empires of modernity (Great Britain, France, Germany) that comes forward in the shaping of subjectivity of both the colonizer and the colonized. On the global scale this imperial difference mutates into the colonial one, as Russia becomes an example of the external imperial difference, a country that allows the Western philosophy, knowledge, culture to colonize itself with no blood shed. The Russian imperial discourses of the nineteenth century demonstrate the Janus-faced nature of this empire that always felt itself a colony in the presence of the West and, at the same time, half heartedly played the part of the caricature "civilizer" in its non-European colonies.[2] Taking into account these specific conditions of Russia as an intellectually colonized empire with the stressed imperial difference, let us see how Orientalist discourses have been reshaped and transmuted in secular modernity as specific ways of representation and interpretation of the non-European colonies of Caucasus and Central Asia, which were used as replacements of the missing Orient and coded as such. Gender discourses were a crucial part of this problematic as they intermingled with race, class, and religion. Coloniality of power intersected with coloniality of being, of knowledge and of gender to shape a peculiar phenomenon of Russian and later Soviet modernity in its imperial and colonial forms.

In Europe, Orientalism was a product of secular modernity which nevertheless was a successor of Christian modernity in its xenophobic tendencies and a skillful legitimating of violence against the fallen out of history. Russia by contrast was infected by Orientalism as a manifestation of the secular modernity rhetoric, rather late. In Russia, Orientalism did not have a previous model to build its continuity upon and had to start from zero. What I mean is that before borrowing the Western Orientalism Russia did not have a developed tradition of othering the East. On the contrary, various links with the East, up to the blood links, were regarded quite favorably.

As Kalpana Sahni points out, "for centuries there existed regular cross-cultural assimilation and cross-cultural transference of dress, food, living habits and language between Russians, Turkic, Persian, Caucasian and Finno-Ugric" peoples (Sahni 1997, 5). Only the late seventeenth century brings together with the split into two cultures the first unclear beginnings of Orientalism which in the eighteenth century would result in the active orientalization of Russia by the West and also by the Russian aristocracy, who was brought up and transformed by Western teachers. As a result the history of Russia would be rewritten by mostly foreign scholars and repeated by their local intellectually dependent clones. While in the nineteenth century Russia would finally attempt to point the newly acquired Western weapon of Orientalism against its own internal colonial others.

Let us now look at the main elements of Russian secondary Orientalism and its subversion and manipulation in the colonies through the decolonial lens with an accent on gender and race as its constitutive parts. I am not attempting to recreate the imperial Orientalist discourse or simply restore the women's voices. This task has been already fulfilled—less successfully by Western (Northrop 2004, Kamp 2007) and more successfully by Diasporic (Sahni 1997, Khalid 1999, 2007) and also by a few local scholars (Tokhtakhodzhayeva 1996, 1999, 2001). What I would like to do instead is to conceptualize their mostly empirical findings and see what is the place of

Caucasus and Central Asian gendered and racialized others within the frame of global decolonial discourse. The most interesting here would be a particular impulse of gender tricksterism as a way of transcending the limitations of colonialist, orientalist, ideological, cultural, religious, ethnic, and sexual nature, and a way of acting beyond and around the dominant power structures, weakening them from a particular gendered exteriority. Therefore a specific attention will be paid to the models of transcultural and transvalue contestation of border-dwellers, avoiding the black-and-white divisions into the paranjee versus the miniskirt and opting for mediation, an ironic play on and a conscious deconstruction of Orientalist stereotypes and a movement towards a positive self-identification.

The inseparable connection between race, class, gender and sexuality in the construction of modern imperial and colonial discourses remains intact in the case of Russia and its colonies, though it acquires a number of specific features, changing at various stages of Russian and Soviet expansion from romantic Orientalism, through quasi-scientific positivist racism to commodity racism and to Soviet pseudo-internationalism with its underside of transmuted racism and finally, to the post-Soviet revenge of zoological racist discourses. Any attempt to analyze gender-racial-class intersectionality in Russia and its colonies shows that coloniality of power is wider than capitalism and cannot be taken to economy. Although in the Western world it is closely linked to and starts from capitalism, in the case of Russia coloniality of power is borrowed in secular modernity as an already established and naturalized ideological and cognitive system, with racism at its core, which has never been properly conceptualized by the Russian minds. Racial discourses were unconsciously borrowed from the West together with the whole package of the rhetoric of modernity, finding their way into the Russian scholarly, scientific, literary, intellectual discourses and quickly generating violence, humiliation and in some cases, like in Caucasus, genocide.

The ethics of war played an important part in the annexation of Caucasus and Central Asia, yet it was not linked directly with race as a manifestation of the closeness to violence and murder, but rather with specifically interpreted and essentialized ethnicity and a more and more racialized religion (Islam) which came to replace the racial discourses in Russia and its colonial spaces. Here the Russians were far from being original but the configuration itself was different, say, from the Muslim Arabic colonies of the West due to a different nature and role of Islam in Central Asia and particularly in Caucasus, where Islam was a relatively new and hybridized religion, while remnants of earlier Christianity were not a result of Russian colonization but rather an old Byzantine influence. Hence there was no direct connection between colonization and Christianization. The aboriginal polytheistic religions and cosmologies continued to be influential, while Islam was incorporated into the local cosmology in a similar way as it happened with Amerindians a few centuries before. Instead of the linear scheme, according to which the aboriginal religion was replaced by Christianity, first forcefully imposed and later incorporated into the local cosmologies, in Central Asia it was Islam that was first overlaid onto the local religious systems and in Caucasus it was Christianity in its Greek form which was partially replaced with Islam much later and often parallel to Russian colonization. The latter was relatively secular as religion was translated into ethnicity and the ethics of war had a civilizing and modernizing and not an openly religious justification.

Misanthropic skepticism played an important part in the colonization of Central Asia and Caucasus, as secondary racism here mixed with Orthodox Christian othering of even the same, taking it to a subhuman status. The Russian Empire can be defined as theocratic, at least in its intentions, if not in reality. One of its manifestations was providentialism which added specific shades to Russian xenophobia. Within this frame the other was seen as hostile to the great theocratic project. Territorial expansionism has been motivated primarily not in strategic or military or much less economic terms, but in terms of rather aggressive Russian Orthodox universalist ideal of a particular spirituality, destined to take over the whole humanity, of the specific universalist Russian Orthodox vision. In F. Dostoyevsky's words, written in 1877, "Europe is almost as dear to us as Russia, in Europe there resides the whole Japheth race, and our goal is to unite all the nations of this race and even further, to Sem and Ham" (Dostoyevsky 2002, 161). As a modern Russian philosopher A. Davydov pointed out, "taken from Byzantine tradition and linked with the Russian authoritarian collectivist ideal of 'sobornost,' monotheism created in Russia a different religious and moral basis of culture—a communitarian religion with its special kind of anthropology which did not correspond to the New Testament and could be summarized in the formula: 'I am a worm, not a man'" (Davydov 1999, 31).

Intersectionality then was more complex and multilayered in Russia and its colonies from the start than it was the case in the New World. One of the reasons was that the economic exploitation was not directly linked with race in the colonization of Caucasus and Central Asia. The devious ingenuity of Western modernity consisted among other things in making a perfect move—linking directly the economic exploitation with racial discrimination and presenting it as natural. The first (Pre-Soviet) stages of Russian colonization were not marked by this element even if later it gradually crawled into the socialist division of labor and the logic of Soviet modernity.[3]

As mentioned above, in early European colonialism the colonizers did not always apply gender dimorphism to the interpretation of the colonized (Lugones 2007) while secular modernity brought with it an imposition and a strict policing of gender binarity of the colonized and their education into bad copies of European gender system. Both Caucasus and Central Asia were annexed during secular modernity. Therefore the "pornotropics" discourse as defined by Ann McClintock (McClintock 1995) did not work in this case although the cannibalistic imagery was to be found in the earlier colonization of Siberia and the Far East—the Russian variants of the New World.

Caucasus was colonized during the Orientalist stage of coloniality, Turkistan was annexed in the positivist stage, both of which were marked rhetorically with a less radical othering. However this did not prevent the empire from taking humanity away from the colonized, by using cultural (instead of natural) arguments. Similarly to European colonialism in the New World condemning transgender and other-than-gender Amerindian identities, such as *berdache, alyha, hwame,* the British misinterpreting of the Hindu Indian *hijras* or the Polynesian *Mahu* as eunuchs or "sodomites," in case of Russian colonialism gender dimorphism of the European and, by association, Russian type was automatically imposed onto the colonized spaces. As a result, all transsexual and transgender forms existing in these societies before colonization were condemned, ridiculed and eventually destroyed by Russians/Soviets. This is what happened to the transsexual tradition of *Bacha* (adolescent boy) cult in Central Asia which could take both male and more rarely female forms. Its presumable homosexual overtones infuriated the hypocritical colonial administration and were used as a justification for its racist demonization of Central Asian customs and morality.

Caucasus was the first of the conquered territories which joined the Russian imperial cultural imaginary in the role of the Orient. Yet from the start its interpretation combined the civilizing Orientalist mission with the earlier colonialist discourses on Amerindians which allowed the Russians to add to their self-proclaimed image of the "pioneers of the South" and justify their genocidal treatment of indigenous people. Speaking to an American, a Russian prince Kochubei, a Tatar by origin, would say: "These Circassians are just like your American Indians—as untamable and uncivilized, and, owing to their natural energy of character, extermination only would keep them quiet" (Broxup 1992, 80). The colonization of Caucasus coincided with and contributed to the proliferation of Orientalist discourses among the Russian intelligentsia. According to Ronald Grigor Suny, in "perception of the Asian "other," Russians conceptualized ideas of themselves...Emotional intensity and primitive poetry mixed with macho violence. For some, the civilizing mission of Russia in the South and East was paramount, for others...adventure and a "license to kill" were what they sought" (Suny 2001, 46).

The very encoding of Caucasus as part of the prototypal Orient— biologically inferior, culturally backward and forever fixed and fallen out of history signalizes a deep interiorization of the borrowed European Orientalist clichés. The latter were often overtly libidinous. Cruelty and eroticism as the main signifiers of the colonized body— the desire to possess and to destroy—were clearly present in Russia as well. But if in the Western mind it has been often depicted in terms of submissive feminine Orient dominated and inseminated by the European colonizer, in the Russian version of early romantic Orientalism this model was impossible, because of the inferiority complex vis-à-vis Europe, which was partially compensated by the caricature secondary Orientalism in Russia's colonies. It was also connected with the general orientalizing of the Russians themselves by the West. Thus, lord Curzon called the colonization of Central Asia by Russia, which created a constant anxiety in Britain's imperial ideologues, "an annexation of Asiatics by Asiatics" (Curzon 1967, 392) to draw a clear line between the Western style colonialism and the Russian mimicking one. Typical Western descriptions of the Russian or wider, Slavic character mostly saw it as inferior to European, often feminine, soft and submissive. Later it also became firmly ahistorical. The imperial difference which Russia was marked with generated its secondary status in European eyes and hence, an open or hidden orientalization.

Within this complex and contradictory configuration the Russian orientalist discourses could not be simple or straightforward as they were based on the interplay of the colonial and imperial difference. The Western image of Russia as the Janus-faced combination of Asiatic and Germanic characteristics, where the aggressive despotic demonic elements of the Orient dominated over the exotic and erotic ones, was further on interiorized and reinterpreted in Russia's own intellectual tradition, particularly in religious philosophy. If in Europe Orientalism was a rather late appearing tool for the positive self-semiotization as opposed to the fallen out of time, irrational, devious Orient, in Russia the configuration was different. A representative of the Russian elite clearly coded himself/herself as a European, albeit a second-rate one. Here they were assisted by an army of foreigners from Adam Olearius to Marquis de Custine, who resided in Russia in the capacity of the champions of modernity and the bearers of the monopoly of knowledge and education, projecting onto the Russians, the racial epistemic taxonomies as a basis of Orientalism.

Even the presumably progressive Russian thinkers of the nineteenth century such as V. Belynsky, N. Dobroljubov, N. Chernyshevsky, A. Hertzen, demonstrated what can be called a darker side of Russian democratic liberalism and socialism. It is racism and Eurocentrism marked by simplified social Darwinism and Hegelian philosophy of history, in the interpretation of the orientalized others from Eurasian borderlands. One of the recurrent motifs was the comparison of the colonized peoples with animals, thus reducing them to the sphere of *anthropos* (Hertzen 1957, 526).

Caucasus as an uncomfortable, relatively small space covered with steep and high mountains and populated with proud and skillful warriors was far from the Orientalist tale drawn in Europe and imported into Russia, based on the idea of the Orient as a manifestation of feminine penetrability and supine malleability. However, the stereotype of the female nature of the colonized space required to edit the nonmatching reality on the way. So Georgia was chosen by the Russian elites to represent the feminine which is expressed in Russian romantic poetry. Yet, this was a special kind of femininity—a sensuous but dangerous one, always capable of murder. Therefore "she" was in need of Russian disciplining for her own benefit.

Secondary Eurocentrism that poisoned the sweet flavor of annexations for Russia was responsible for the fact that even in the relatively "favorable" years of Russian imperialism its ideologues felt that the Orient that the Russian Empire was getting through its colonizing efforts was somehow second-rate, not like the bright and exotic one of Europe. The Orient in the Russian interpretation of the late nineteenth and early twentieth century somehow redoubled and there were also two possible ways of its interpretation. The first consisted in turning to the real (European) Orient instead of paying attention to the second-rate Russian Asia. Fascination with the Orient and the primitivist and exoticist tendencies in the early twentieth-century Russian literature and art were expressed not only in the quest for their own Asiatic roots (often imagined and stylized), in a limited attention to Caucasus and particularly Turkistan as Russia's secondary Orient, but also in turning to the real (first-rate European) Orient, such as India, China, Egypt, Muslim Africa. This tendency can be illustrated by the works of the master of Russian *akmeism* Nikolay Gumilyev. Sometimes this alien non-Russian Orient was recoded differently. The second type of Orientalism consisted in editing Russia's own Orient on the way and making it look more like the Western Orientalist stereotype. The only way to do it for Russians was to cling even more to the false European identity which was precisely what they did, compensating their inferiority, both with respect to Europe and the newly acquired colonies with an exaggerated assertion of Europeism, Whiteness, civilizing and *Kulturtrager* discourses.

3.2. The Romantic Orientalist Stage

The double nature of Russian Orientalism was clearly expressed as early as in Romanticism based on a contradictory mixture of copied Western models and the necessity of corresponding to the Russian imperial rule of co-optation the intellectuals and making them serve the empire in the fear of repressions. Hence emerge the schizophrenic tendencies of Russian romantics in the interpretation of Caucasus and Turkistan. Romantization of topos went in accordance with the Western logic of colonization, when the territory was regarded separately from its inhabitants. The latter are demonized or exoticized and classified as fallen out of modernity. Their way of life and system of values can be interesting for the artistic colonizer (a poet, a painter, or a writer) as a curious document of the past which can be used as a source of theatrical change of clothes and playing the other. For instance the Russian officers were partial to Circassian dress and armaments and imitated the Caucasus caracole, continuing to dehumanize the contemporary Circassians.

One of the interesting examples was the famous Russian poet Alexander Pushkin who in his *Journey to Erzurum* demonstrates a sensibility of the "Russian Frenchman" as opposed to "Asiatic" Turks and goes on to describe a typical orientalist experience copied mostly from the Western sources—from the exotic baths to the necessary trip to harem (Pushkin 1934). His pronounced Eurocentrism is particularly amusing if we remember Pushkin's own mixed racial origins (Pushkin 1934, 766). In Pushkin's case race played an important role not in the sense of the purity of blood or the color of skin, but as a set of European cultural, ideological, and epistemic categories. As it was a borrowed discourse its logic was distorted from the start and based on associating the wrong ethnicity, religion, or culture with often imagined improper physical characteristics. Russia interpreted race post-factum as many other European discourses but in the end it used race to reestablish and confirm its own quite dubious racial status within the global configuration.

When Pushkin wrote his poem "To a Kalmyk Woman" he defined her negatively, similarly to William Shakespeare in his sonnet 130, which was based on ridiculing the ideal of feminine beauty of the time. In Pushkin's case it is the racially marked juxtaposition based on the cultural training that teaches the eye not only how but also what to see, as R. Wiegman points out in her discussion of the economies of visibility (Wiegman 1995, 22). The Kalmyk woman is pictured as an inferior, uncultured, but sexually attractive (if only for half an hour) creature who does not speak French, does not read Shakespeare, does not dance European dances or copy English manners. She is defined entirely within the racial stereotype: her eyes are predictably narrow, her nose is flat, her forehead is wide, and her beauty is savage.

However, the reality of the Russian conquest of the non-European spaces often resisted this borrowed racial matrix, even if the Russian mind was zombified by the Western principles of human classification and was automatically looking for ready-made signs of bodily difference that signified a more fundamental divide. That was why in 1837 a lieutenant N. Simanovsky commented on the surprising whiteness of the captured Cherkess princess in his personal diary: "After the restaurant I dropped by to look at the captured Cherkess. Among them there was a princess, quite attractive and—what was most strange—quite White" (Simanovsky 1999). Since in his reference system she belonged to the "savages" she had to be non-White. A similar attitude we find in the relatively rare women's sources where the Russian noble women were trying to play the role of the European ladies in their condescending attitude to the Caucasus gendered others.[4]

As early as the 1830s the Russian Empire had already fashioned a strict racial hierarchy which often clashed with religious and linguistic markers of identity. As Azade-Ayse Rorlich points out, "definitions and practices of citizenship varied in the vast lands of a multiracial empire. This should come as no surprise. What is surprising is the resilience of the racial marker of identity as a boundary of otherness that, at times, could not be obliterated even by religious otherness. When in 1833 Russian imperial legislators divided the population of the empire into *prirodnye obyvateli* (natural inhabitants) and *inorodtsy* (those born others), they cast a disjunctive representation of the imperial social self whereby the concept of *inorodets* as a notion of identity based on negation of ancestral racial affinity with the Russians, was at once exclusive and judgmental...Even for Russian Christian religious scholars and missionaries, race superseded religion as the defining identity marker of non-Russians" (Rorlich 2004, 40).

One finds traces of mutant Orientalist discourses in the majority of Russian romantic works—from A. Pushkin, M. Lermontov, partly L. Tolstoy to erotic orientalist tales of A. Bestuzhev-Marlinsky, the author of the Caucasus novelettes "Mulla-Nur" and "Amalat-bek" and even to Lermontov's killer N. Martynov's long poem "Guasha" where the interpretation of the colonized women went in accordance with Eurocentric exoticist stereotypes. Here we find typical notions of extremely early puberty, heightened sexuality and relative social freedom, and unscrupulousness of the local young girls which helped justify the pedophilic inclinations of the Russian officers. The Caucasus "savage" women were compared to animals and denied any rationality, spirituality, and ultimately, humanity. While the voices of the orientalized themselves then and now remained largely undocumented or neglected, because for the Russian colonizers, as well as for their Western counterparts, subjectivity as such remained White, to paraphrase F. Fanon (Fanon 1967, 109–110).

In spite of the lacking porno-tropic tradition, in the wider Russian cultural imaginary sexual Orientalism obviously flourished as early as the second half of the nineteenth century, albeit undocumented. Indirect traces of these notions can be found in the well known literary sources, for example, in Leo Tolstoy's *Caucasus Captive* where the main character comes to Caucasus with the popular and common dream of acquiring a beautiful Cherkess slave. Yet there was an important difference with European porno-tropics. McClintock stresses the importance of Renaissance and Enlightenment in the genealogy of porno-tropics when the idea of dominance in the sphere of knowledge production came into the center of the erotic experience of appropriating the new territories. Coming to know the new and unknown world meant its ordering by means of taking out the unruly erotic element and, at the same time, the possibility of setting free the European suppressed impulses and erotic drives. Then knowledge became a "metaphysics of gender violence and not an acknowledgement of cultural difference" (McClintock 1995, 23). After the Enlightenment this logic was further sanctioned by the established sacred private property and egology. The world became feminized again and crucified for the male investigation and conquest—this time in order to bring all its elements together in a new way, and make them serve the interest of the imperial male power. Now the male dominance acquired the form of knowledge expansion as predominantly natural and strict sciences. Man became the master of nature and woman became its part, particularly a non-White woman.

In Russia the acquisition of new lands took place differently and the contrast between the motherland (metropolis) and the colony (an eroticized space of internal porno-tropics) was less pronounced. One of the reasons for that was the geography of the conquest—there was no ocean between the metropolis and the colonies as an important marker dividing the same from the other. In Russian literary romanticism the dominant exoticist and ornamental stylized element favored the description of clothes over the strange bodies, although the schizophrenic duality was expressed in a sharp contrast between the artistic works and the documentary sources, for example, between the romantic poetry and the letters and diaries of the Russian romantics conquering the Orient. A good example is M. Lermontov's novelette "Bela" from the *Hero of our Time* where the objectification of Bela by Pechorin is balanced with Maxim Maximych's strive to see her as a human being, not an exotic sexual beast.[5]

Russian nineteenth-century fiction and fine arts were much less erotic than European tradition in the depiction of alien spaces. Even the most sensuous of Russian romantic writers Bestuzhev-Marlinsky was more clichéd in his Orientalist love tales than openly erotic. Consider, for instance, this almost ethnographic portrait of the Caucasus beauty: "Her braids, black as tar, were covering her entire face; but every once in a while they were parting on her open bosom which was restrained by a jealous chain with golden pendants and coins; her breasts were still clearly seen through the opening of her pink taffeta shirt and were striving to cut through the brocade of her top dress, that embraced fiercely her slender waist as a lover would do..." (Bestuzhev-Marlinsky 1958, 340).[6]

A similar logic is to be found in fine arts. Take, for example, Orest Kiprensky's 1813 portrait of the Kalmyk woman Bayausta which in all its Orientalist fairytale overtones, almost completely lacks a sexual element, or the 1873 Vassily Vereshchagin's ethnographic depiction of a veiled Uzbek woman as a walking manifestation of Oriental impenetrability. None of the traditional sexual irritants normally stressed by European female attire were present in the dress of Central Asian woman thus making her a non-woman in European or Russian eyes. By contrast, much more overtly erotic Orientalist features mark the portrait of the Cherkess exile to the Ottoman sultanate by a famous French Orientalist Jean-Leon Gerome who was Vereshchagin's teacher if only for a short time.

Vereshchagin's art clearly demonstrates the difference between Western and Russian second-rate Orientalism. A professional soldier and globe-trotter, he was attracted to wars (most of which were imperial wars for the new territories) if not obsessed with them, as his biographers reveal (Lebedev and Solodovnikov 1987, Brower 1993). His enchantment with cruel, bloody, and sensational subjects, betrays a serious psychological complex which could be connected with the general obsession with the demonic other, which Vereshchagin saw as cruel and impenetrable, not exotic or noble, as was often the case with Western European art of the time. This could be why he never liked to be the pupil of Jean-Leon Gerome. Vereshchagin's decision to go to Europe was prompted by the typical Russian ambivalence between the veneration for and annoyance with Europe. He would work fifteen hours a day striving to catch up and leave behind the European teachers developing, his own idea of the Orient which did not match the French school.

A son of a provincial small landowner from Cherepovets, Vereshchagin was longing for a European acknowledgement. In order for that to happen it was necessary for his paintings to start speaking in the language familiar to Europe, that of Orientalism, both military and ethnographic. He wanted to acquaint the West with other variants of the Orient yet unknown and mysterious. Indirectly Vereshchagin was trying to take a higher place in the human and imperial hierarchy—to turn from the orientalized Russian into an almost European, with his own no less exotic Orient. The other thus helped the positive self-identification of the artist and the translation of the "savage" Russian Orient into the language of Western Orientalism. This is what Vereshchagin accomplished in 1873 when he organized an exhibition of his Turkistan *Barbarians* series at the Crystal Palace in London.

His position was a typical expression of the imperial mythology gone wild as well as an anti-imperialistic criticism from within. He was a conscientious colonialist, in A. Memmi's terms (Memmi 1991) desperately striving and failing to grasp both view points, both sides. However, the Russian Empire was not ready to accept even such lame criticism based on the poorly hidden inclination to sensational and sadistic. It wanted to see itself in exclusively heroic terms and to depict its enemies—simply and straightforwardly—as savages who must be exterminated. Vereshchagin's deviation from the official imperial position was not that he humanized his Orient. On the contrary, its inhabitants remained barbarous and savage. The deviation was only that the Russian army and particularly its top officials were not presented in a heroic way as it was expected. Instead of that the Russian soldier, the cannon fodder of imperial wars, who was regarded as sub-human and expandable life, became the real hero of Vereshchagin's works. His deheroization of the military face of Russia and the excessive demonization of the enemy who seemed impervious to Russian military endeavors—looked unpatriotic in the context of hysterical discourses of Russian imperialism. Yet Vereshchagin suffered from the typical imperial disease of double standards. On the one hand, he openly condemned the colonizing wars, on the other hand, he took an active part in several of them always coding the Russian invasion as a civilizing, modernizing, and sometimes liberating mission.

In case of his ethnographic paintings, the characters were seldom presented as people. They remained frozen dehumanized images of the Orient—demonic, impenetrable, sinister, feudal, religiously fanatic, retarded, pedophiliac, homosexual, and addicted to drugs. The way of life and the every day exist in these canvases separately from the people, as if it were a museum exhibit, a theatrical props fallen out of time and not a part of the real life of his contemporaries. Otherwise there would have been a danger of making his characters too human. For this reason Vereshchagin is constantly in quest of dramatic events, sensational scenes, and walking stereotypes—always seeing what his eyes were trained to see yet claiming to depict the typical.

In contrast with Gerome and other Western orientalists who were fascinated with the erotic, Vereshchagin seldom depicted the sexual side of Asian exoticism. In his Turkistan series we find *Beggars in Samarkand, Politicians in the Opium Shop, Dervishes in Holiday Clothes, Dervishes Begging in Chorus, Entrance to Samarkand's Zindan (prison)*, etc. Among them the modest *Uzbek Woman in Tashkent Street* seems to be the least sensational and sinister. The sexual connotations were invariably presented in the form of indulgence in painful and forbidden details as it happened in *Selling of a Slave-Child* and in less known canvases depicting the *bacha* dancers, some of which were later destroyed.

3.3. The Paradox of Colonial Masculinity and Femininity and the Vectors of Colonial Gender Suppression

This brings us to the ways the paradox of colonial femininity and masculinity discussed in part I in relation to Western modernity was altered in the subaltern Russian Empire and its colonial spaces. The Western paradox of colonial femininity and masculinity based on blaming the colonial others for mutually exclusive vices, intensifying their negative self-identification, has been thoroughly discussed by many scholars (Alexander and Mohanty 1997, Espiritu 1997, Sandoval 2000). In this case racialization worked through gender, and colonization itself came to be symbolized as an act of violence. However this is typical of the confident empires with a positive masculine identity while Russia was far from being confident. The gap between the Orientalist European fantasy and the reality of Caucasus and Turkistan conquest was too obvious and based on secondary Orientalist ideologies, always poisoning any victory for Russia. The same way as the officers of the Russian army complained that the war in Caucasus was not interesting or educational enough as a war in Europe could be, when it referred to the Orient they constructed out of Caucasus and later, of Central Asia, it also turned out to be inferior: the women were not beautiful, submissive, and exotic enough, the luxury was lacking, the entertainments and pleasures were not refined as the ones in the European image of the Orient (Simanovsky 1999).

The situation in Caucasus was different from Central Asia due to a different role of Islam. The women in Central Asia were well protected by Muslim and local ethnic-cultural custom and could not possibly act in the role of the non-White women in the European colonial imaginary, although the Caucasus women played for a while a part of the exotic sexual slaves (objects of rape) and even profitable commodity, both for the local slave-dealers and for the Russian and even Soviet army. Thus, the tactic of general Yermolov's punitive expeditions as a result of which whole villages were burnt and their inhabitants massacred, had a clear sexual element (Broxup 1992, Gorky 2008).

In the case of the Russian Empire sexual violence as a form of colonization was a poorly documented story, but what the sparse sources allow us to see is how closely the evolution of sexual violence rationale in various periods, was linked to the changes in the interpretation of racism. In the case of Caucasus we encounter the typical poetics of sexual adventures, yet there is no clearly expressed racist squeamishness, no physiological disgust which would develop in the late nineteenth century in the time of the proliferation of racial taxonomies and scientific racism. Here often the official imperial racism that did not see the colonized and particularly women as people, and did not allow for the possibility of a Russian colonist male's interest in local women, clashed against a more nuanced position of the clergy, which stressed that instead of the swaggering assuredness in the impossibility of a marriage between a Russian orthodox Christian and a downtrodden illiterate local woman, the empire needs to think of a law that would ban and regulate the racial and religious mixing (Rorlich 2004, 43). In the Russian Orientalist phase the exotic appropriation, often in the form of violence, clashed against the open ethics of war.

The local men could hardly be interpreted within the Orientalist docile stereotype and any comparison with them was not to the advantage of the much more tepid Russian masculinity. The erotic element of Russian imperialism was expressed in the male form and extrapolated into the Russian male anxiety and fear of the Caucasus machismo in war and in sex (Sahni 1997, 33–69; Tekuyeva 2006). Feminization of aboriginal males was never widely used in the colonialist interpretation of Caucasus and hard to find in Central Asia either with an exception of transsexual cases. In Russian colonization only one side of the colonial gender paradox was at work—that of the association of the local men with violence. As in the case of the British in India that presented the widow burning as an example of Hindu barbarism and savagery, gender and sexual problematic were used by the Russian imperial rhetoric in its justification of colonization coded as emancipation of the local women from the horrible male dictate. Russia was then presented as an enlightened and modern empire.

The post-Soviet society retains the stereotype of the Caucasus male which today is used as the basis of the standard racist accusations of his desire to possess a Russian woman. But during the colonization this would be unthinkable because they never encountered each other in reality. In the nineteenth-century Russian society the upper class women seldom found themselves in "hot Siberia" as Caucasus used to be called. However starting from the second half of the nineteenth century the Russian army conquering Caucasus began to be accompanied by prostitutes who did not belong to Caucasus ethnicities.[7] The encounters of local men and upper-class Russian women vacationing in Caucasus spa resorts were relatively rare, and judging by indirect mentioning in letters, diaries and fiction of the time women diligently faked a fear of the mountaineers. A classical illustration is Lermontov's princess Mary from *The Hero of our Time* who sees Pechorin dressed in a Cherkess attire, takes him for a "savage," assumes that he wants to kidnap her until he speaks French demonstrating his belonging to the civilized world. However there is evidence that the more emancipated Russian ladies were not against the advances of the Caucasus "savages" provided that they were from upper class families. Some Russian women were not stopped by the stigma of racial mixing, but on the contrary, were attracted by the exotic erotic difference of a forbidden sexual partner. Tekuyeva gives a detailed account of an extra-marital affair between a Kabardin noble man Astemir Sheriyev and a Russian estate owner Khomyakova, who bought a house in Caucasus. In this case a certain reversal of roles took place when Khomyakova openly expressed her feelings for Astemir, whereas the married prince tried to hide their affair and in the spirit of conventional romanticism, dug an underground corridor from his estate to the house of the Russian woman (Tekuyeva 2006, 75). Such facts shake the accepted image of the stereotypes and gender divisions between the colonizers and the colonized.

The Caucasus male was used by the Russian officers as an attractive sexual role model—they massively changed into Cherkess traditional dress in order to borrow some of the aura of the Caucasus masculinity. In this theatrical metamorphosis into a noble savage there was a clear Rousseauistic touch. In spite of all their borrowed enlightenment discourses, the imperial ideologues imbued the Caucasus people with such inherent and stable (not culturally determined) characteristics as proneness to violence and crime, coded in indirectly racial terms, which would be later reproduced in Bolshevik constructions of the Orient. In accordance with racial theories of the time, the mountaineers were presented as impulsive, courageous machos unable to control themselves and in need of the supervision of the Russian Empire (Jersild 2002, 104–105). Here the two sides of the medal—the light (modern) and the dark (colonial)—merged in the interpretation of the colonies. On the one hand, the Caucasus people were racialized and presented as unreformable, on the other hand, it was assumed that under the influence of the Russian/Soviet civilizing efforts the mountaineers would gradually change and turn into fully humans (Jersild 2002, 9–125).

There was hardly a developed Orientalist exotic beauty stereotype in the interpretation of Central Asia where women images remained largely impenetrable for the imperial gaze. A stricter social hierarchy of Turkistan was supported by the stronger Muslim influence than in Caucasus which led to an elaborate system of protection of the socially and culturally valuable women from the unwanted attention of the colonizers. In veiling practices which were later incorrectly labeled as medieval, there are certainly traces of the common Muslim ethical model according to which women stand on the verge of the clean and the dirty and are always in danger of crossing this boundary. The veiling practices were used as a means of dividing the proper pious Central Asian women—usually upper class and urban, from the easily sexually accessible and "sinful," Europeanized and modernized Russians and from the local lower classes and sexually available prostitutes. The clothes were meant to protect the women in the difficult conditions of external invasion rather than to simply restrict their freedom. Thus it was becoming a form of resistance. Muslim conservatives practiced mostly a passive resistance to colonization. One of its central tactics was the inviolability of the private sphere, family, and women as a guarantee of the successful maintenance of the local society. This argument as a form of cultural self-protection was used by the Russian Empire and later the Bolsheviks as a proof of Muslim culture's deficiency. What is important is that from a rather relaxed veiling the local urban cultures gradually switched to paranjee and chachvon, which, according to some scholars (Northrop 2004, 44–45), came forward as a reaction to colonization. The latter caused a major reconsideration and elevation of traditional practices as signs of Muslim and ethnic identity which acquired a symbolic meaning.

The urban society of Turkistan was becoming more stratified and its well off strata did not want to be associated with either the colonizers or the lower classes, including the way their women looked like and behaved. As pointed out by A. Khalid (Khalid 1999, 223), polygamy in this period turned into a hidden form of consumption together with the development of prostitution which made it necessary to divide the women according to social groups and status.

There is no access today to the erased voices of the nineteenth-century Central Asian women. We can only guess if they were against the stricter veiling or considered it a part of their passive resistance. A complex combination of social, cultural, religious, and economic factors that lay in the basis of veiling controversy was erased or distorted in colonialist discourses of the time—Western and Russian alike. They both stressed the downtrodden status of Central Asian women treated in a primitive wholistic manner, and judged their lack of rights using the Western measuring rod. Additionally, for a Russian colonist, priest, or officer it was symbolically important to dismiss the local upper class and drag it to the lower status in order to elevate their own position.

In the colonization of Central Asia the logic of blaming the victim for her own raping could not work, neither did the gendered variant of the "black legend"—an accusation of Islamic cultures in sexual deviance and lack of morals. Soon the colonizers brought to Turkistan all the vices of modernity, including the brothels which along with alcoholism came to be regarded by the local population as the true signs of Russian modernization. The works of the Russian ethnographers—husband and wife Nalivkins, writing in the end of the nineteenth and beginning of the twentieth century, already manifested a typical quasi-scientific mythology which blamed the victim for the crime committed against her. They would repeatedly state that Central Asian women became prostitutes of their own will due to their natural inclination to erotic adventures and unhealthy sexuality, as a result of its constant restraint (Nalivkin and Nalivkina 1886, 235–244). Another exception was an Orientalist interpretation of homosexual problematic, particularly, male homosexualism between grown ups and young boys, presented as a manifestation of Central Asian perverted morals, yet never directly linked to Islam. Lesbianism figured in these accusations less frequently although it was also regarded as a direct and unhealthy result of female seclusion (Polovtsoff 1932, Lykoshyn 1916, Logofet 1913, Ostroumov 1880, Northrop 2004, 41).[8]

The Russian and Soviet Empire did not go as far as to accuse the Muslim women in Turkistan of sexual dissoluteness. Any erotic relations of the Russian males with the colonized women remained adventures outside the realm of the metropolis morale. These women were not turned into an important part of the economy of sexual and labor exploitation. So the gendered black legend took a more restricted form of associating the Oriental women with backwardness, illiteracy, and lack of hygiene. As neither in Caucasus nor in Turkistan there was a system of direct colonial slavery, it was difficult to create a unified and coherent system of labor and sexual exploitation of local women. Particularly because in Russia's case the Western logic of effective exploitation of dehumanized locals was much less developed or consciously taken into account. On the contrary there was a clear inclination to destroy or expel the locals and populate the vacated lands with Russian colonists.

A Western myth of the White woman as an innocent, submissive, and sexually passive being, who is in constant threat coming from the non-White and non-European males, and has to be defended from them, was transformed in the non-European colonies of Russia almost into its opposite. Except for the Russian romantic fiction, there was hardly any developed image of the colonized woman, typical for Western Orientalist tradition and pictured as a sexually accessible and deviant creature who could be opposed to the White European lady, standing for Christian or later secular, for instance, Victorian values. One of the reasons for this was Islam and also, the degree of modernization. In Central Asia and in Caucasus up to today it is the local woman that manifests purity, sexual passivity, and piety, while a more modernized Russian one or an over-emancipated local, often stand for the stereotype of aggressive sexual promiscuity. What is at work here is a peculiar reversal of roles and a projection of negative gender characteristics onto the Europeans and Russians as their caricature followers. Paranjee in this case was precisely a way of positive marking of the native morality as opposed to the alien new one. Yet on the basis of this seemingly different configuration there lied the same ideology of modernization with its essentialist interpretation of race and cultural difference. Symbolically a Russian (that is, more European) woman was and is forgiven her dissoluteness precisely on the grounds of her being Russian (that is, superior).

In the Russian and early Soviet Empire the colonizers demonstratively ignored possible sexual partners from the group of the colonized women as being below their status. In Northern Caucasus and Central Asia gender aspects of modernity and the mixture of culture and biology in the interpretation of race came forward in the 1920s when representatives of the local elites, freshly educated in the new Soviet mode, began to demonstrate at every step their loyalty to the empire and found it important to marry Russian women. This was a symbolic communion from the Soviet modernity which helped to elevate one's status by means of getting a more prestigious (White, European, civilized) sexual partner. If changing of the local wife was impossible for whatever reason, she had to be at least remodeled in order to correspond to the requirements of the Russian/Soviet modernity—from changing of her name to changing of her clothes and the way of life. D. Northrop quotes an Uzbek Yoldosh Akhunbabayev, a representative of such freshly made local Soviet elites who openly justified divorcing local wives and marrying Europeans using the arguments of dirtiness, ignorance, and general backwardness of Oriental women (Northrop 2004, 62).

Roughly by the mid-1960s the situation started to reverse in the sense that the local elites and the middle class began to regard Russian women as sexually accessible and socially emancipated, but preferred to marry local (Muslim) women from good families who were educated and modernized to some extent yet continued to act as the bearers of the sanctified local tradition and of the local brand of modernity. These local modernities gradually worked out in-between negotiating versions of women's appearance and behavior and subtler ways of marking the difference that have acted as a "virtual hijab," to use Mekhti's metaphor (Mekhti 2005), and have created specific parallel negotiating identities.

The nature of the subaltern empire and a specific subjectivity of the colonizer who is himself/herself colonized by Western modernity, complicates the power vectors of the colonial suppression in Eurasian borderlands. Some of these vectors are indirect and work only in the sphere of imagination, the bodily gender stereotypes, etc. Such are the vectors directed from the European males and females to men and women of Russian colonies. These vectors were always mediated by the Russian subaltern colonizers. What is clear here is the dubious status of Russians and their mediating dependent role in the spread of the global coloniality.

There was one more redoubling of gender-class-race problematic in the Russian Empire worth mentioning. It is connected with a gradual polarization in the eighteenth and nineteenth centuries of the higher and folk cultures in Russia. In this context a Russian serf woman performed a number of functions typical of the African slaves in the New World. If in Western modernity/coloniality representatives of the non-Western world were excluded from the human and feminine realms in order to facilitate their discrimination, exploitation and objectification (Lugones 2007, McClintock 1995), in Russia the picture was different. The role of the sexually, economically, and psychologically exploited woman associated with animals and taken outside the realm of gender, was played by an ethnically same and only socially other serf woman.

In Russia and later in the Soviet Union the paradoxical tactic of internal racialization and othering was justified by the elites' claims at belonging to European culture or, as a variant, to communist ideology. This resulted in efforts to build a Chinese wall between themselves and the Russian people, that in the minds of the elites were excluded from European-ness. In communist discourses the same logic referred not just to peasants, but to all enemies of the Soviet power. This led to extreme cruelty in the treatment of women political prisoners in Soviet camps who were divested of their human, civil and gender status and hence allowed to be raped and killed. A totalitarian ideology in this case was a specific manifestation of coloniality of power.

3.4. Caucasian Slaves, Circassian Beauties, and the Discourses of Whiteness

The coding of aboriginal women as animals was clearly expressed in the way the Russian Empire saw its Oriental gendered others. The Caucasus women in contrast with African slaves in the Americas represented the exotic erotic extreme of Orientalist racist hierarchy in which sexual exploitation was not directly linked with a labor one. There was a clear difference in the degree and nature of dispensability of human lives in Western modernity, in the Ottoman Sultanate and in Russia. In the Ottoman Sultanate there was a specific understanding of the slave status which did not rob him/her of rights and humanity. A slave could change his/her status and it was easier for women due to the possibility of marriage.

The Turkish-Caucasus slave trade that persisted for many centuries clearly demonstrated not merely a constructed nature of race and gender discourses but also their extreme commercialization. Slave trade in this case must be considered within the wider context of commercial relations of Caucasus and the Ottoman Sultanate, as well as Russia, and, indirectly, Europe. Circassians, even if they were seen as fallen out of modernity by both the West and Russia, did take a modest part in the capitalist market. Their main profitable articles were the natural resources[9] and women and children. The lively slave trade between the Ottoman Sultanate and Circassia even if it looked as a remnant of earlier economic and social relations in fact was firmly grounded in racial discourses as a fundamental part of modernity and capitalism. These discourses were internalized by both the Ottoman Turks and Circassians, who were and remain to be both the victims and the perpetrators of the Whiteness myth. The Turks were interested in buying a White sexual partner even if this was just a substitute of a true European. By the mid-nineteenth century Circassians were the closest to European embodiment of the White race available for Turks.

In the course of the nineteenth-century Russia was repeatedly trying to either ban the Black Sea trade between the Ottoman Sultanate and the mountaineers, claiming it was a source of armaments for the insurgents, or control and surtax it. Here the economic interests were linked with military and geopolitical ones. As for the slave trade, Russia as usual took a dubious position. On the one hand, it applied human and particularly women's rights rhetoric and condemned the slave trade. On the other hand, the rights of Circassian women were of much less interest to Russia than the possible profits that it missed. A. Chechuyeva quotes a late nineteenth-century commentator T. Lapinsky (1876) who claimed that "having completed a few journeys with live goods a Turkish merchant could sustain himself for the rest of his life. A boy cost a hundred silver rubles and a girl—three hundred to three hundred and fifty rubles, women for the rich harems cost between fifty and hundred thousand piastres" (Chechuyeva 2007, 115). The indignation of the Russian commentator here is caused not by the horrible condition of women and children slaves but by the quick enrichment of the Turks.

One such case is analyzed by a Diasporic Circassian anthropologist Setenei Shami in her article "Pre-histories of Globalization: Circassian Identity in Motion" (Shami 2000), offering an unexpected approach to the interpretation of the Adyghean Diaspora after the exile from Caucasus which allows us to make a parallel with Atlantic modernity and the destiny of African slaves. In this case a symbolic transit, turning the human identity into a mobile and changing one, balancing between memory and forgetting, takes place in the Black Sea instead of the Atlantic Ocean. The focus in both cases is on the problem of the imagined past of the diasporic nations that found themselves in the situation of prehistory of globalization and involuntary uprootedness.

Shami reproduces the story of Shemsigul—a nineteenth-century Circassian girl who was sold into slavery by her relatives and made a journey from her native village first to Constantinople and then to Cairo. Her story was reconstructed by Ehud Toledano (Toledano 1993) using the available police interrogation. We find out about her rape by the slave owner on board of the ship. According to the Ottoman law, the price of such a slave automatically dropped, while the owner was forbidden to sell a pregnant slave. Shemsigul's owner unsuccessfully attempted to get rid of her fetus and later his wife adopted the new born baby to avoid a possibility of Shemsigul's becoming a legitimate wife. Shemsigul was saved by an external interference: there was a complaint to the head of the slave dealers' guild and the police accepted Shemsigul's account and passed its opinion to the court. This was an exception rather than a rule. Moreover, even upon proving their right to be a free citizen many ex-slaves in fact did not get anything in return. In patriarchal Ottoman society the status of the free unmarried woman without her family support and with a slave stigma in the past was not enviable.

There is a clear difference between Circassians as an object of Orientalist mythology in the West and in Russia, and a Circassian discourse in the Ottoman Sultanate which was going through its own adaptation of civilizing enlightenment ideals at the time. This difference can be summarized as follows: for Russians the Circassian myth was based on complete othering and annihilation, for the West it was based on commodification and exotization. Both regarded the Caucasus people as dispensable lives. For the Ottomans it was not the case because the Turkish rendering of the Circassian slaves was not marked by Western misanthropic skepticism. They were not taken outside of humanity.[10] The mid-nineteenth century massive migration of Circassians to the Ottoman Sultanate did not come to mainly slaves and aristocrats as before but to a much wider strata of common people who later created the peasant and merchant communities of Anatolia and wider, the Middle East, many of which still exist. Some of these people trying to secure funds for resettling in new territories sold or pawned their own daughters or sons to the Ottomans. This was a peculiar combination of capitalist discourses of the second modernity and an earlier local tradition in interpreting kinship, race, humanity, ethnicity, gender, and caste. Circassian parents, particularly poor ones or slaves in their own land, when selling their children to slave traders were hoping that they would become happy in the Ottoman harem.

The Ottomans used the rhetoric of modernity in a peculiar way, justifying the continuing slave trade with Caucasus. They claimed that through slavery the Circassians could rise from barbarity to civilization and from poverty to happiness and well being (Shami 2000, 194). As Shami points out, in this respect the Ottoman discourse was mixed, as it combined the old understanding of slavery as a religiously sanctioned and eternal institution and status, given once and for all and regulated by a number of strict laws, and the European enlightenment interpretation of freedom and humanism (Shami 2000, 195). The closing decades of the nineteenth century brought precedents of legitimate struggle of Circassian women-slaves for their freedom using the Ottoman law and judicial system. They appealed to official organs asking to revise their slave status and there were cases decided in their favor if they could prove that they were free people before. The Ottoman state had to take care of migrants, if only minimally (Shami 2000, 196) until their free status was proven or disproved. There emerged a system of detention migrant centers which had become a real destination of Circassians' Ottoman transit by this time, instead of the imagined exoticist mythology of the harem (Shami 2000).

In other words, there is a not very well studied gap between the under-expressed identities and dead-end aspirations of Circassian women and the role imposed on them by their families, the economic, social, and political conditions of the forced exile, often making these women into a commodity, sacrificing them to diaspora, to empire and later, to nation-states which were founded on the remnants of the Ottoman Sultanate. However, Shami does not speak of the imperial-colonial difference and coloniality at large. Neither does she touch upon the racial side of this problematic. If we do this we will see that in the history of Circassian slavery there merged the rivalries of the Western empires of modernity and the non-Western or not-quite-Western subaltern ones. The latter abandoned their previous discourses of sameness and otherness, and in the nineteenth century found themselves simultaneously forced and talked into being enchanted with Western modernity/coloniality in the interpretation of race, slavery, knowledge, being, gender, etc. Before the coming of Western modernity the Ottoman Sultanate social system was not based on European White superiority or dispensability and dehumanization of others. But during the Circassian transit the Ottomans were already infected by modernity—although not to such an extent as in the twentieth century. This referred to the discourses of Whiteness which resulted in the humiliation of African slaves, and also to Western talk on human rights and civilizing mission, which the Ottomans appropriated and adapted to their own conditions. The Ottoman Sultanate had to cut on the African slave trade because the Western powers demanded to observe the Africans' rights and it is at this moment that the Circassian girls, imported en mass, took the place of the Africans in the Ottoman markets. Defending the rights of the African slaves, the Western empires were not interested in the fate of Circassians. Neither were they preoccupied with the opposite effect that their claim had in the end—a mass of African women often with children, thrown out to the street because their Turkish masters changed them to Circassians as more attractive (according to Eurocentric principles) sexual partners and producers of White progeny.

Let us look at the image of Circassians in the West. In the nineteenth century they acted in the Western imaginary as exotic internal noble savages of the South of Europe, fallen out of modernity, who could be protected by the benevolent humanistic West from the barbarous Russian Empire and the devious Ottoman Sultanate. A typical manifestation of this rhetoric is to be found in the 1851 book written by an American popular writer and publisher Maturin Murray Ballow (lieutenant Maturin Murray). It is an exoticist tale *The Circassian Slave, or the Sultan's Favorite* (Murray Ballou 2006). The racial, cultural, and religious model presented in this book is built on the imperial rivalry between the West, Russia, and the Ottoman Sultanate which shares Russia's status of imperial difference.

Books like this confirmed popular Western racial stereotypes, according to which the author builds his human taxonomy: the Nubians are regarded as subhuman and used as servants, even among the slaves in the harem. For instance, they serve the beautiful

Circassian Komel but they are not regarded as an interesting sexual object by the sultan. The Arabs are seen in quintessential Orientalist frame. Sinister and cruel, they appear in the book for the single purpose of robbing and attempting to murder the sultan. The Turks are presented as more complex and even prone to nobleness due to the fact that their blood was diluted over the generations by Europeans and Christians. Yet the Asiatic cunning always wins. Since we are speaking here of a secular version of racism, ethnicity, and the color of skin often stand for religion, so that Asiatic (Muslim) is opposed to European (Christian).

But Circassians seem to destroy this simple opposition. According to Murray, they are Christians deep in their hearts, even if they forgot their Christianity, while Islam for them is a delusion that can be easily corrected by a good Western/Christian guidance. In his racial-gender taxonomy the Circassian slave stands higher than the Turkish beauties because of her Whiteness, closeness to Christianity, and natural intellect. Murray stresses the whiteness and fairness of Circassian slaves in opposition with the dominant Russian view of them as Asiatic savage girls. Circassia is presented by Murray as an enchanted happy Arcadian and yet, unmistakably (Southern) European space between the exotic and cruel Ottoman Sultanate and dangerous Russia. It is stereotypically comprised of arrogant men who Russia cannot defeat for a century and the most beautiful women dreaming of becoming the Turkish slaves. Until the end the author does not say openly that his Circassians were once Christian. But for the reader it is obvious by the way they are described and presented in the book. When the conventional plot predictably reveals that the Turkish captain Selim was the lost (and sold into bondage) brother of the beautiful Cherkess Komel, we find out that Christianity by the author's design was too strong to be forgotten even at the service of the sultan.

This highly conventional tale, full of unbelievable coincidences, starts with the typical description of the slave market—"the sale of humanity," where greedy lusting Turks look for young innocent Circassian girls. It is here that we first see Komel, whose features are compared to that of the Grecian cast to elevate her racial status. The author mixes romantic and sentimentalist clichés with biased ethnographic and historical details. As in case of "black legend" which created a mythology of imperial rivalry, in this tale there is a subdued version of a similar sentiment juxtaposing the Russian or Ottoman (evil) empires with the Western view that whitens itself by blackening the rival. In this peculiar version of the "black legend" logic the Russian Empire is painted black, when the author reveals its ignoble goals in preventing the Circassians from their long-existing slave trade with Turks. As in the case of any "black legend," it was important to present the resisting side—in this case the Circassians—in romantic elevated terms, as opposed to dangerous demonic barbarians or the residents of the Western Orient. This inconsistency is repeated in any imperial mythology—British, Spanish, French, or Russian alike.

In Murray's taxonomy the main character clearly takes the place of an exotic and delicate, sexually attractive other with a capacity to be enlightened and brought to reason. Alas, in this tale there is no Westerner to perform this task. The only shadowy presence of the West is that of America. This presence is symbolized by an American ship. Murray could not write a popular tale without an element of propaganda and patriotic didacticism. So the reader comes upon the most artificially constructed passage—a conversation between captain Selim and his Turkish lover Zillah who cannot get married because of religious differences and dream of going to America where religious belief is no bar to the union of heart. Even writing about exotic people and places, Murray finds a place to mention in laudatory terms the American ideals of freedom and democracy, putting these words into the mouth of a Turk who later would turn out to be a Circassian. Finally he brings his romantic heroes to Circassia—a fairy-tale eternal paradise that somehow escapes the dangers of Russian colonization.

In 1856 the *London Post* published a report (later reprinted in *New York Daily Times*) where the pre–Civil War Anglo-Saxon anxiety about the intersections of class, race, gender, and slavery comes forward. The report speaks of numerous Circassian women slave dealers in Constantinople: "Perceiving that when the Russians shall have reoccupied the coast of the Caucasus this traffic in white slaves will be over, the Circassian dealers have redoubled their efforts ever since the commencement of the peace conferences to introduce into Turkey the greatest possible number of women while the opportunity of doing so lasted. They have been so successful, notwithstanding the prohibition of the trade by the Porte, and the presence of so many of Her Majesty's ships in the Black Sea, that never, perhaps, at any former period, was *white human flesh* [italics mine—M.T.] so cheap as it is at this moment" (Horrible Traffic 2006).

Further on the reporter introduces an opposition of Circassian and African slaves, with a social touch, saying that due to the cheapness of the White women, the low class purchasers started to sell their African slaves and buy the cheap Circassians instead. It is implied that before the slave-holding status was for privileged people only, while now the low class claimed it together with the possibility of buying a White woman. This is rather hypocritically presented as immoral, inhumane, and unchristian. The journalist goes even as far as to speak for the rights of the Black women-slaves who "after being as many as eight or ten years in the same hands, have lately been consigned to the broker for disposal." But soon we learn that this is because a "respectable slave-broker" told him that these discarded women are difficult to resell. The article ends with the standard rebuke of the Turks who are blamed for their racism (!) and infanticide. In the core of this newspaper article there stands a familiar opposition of the civilized West which presumably would not sell a White woman or kill a Black baby, and the barbarous Turks.

A German anthropologist J.F. Blumenbach's popular racial quasi-theory presented Caucasus as the origin of the purest Caucasian (White) stock (Blumenbach 1865).[11] The story of the White (Caucasus) slaves was particularly interesting for Americans because in this case slavery did not go hand in hand with race but rather contradicted the established racial hierarchy. The whole controversy around Circassians was a good example of the highly manipulative and completely symbolic nature of racial discourses. In its basis there was demonization and racialization of Islam and of Turkish slave-holders who were associated with the "White slavery" black legend. For the Western audience the dramatic and sensational voyeuristic stories of Circassian girls liberated from Turkish harems invariably carried an element of fundamental illegitimacy of racial mixing between these presumably Whitest women on earth and the racialized Muslim Turks.

However the Circassians' role of live exhibits in America was not interpreted as humiliating by the public. Of course no one would demonstrate an English lady in a dime museum, playing the part of the English lady who escaped from the Turkish harem. But it was acceptable to demonstrate an American girl if she was hired to play the role of a Circassian beauty. In other words, there were many degrees, shades, and qualities of Whiteness which turned Circassians into erotic exotic objects, representatives of pure biological race, who nevertheless lacked human rights and were in fact dehumanized. Race as well as the color of skin in this case was already reconsidered through belonging to (the center) of Europe, to Christianity and modernity. At the same time, it was commercialized and virtualized in the frame of "commodity racism" (McClintock 1995).

Americans easily forgot about the whiteness of Circassian beauties and tended to exhibit them side by side with other exotic human and animal freaks in medicinal shows, circuses, and dime museums. A famous American entrepreneur P.T. Barnum, the owner of several circuses and, most notably, the American Museum, displayed the first fake "Circassian Beauty." When Barnum's assistant failed to purchase a real Circassian in Constantinople, he had to satisfy himself with a local girl with exotically teased hair whom he named Zalumma Agra—the Star of the East (The Circassian Beauty Archive 2006). The "moss-hair" from then on came to be patented as Circassian but in fact had nothing to do with the real hair styles of Caucasus women. Such "medusas" or "moss-haired" girls became a staple in every provincial circus show and the interest in them quickly died. Commodity racism in relation to Circassians finally deteriorated in the United States and England into its basest forms in a specific line of cheap beauty products which exploited the image of Circassian beauty (Circassian hair dye, Circassian blush, etc.).

Commercialization of race in case of Circassians did not just come to the Ottoman Black Sea transit, but had a more global nature long before anyone started to discuss globalization. In a more or less virtual way this racial commodification stepped into the New World and acquired in the United States its final forms of commodity racism typical of commercially oriented Orientalist discourses of the late nineteenth century, in the wider space of the rapidly developing capitalism where race was becoming completely commodified.

Chapter Four

Quasi-scientific Racism and Gender in Russian and Soviet Discourses

4.1. Colonial Modernities, Colonial Nations, and the Beginning of Women's Activism

The end of the nineteenth and the beginning of the twentieth century in Russia was marked by a quasi-scientific positivist stage of racial and gender discourses in the interpretation of colonial others. It came later than in Europe and America where knowing the Orient, studying and observing it through comparative racial hierarchies and biological taxonomies went hand in hand with colonization as such. By contrast Russia acted reactively in the sense that it began to study when it was too late and it did not fully realize the importance of knowing for owning. The instruments for this study were also borrowed from the West with the usual distortions. Thus, by the time the scientific apparatus was ready to create the description of the Caucasus way of life this world in its precolonial form had already vanished.

Yet, the late nineteenth century brought the first Russian colonial administration's efforts to use science for a more successful colonization. It included an invention of ethnic and racial taxonomies, which was in itself a difficult task as an ethnic understanding of the national was largely alien to colonial spaces of Caucasus and Turkistan. People coded themselves differently—through religion, social status, clan system, gender, but not through ethnicity or nationality. As in the case of many other societies it was the Western modernity mediated by the Russian and later the Soviet empires, which brought such initially foreign concepts as ethnic and linguistic nationalism, religious and linguistic purism and intolerance, racialization, and ethnization, artificial divisions into major ethnicities and minorities, into Aryans and Mongolians, etc.

The Russian imperial ideologues realized that in Central Asia or Caucasus there were no convenient classifications of people based on the purity of blood. The first Turkistan general-governor von Kaufman lamented that the local population is mixed and often impossible to define in ethnographic terms (Abashin and Bushkov 2004, 49). By the early twentieth century, due to interference of quasi-scientific racial discourses, Orientalism had finally lost its romantic element. The local population became the untouchables. This racist squeamishness would go away from the Russian imaginary for a while in the Soviet decades in order to come back in a forceful way after the collapse of the Soviet Union. The Russian and Soviet imperial ideologues attempted to create ethnic nations which would be easier to work with, a classification of the colonized people on the scale of humanity and, what was particularly important, an opposition of the Russians as more developed, White and civilized to these newly invented ethnicities. Besides, it was easier to control the separate nationalities, opposed to each other and devoid of any ability to unite on Muslim, pan-Turkic, or pan-Caucasian terms. So the imagined communities of Central Asian or Caucasus ethnic nations had to be quickly turned into reality. This work was started by the Russian empire and successfully accomplished by the Soviet one.[1]

In the closing years of the Czarist Empire, race was interpreted in a complex and contradictory way and did not come to merely the color of skin. In spite of the overtly lacking racial discourses in comparison with America and Europe, race did creep into the colonial ethnic-national contexts in the end of the nineteenth and beginning of the twentieth century. An interesting analysis of the quasi-scientific racism in anthropological studies of Central Asia is offered in Sergei Abashin's *Nationalisms in Central Asia* (Abashin 2007). The scholar compares a book on Turkistan written by a Russian eighteenth-century traveler and a nineteenth-century anthropological study of the same region. There is a gradual emergence of racism and grounding of any research in clear and unquestioned human taxonomies, based on object-subject duality. The first book is called *The Journey of Philip Yefremov* (1784) and can be defined as a captivity narrative. After a heavy editing this work was made to look more scientific and imbued with a strict hierarchy of nature/versus society opposition. From the description of nature and geography the author turned to economy and population, after which he wrote about family, customs, diseases, religion, education, and politics. He followed the logic of historical linear progress from natural to cultural lying in the basis of the social sciences and the humanities.

Abashin points out that the chapter on Central Asian population comes between geography and economy, on the one hand, and the way of life, politics and history, on the other (Abashin 2007, 78). This signifies a double (biological and social at once) interpretation of colonial others.[2] The fact that the colonial population description was put in between nature and society would be repeated and naturalized in all future studies of Central Asia. Having said all that, Abashin does not come to an obvious conclusion on epistemic racism lying in the basis of the emerging scientific taxonomies. He points out the vague opposition (not yet ideologically shaped) between the Uzbeks and the Tadzhiks (Abashin 2007, 80), which would be developed later in the vein of evolutionary anthropology into the opposition of the Uzbeks as the mongoloid savage newcomers to this land, and the Aryan local Tadzhiks who were presumably pushed out by the invaders.

Abashin analyzes an interesting example of the late-nineteenth-century ethnographic taxonomy. It is N. Khanykov's book *The Description of Bukharian Khanate* (1879), where again, a chapter on population is placed at the boundary between nature and society, or rather, as Abashin says, this chapter itself is the boundary because both biological and social characteristics are to be found in population (Abashin 2007, 82). Analyzing Khanykov's book Abashin more clearly shows his critical approach to such scholarly methods, when he sarcastically says that Khanykov was as little interested in the way the Bukharians called themselves as biologists would be interested if butterflies agreed to be called so. "For him the tribes are the same kind of biological and social unions whose representatives lack their own selves and are in need of urgent classification" (Abashin 2007, 83). Abashin even offers that the term Tadzhik was invented by Khanykov for the sake of the elegant classification and scientific systematicity. The scholar clearly opposes the constructed notions of Uzbeks and Tadzhiks. Both are regarded in Orientalist terms in points of appearance and moral qualities. Abashin is interested here in deconstructing comparison as a method of scientific analysis. He stresses that in the invented oppositions there was already "a conflict at work which could act as a convenient explanatory model for the historical and political events" (Abashin 2007, 84). This is how the Uzbeks turned into the winners and the Tadzhiks into the conquered, and the Mongolian tribe replaced the Aryan cultural aboriginals. Abashin shows how this quasi-scientific myth was born, though he does not analyze the epistemic racism at its base.[3]

The anthropological intrigue based on the replacement of Aryans with Mongolians was complimented in Soviet time by an additional political element. For a few months before the Bolsheviks took over, the power in Central Asia was in the hands of the Young Bukharians that is, the Jadids[4] who saw revolution as a national revival and the beginning of enlightenment, and linked it to the development of national language (the so called *Chagatay*) and literature. This became synonymous with the Turkization of the Farsi-speaking population of the region, as one of the first steps of the Young Bukharians was to replace Farsi with Turkic as a state language. Later the Jadids were condemned as Bourgeois nationalists and pan-Turkists and almost entirely destroyed. In this context the proliferation of scholarly discourses based on a negative interpretation of Turkic peoples and their presumable expansion into the regions earlier populated by the Aryans, was only natural.

However Muslim peoples of the Russian empire did not tacitly agree with their role of objects of analysis and application of pseudo-scientific myths and taxonomies. By the beginning of the twentieth century the colonial others had already started to discuss this problematic in public discourse. They were attempting to have a dialogue with the state and with the scientific authorities. These efforts were mostly ignored. Yet, the degree of zombification and self-orientalizing was lower in the Czarist Empire than in the Soviet Union which radically destroyed any traces of alternative thinking. In the 1900s the Russian Muslims became more articulate in their opposition to Orientalist tendencies of missionaries and colonial bureaucrats who liked to use the notorious women's question in order to blacken Islam. Rorlich gives an example in her analysis of the 1912 polemics between the director of Tashkent seminary for the indigenous people, a graduate of the Missionary anti-Muslim department of Kazan Religious Academy Nikolay Ostroumov and A. Mustafi who blamed Ostroumov for his Orientalism and readiness to regard Muslim women as frozen and fallen out of time and modernity. Mustafi successfully deconstructed the typical imperial racist taxonomy of cultures and peoples of the world which was presented by Ostroumov as natural and given once and for all (Rorlich 2004, 43).

In this article there also emerges an important crack between the Russian orientalists studying the other, even if with good intentions, and the colonial Muslims themselves. Rorlich speaks of Olga Lebedeva, a Russian Christian woman who devoted her life to Turkic and Islamic studies. Yet, even if her goal was gender equality and education of Muslim women of Russia the ways of its realization could not be the same as envisioned by the Muslim women themselves. Lebedeva saw the main problem in conservative religious circles, while the women's enlightenment and education for her were the answers to all questions. This discourse was incomplete and distorting as it ignored the fundamental element of colonial-imperial asymmetries, outside of which it was not possible to speak of any liberation, much less freedom (Rorlich 2004, 46).

A.-A. Rorlich shows that a number of Muslim women in the late Czarist Empire fought for their rights using legitimate means and trying to combine their Muslim values with a loyalty to the Russian empire as its citizens. The situation was somewhat similar to today's European conflict with Muslim migrants, who after gaining a European citizenship start to use liberal democratic means to restate their rights, not always realizing that the very rhetoric of modernity automatically excludes them from those who are entitled to such rights. In 1915 a Tatar women's magazine *Soyem Bike* published a discussion on the possibility of combining the Muslim and the Russian women's identity. As Rorlich demonstrates, Muslim women who took part in this discussion were far from that negative image that was nourished by Russian missionaries, colonial administrators, and feminists. What was crucial here was the ability and willingness on the part of the women to keep their Muslim identity at the center yet also make it modern and Russian. These women took a border positioning marked by a double critique of themselves, the society where they lived, and the double standards in relation to European and non-European women. The Tatar women activists saw a more complex picture from the start than their Russian or European counterparts, who continued to condescendingly speak of backward Muslims, remaining blind to their own secondary status and lack of civil, political, economic, or human rights. In this respect the Tatar women activists had an epistemic privilege as they thought and wrote from a specific threshold transcultural state of *dihliz,* to use Abu Hamid al-Ghazali's metaphor (Moosa 2005), based on dialogic imagination and on balancing between the inside and the outside, enriching them with freedom both from the missionary zeal of Russian feminists and Muslim fundamentalists.[5]

In the late nineteenth and early twentieth century within the Muslim communities of the Russian empire there emerged a sharp division into the champions of those values that were presented as traditionally Islamic and meant to maintain the existing order of things, and various Muslim and national reformers among which the most prominent were the Jadids—the carriers of the contradictory ideal of national and, at the same time, reformed Muslim modernity. They can be regarded as a part of the global Muslim turn to reformism of the time.

The influence of Western modernity was multiplied and distorted through a large number of sources. The Western discourses of hygiene, culture, new morals went through Tartar, Turkish, Arabic, Afghan, Iranian influence before landing in Central Asian soil. They were marked by a constant comparative drive and competition which the Bolsheviks later had to also take into account. A good example of such an adaptation was Turkey. As N. Göle points out (Göle 1996), veiling demonstrates the importance of gender questions and sexuality in the Islamic criticism of the Western project of modernity. Politicization of women generates a shaping of the public collective identity which abstains from any definitions of separate gender roles in the private sphere. The chador penetrates the power relations between Islam and the West, secularism and religion, men and women, and also between women themselves. Göle stresses that gender question has remained central in the nation-building period when the public and the private spheres clashed in the quickly changing attitudes to women, and also today, when the politicized Islam offers its own reading of the social history of Turkey. The emergence of civil society in Turkey was directly linked to the beginning of perception of women as fully human and with their specific socialization which went hand in hand with Turkish modernization. The women of Kemalist Turkey were the real symbols of civilizing, modernizing and at the same time national project (Göle 1996, 131). Something similar—although with a different communist ideology instead of nationalist one and the outward atheism—one finds in Soviet Turkistan during the infamous campaign for the liberation of the women of the East, and later, when these colonies shaped their own model of secular educated and socially active working mother, linked with the Soviet state colonial gender discourse. There is a difference between the Soviet atheistic modernization that interpreted Islam as archaic backwardness, and the Kemalist one, which did not deny Islam altogether, letting it exist in certain spheres, however symbolic.

When Reza Khan came to power in Persia in the 1920s he proclaimed himself the head of the Pahlavi dynasty which went back to the ancient pre-Islamic layer of Persian culture. As a result there developed peculiar double discourses of modernization desperately trying to save the tradition as well. The shah copied Ata Turk in his new role of the enlightened ruler, yet retained the monarchy with its feudal prerogatives. In the vein of specific modernization logic he not only sent his compatriots to France and Germany, but also, attempted to change the gender relations, albeit externally, ignoring Shia fundamentalism: in the 1930s the veiled women were banned from public spaces in Iran.

A similar story is to be found in Afghanistan where a reformer Amanulla Khan came to power after World War I. He presented himself as a king, not an emir and, in the spirit of the time attempted to make Afghanistan into a nation-state. The difference was that Amanulla looked for the role model in the Soviet Union, although his views and logic rather corresponded to those of Ata Turk. The Afghan traditionalists were infuriated with his opening of Western style schools and modest measures for the liberation of women. Modernization leap finished with the displacement of Amanulla in 1928. As in case of Persia, this coincided time-wise with the Soviet campaigns of Oriental women liberation, while the very presence of such an alternative model made the Bolsheviks take more active efforts in persuading the local population in the advantages of the Russian/ Soviet modernization.

Both the Jadids and the conservatives reacted to the excesses of modernization/colonization, although they did it in opposite ways. The first wanted to create their own local modernity, the second wished to destroy the very possibility of modern ideology's penetrating local life. In the end the Soviet modernity crashed both, at the same time appropriating much of what they created in transmuted forms. The local intelligentsia's skepticism about modernity is understandable in the case of India, Central Asia, or Caucasus. Its reasons lie in colonialism with which the history of modernity is entangled. It was this side of modernization that turned the colonial intellectuals into the skeptics who did not believe in the possibility of any universal sphere of free discourse unmarked by racial or national differences. As Partha Chatterjee points out, the colonial intelligentsia could guess that under the agreement between the modern knowledge and modern power regimes it was bound to remain in the condition of universal modernity's consumer and not producer. Nationalism marked by anti-colonial pathos was linked with the striving to create their own modernity. It took the colonial elites some time to realize that the Western principles they were copying did not refer to everyone, that in the public discourse of the colonial state there were crucial racial differences as well as differences in the political status of the nation and national, and that the freedom of expression was the right of the colonizer, not the colonized (Chatterjee 1997).

The idea of other modernity was unacceptable for both Russian and Soviet colonizers. The local reformers who turned to Muslim, European, Russian, and later Soviet forms of modernity, did not meet with a reciprocal movement except in the form of militant missionary syndrome. In spite of the fact that Muslims were ready to be loyal Russian empire citizens the Russian elites and common people were not ready for that. That is why, as Rorlich shows, in the first decade of the twentieth century the scholars, the government, and the missionaries were busy proving the insuperable impediments in uniting Islam and modernity. Such proofs were looked for in racial, religious, and civilizational spheres. Even if the Russian (Soviet) empire was secondary, it was not ready and is not ready today to lose its prerogative to preach modernity in the (post)colonial spaces of Central Asia and Caucasus. Any attempts at modernization from below in local forms would be destroyed as potentially dangerous. In spite of the 1905 Decree of religious toleration, the late imperial Russian politics tended to remain intolerant in its interpretation of Islam and in many ways, paradoxically coincided with the most conservative versions of Islam. The imperial government preferred them to integrational yet independent views of the Jadids (Rorlich 2004, 42).

A typical accusation of the colonized (and particularly women) was ignorance spread into educational, hygienic, religious, and other discourses. Rorlich quotes a few of the participants of the Missionary congress in Kazan in June 1919 who discussed the problem of education. Russian clergy who had dealt with Muslim colonials before admitted that the success of the dynamic Muslim women missionaries was linked not only to their faith but also to a high educational level and a system of values they were exposed to from childhood. This resulted in very high figures of Muslim children, including the girls, attending schools and graduating from them (Rorlich 2004, 43). But the official Russian propaganda then and now has always promoted a different view, according to which a Muslim woman has been presented as a downtrodden and uneducated justification of the civilizing mission of the Russian and Soviet empires.

In the complex interplay of various political actors with different interests the Russian and the Soviet government was only one of the players along with the local forces—from Muslim traditionalists to the Jadids and Russian colonists in Turkistan. The relations of these groups were not simply based on a hierarchy of the metropolis and the colonized, but rather on a complex transcultural interaction and tactical unions for the sake of survival and establishing power and influence as well as building of wider coalitions. The Jadid nationalism was close to anti-colonial nationalism as defined by Partha Chatterjee and cannot be regarded outside the imperial-colonial relations and the logic of coloniality. According to this model, members of the colonized societies who get an access to education, and elevate their status in the colonizers' eyes, immediately become a threat to the grounds of colonialism. Its claim to be a modern regime of power is that it can incite colonial subjects to self-improvement and development, so that they become more rational and leave primitive superstition behind. But to grant them such a status would mean to threaten colonialism as a rule of colonial difference. Therefore colonialism despises the products it creates—the people of the mixed cultural heritage who form the elites of the colonized societies. For the colonial administration it is easier to deal with presumably traditional populations who would not question the contradictions of colonialism. But the longer colonialism exists, the greater becomes the number of local intellectuals who challenge the legitimacy of the rule of colonial difference (Chatterjee 1988, 1993). Anti-colonial nationalism achieves what Chatterjee calls after A. Gramsci, a passive revolution, when the new colonial middle classes take over the state with no blood shed. The space which was occupied by the civil society institutions under colonialism, comes to be occupied by the political society with a close affiliation with the state (Chatterjee 1993, 2004). Anti-colonial nationalism and colonialism share the notion of progress toward modernity and reason, and the negative interpretation of tradition.

The Jadid nationalism also accepted the idea of progress and development toward the universal reason as the main myth of modernity. But they offered to put it to life in their own specific forms including the reformed Muslim vision. The Soviet power intensified the process of Jadids's disillusionment in modern (Western) values. Its lack of justice allowed them to feel that even if certain progressive values were to be translated from modernity to the colonial world, one could not avoid racism and the colonial asymmetry, the darker side of modernity. As soon as they realized that the Soviet Union was not about to end colonialism they turned away from the Bolsheviks as before they became disappointed in European modernity and its Orientalism (Fitrat 1919).

As early as 1920 a Bashkir leader of anti-colonial national liberation movement Zeki Velidi Togan clearly expressed his disillusion with Bolshevism, pointing out in his letter to V. Lenin the cynical and manipulative Bolshevik tactics: "You accept the ideas of genuine national Russian chauvinism as the basis of your policy...We have clearly explained that the land question in the East has in principle produced no class distinction...For in the East it is the European Russians, weather capitalists or workers, who are the top class, while the people of the soil..., rich or poor, are their slaves...You will go now finding class enemies of the workers, and rooting them out until every educated man among the native population...has been removed" (Caroe 1967, 112–113). Indeed, the beginning decolonization of the mind opened the Jadids' eyes to the darker side of any modernity.

However, it was not to develop fully due to the quick defeat of Jadidism.

Jadids' opinion on gender relations, have not yet been sufficiently studied. In general, the male Jadids tended to uncritically borrow gender stereotypes of modernity, and the degree of their radicalism in gender questions has always been a bit overestimated. The Jadids enlightenment bias included the Western concepts of justice, equality, women's rights and woman as the "light of civilization," the technocratic terms and the sanctification of sciences and progress. Along with the Western basis the Muslim reformers also incorporated the Western and middle class understanding of women's roles mainly as mothers and educators of children. A good example of the latter is a series of articles on family health by Mahmud Khoja Behbudi (1914), who followed modern Arabic and Turkish sources, which in their turn were based on Western science of the time. It is through this unconscious Western influence that we can explain the clear accent on the social importance of the family and the disciplining of sexual instincts through particular requirements of social morality, which were presented in the Quranic form but still, in A. Khalid's words, remained the products of Western modernity (Khalid 1999).

In the closing days of the Russian empire in Turkistan the local women continued to remain in the grip of patriarchally distorted Quranic notions. Similarly to other Muslim countries, the men distorted Quran, because it was in their interest to define women as weak and lacking the ability to think rationally. Taking into account the intensified women's isolation with the beginning of Russian colonization of Turkistan the Jadids' active defense of women was seen as one of the most shocking elements of their program of national renaissance. In this sense they represented a double critique questioning both colonialism and Islamic traditionalism, applying the modernizing tendencies brought from Turkey, the Arabic countries and the Tatar provinces of Russia, where a rethinking of gender relations had started earlier.

The critique of miserable women's condition in Central Asian society stood in the center of the Jadids attention from the start and to the end of their movement. They thought that the women's rights and the growth of their influence upon the society were necessary conditions for the successful development of a nation. This logic was used in many projects of Muslim modernization. The Jadids spoke against polygamy and criticized the women's lack of rights and their ignorance. The restoration of the true Islam and its teaching in the new method schools along with secular subjects was regarded as one of the important means in the struggle for women's rights, as a necessary condition for the successful national project. The veil was not regarded as the source of ignorance and filth as it had not yet become an emblem of vice. This would happen later in the Soviet discourses. For the Jadids it was not the paranjee as such but rather a lack of education that presented the main problem, while under the paranjee one could find any morality and any education or lack of them.

A more complex and contradictory position was expressed in a number of fictional texts created by the Jadids, particularly those which were not meant for publication. This answers the colonial rule according to which the philosophy of history, ontology, and existential revelations in colonial spaces are often "buried under the art of imagination" (Harris 1995, 378). I mean, for instance, an unfinished and unpublished novelette written by a prominent Uzbek Jadid writer A. Kadiri (Dzhulkunboy) *Notes of Kalvak Makhzum* which became known thanks to a recent performance of Tashkent theater *Ilkhom*. In Mark Weil's stage interpretation this text turned into a wonderful play *White White Black Stork* (1998). If in case of the Russian romantics the well known literary version leans to the lighter side of modernity, while the letters, diaries, and notes allow to see its darker colonial side, in case of the Jadids the logic was different. The official image of Kadiri, emblematically exploited in modern Uzbekistan, is based on his canonization. The author, who was repressed in 1938 together with the remaining Jadids, is presented as a poetic singer of the olden days, and a founder of the novel genre in Uzbek literature, a devoted lover of traditional Uzbek culture and values nostalgically re-creating them in his works. However, along with his well known novels *Days Gone By* and *Scorpio from the Altar* which were usually presented within the motif of the struggle of the new and the old, Kadiri was the author of unpublished *Notes of Kalvak Makhzum*, which allow us to glimpse into his restless and questioning side, and transvalue and transcultural double critique both with respect to the suffocating local tradition and to modernity seen more and more as alien and forceful. The central and forbidden motif of the novelette is the love of one of the main characters—a poetic and delicate Makhsum—for his Madrasah peer, which ends up in tragedy. The main characters Makhsum and Makhichekhra are sixteen-year-olds who are forced into marriage in order to hide Makhsum's homosexual tendencies and make money by selling the daughter into a good family. Both teenagers are others who do not want to live according to accepted rules. In the play there are two variants of authority, power, and law—the traditional local law and the Russian empire's court, which both families alternatively take their suits to after the teenagers' unsuccessful marriage. Both variants are presented by Kadiri and Weil as being far from real justice or respect for human beings. Makhsum and Makhichekhra are doomed in this world and they have nowhere to go. Behind the ethnographic details of the old Tashkent way of life and colorful historical characters, there emerges a serious conflict—the human struggle for dignity, for his or her right to be himself or herself even if you are different from others. The tragic death of Weil himself (he was killed in 2007) proves that nothing has changed today (Antelava 2008). It is from this impulse that the decolonial ethics and aesthetics is being born.

Muslim women's discourses of the early twentieth century in the Russian empire initially lacked a binary opposition with men, which was to be found in some other locales. Men were considered as potential allies and not enemies. The same way as in anti-colonial movements, in Jadidism and Muslim reform movements in general, the men-women opposition gave place to a more important distinction between the new and the old. Equal citizens of both sexes were seen as builders of the new nation, while the enemies of the new were not distinguished according to gender principle. It was assumed that in the new life gender contradictions would be naturally overcome.

An important role here was played by the first "new" colonial women, who were at once the instruments and symbols of reforms. In the Russian configuration it was first the Tatar women who acted as mediators of modernity and champions of enlightenment. By the second decade of the twentieth century the Tatar women were already publishing a few journals and magazines, such as, for example, the *Woman's World* in Bakhchisaray which was edited by Shafika Khanum, the daughter of an influential Tatar enlightener Ismail Gaspirali.

Later in Turkistan there emerged a separate group of "new women" who were closely linked to the Jadid ideology. A detailed description of their activities is presented in a historical study by M. Kamp *The New Woman in Uzbekistan. Islam, Modernity and Unveiling under Communism* (Kamp 2006). She tells about the first Central Asian women Jadids (for instance, the Koquand Jadid Tazhi, who already in 1906 wrote a letter to *The Woman's World* calling for the awakening of the Muslim women of Turkistan, for their education, progress, and struggle for their rights (Kamp 2006, 36–38); about the teachers and first students of the *Bylym Yurt*—the House of Knowledge for women and girls in Tashkent (Kamp 2006, 86), as well as about the representatives of the *zhenotdels* (women's departments) and the editorial board of the journal *Yangi Yul* (New Way). Many of them came from old Central Asian intelligentsia families, started as Jadids and later accepted at least externally the Soviet model trying to adjust it to their goals of women's liberation and education (Kamp 2006, 101–107). In this artistic and essayistic form, traditionally allowed for the colonized spaces, the discourse of the new Muslim woman was firmly grounded in nationalism and its interpretation of the woman's role in society. The central model was the woman as a mother and an educator of good children—the future ideal citizens of the new state.

They practiced their own gendered colonial tricksterism, which allowed them to survive in the conditions of the starting Soviet repressions against the "bourgeois nationalists." Such were a woman-poet Aydyn (Mansura Sobirova), who wrote a play with a telling title *A Step toward Modernity* (1925), a journalist and writer Kh. Tylyakhanova, who later left her ideologically dangerous position for a safer one in a textile journal, and Jadid R. Nasyrova who refused to agree with the myth that the Soviet power was the sole liberator of women in Turkistan. Colonial gender tricksterism in relation to Russian and later Soviet modernity, could be expressed both in intellectual forms of other modernity, as in the examples above, and in the form of resistance to modernity as such, in maintaining of traditional practices, esoteric and nonrational knowledges, often of pre-Islamic origin. An example of this is the Central Asian institute of *Otins*—the women clerics and readers of Quran, as well as teachers for young children of both sexes. The *Otin* phenomenon was initially a trickster one as it allowed for the women's religious, cultural, health and educational needs to be adjusted to the strict laws of a rather repressive society, yet retained at least a symbolic memory of the previous more egalitarian logic, of women's leadership and power. First the *Otins* were pushed into the periphery of society by the Jadid new method schools. Later they were almost destroyed by the Soviet modernity, which interpreted them as harmful survivals and drove into the underground, eventually turning into healers and midwives.[6]

Thus, national modernity acquires a specific women's face in Turkistan starting from the Jadids' activism onward. Later this tactic continues in altered forms with the coming of Bolsheviks. Even if the Soviet ideologues were rather intellectually derivative, they were also more resolute in their efforts to change the previous model of women's nonparticipation in the public life to the new ones. If before the situation was similar to what Oyěwùmi describes for Yoruba culture, where the European colonizers regarded only men as objects of their ideological, economic, or religious projects (Oyěwùmi 1997, 122), after the October revolt women were put squarely in the center of the Soviet modernizing efforts. Here an earlier conquistador's logic used in the conquering of America stepped forward: a conquering of a people started with the winning of its women. In many ways it was connected with the fear of the success of alternative forces and models of modernizing, both external (in this case coming from other Muslim countries) and internal (coming from the Jadids).

4.2. Hygienic and Medicinal Discourses, Race, and Gender

Modernity in the twentieth century was implemented in two forms—the liberal/capitalist modernity and the socialist/statist one. Each of them had a sunny side and a darker side, each of them had its own kind of coloniality of being and of gender. Many authors have already written on the evolution of the Soviet gender discourses in the metropolis (Navailh 1996, Wood 2000, Ashwin 2000, Posadskaya 1994, Katz 2001). Less studied is the darker colonial side of the Soviet modernity where a second-rate type of the Soviet citizen was constructed in spite of the proclaimed internationalist slogans and an overt goal of racial mixing of the population in order to create a future Soviet Mestizo/a with an erased ethnic element brought up on Russian culture and on Soviet ideology. A metropolitan (Russian) woman was opposed to the stereotyped colonial female who was in need of civilizing and reinvention as the New Woman of the East or a New Mountain Woman. These identities turned out highly problematic and self-negating at times.

As D. Northrop correctly observes, many Bolsheviks' views on Central Asia sounded as much Orientalist as Marxist (Northrop 2004, 39). They reflected the missionary pathos of the people who replaced religion with communist faith and legitimized it as the only correct one. The new Soviet element in the old formula which survived from Czarist times, and linked filth, backwardness, and Oriental women, was the pronounced national dimension. The backward woman now stood for the nation. The colonial national project already at its birth included self-denigrating elements. If filth, disease, and moral degradation were associated with the (colonial) nation then it was the liberation from this nation and the assimilation to the Russian/Soviet norm that became the final goal of the Soviet modernity. The missionary zeal was seasoned with pseudo-scientific element, which used experts with their anthropological and biomedical means to formulate what was the Uzbek or the Chechen nation (sometimes even race) using the woman as the quintessence of all the deficiencies of this nation.

At later stages of modernity medicinal and sanitary discourses as a part of the imperial-colonial relations acquired a crucial role in the interpretation of race and gender. There are interesting parallels in this respect between the Spanish colonies in Northern Africa (Morocco) in the twentieth century and the Soviet Central Asia. In the constructions of early Soviet colonialism the women's question was interpreted through the familiar descriptions of the horrible harem life controlled by Islam and the strict Central-Asian custom. In these discourses one finds common (for this stage of modernity) renderings of race and culture, quasi-scientific civilizing discourses and an accent on environment and education which were additionally distorted in countries marked by the imperial difference, as it was the case with Russia and Spain.

Let us turn to I. Jiménez-Lucena's article "Gender and Coloniality: the 'Moroccan Woman' and the 'Spanish Woman' in Spain's Sanitary Policies in Morocco," which demonstrates the inseparable functioning of androcentrism, colonialism, and class hierarchies in the patriarchal discourse in and for the colonies. Jiménez-Lucena states that the colonial system was not able to exist outside the following contradiction: on the one hand it had to maintain the symbolic and structural distance between us and them. On the other hand, it needed a universal model applicable to the control of all aspects of human life. Hence a constant pendulum movement of imperialism from (the insuperable) difference to common identity and the difficult to fulfill strive for balance between the civilizing of the savage and the keeping of his or her eternal difference (Jiménez-Lucena 2008, 35). Universalism then refers only to the dominant group which creates a special axis of differentiation in all directions, lying in the basis of the world social hierarchical division. This social hierarchy drastically changes in the colonies because the new groups push the former lower classes up from their previous place in the social ladder and allow them to elevate their status. This logic acquires different forms in various imperial-colonial histories. Gender adds other vectors of power relations to this picture, such as a vector between the European and the colonized women or between the colonized males and the European women in particular social roles. Jiménez-Lucena echoes A. Khatibi's position calling for the double critique from the border between Islam and the West. But in her case it is a double critique of the local androcentrism of the Moroccan society and the Spanish colonialist fundamentalism.

The article describes the medicinal stages of colonialist racist discourses when specific attention was paid to the scientific legitimating of natural difference of the other. Medical knowledge combined Eurocentrism and androcentrism and acted as an important part of expansionistic cultural and historical project (Jiménez-Lucena 2008, 36). Medical discourses allowed the power in any colonial space to turn the local into the global, to universalize and naturalize certain categories, justifying the approaches that dismissed the human dignity of others. The local women and the agents of metropolis found themselves equally in the grip of the double game of the universal and the particular.

Behind this pseudo-scientific language it is easy to detect the earlier human taxonomies linked with the opposition of Christianity and Islam including the gender sphere. Something similar we find in Central Asia, but here the Soviet modernity replaced a Catholic one. As in other colonial locales there were two types of women clearly divided from each other—those who played the role of colonial agents and the others. The commonality in their biological nature was balanced with the difference in their imperial-colonial and racial status. Jiménez-Lucena analyzes this problematic in relation to Morocco (then a Spanish protectorate). Therefore her analysis combines the categories common to all androcentric discourses, such as questioning the intellectual abilities of women, the discourse on prostitution, interpreting women as a manifestation of the ethics of care, with a locally determined problem of defining the Moroccan woman as an opposite to the Spanish one.

Within the Spanish culture even in the mid-twentieth century, the Spanish woman was regarded as a creature with only a natural uncultured intellect. While a Moroccan woman was automatically taken down in her status to occupy a position on the verge of the animal. She was accused of superstition, ignorance, and of the fact that she did not speak fluent Spanish (Robles Mendo 1953, 31–37). The Spanish women themselves did not even think of mastering Arabic, following in this respect the general logic of the colonizers. A similar model worked in Russia and the Soviet Union. Practically none of the Russian or Soviet colonizers (with the exception of orientalists) ever attempted to study the local languages. While the locals' lack of fluency in Russian was interpreted as professional incompetence and almost a mental retardation. The colonized women became the objects of forced medical-anthropological studies. And their refusal to act as such was rendered as an animal instinct and as backwardness, never as a conscious resistance.

In the early quasi-scientific racism in the Soviet Union the colonized women were used as an evidence of racial and human deficiency of the colonized people and an object of application of social-evolutionary theories which were later put in the basis of social engineering. Although by this time a developed system of Muslim gender colonial agency had existed in the Russian Empire, the imperial center continued to translate difference not into religion, but into race and national culture, interpreted in primordialist way. A good example was the experts' efforts to define what made a woman an Uzbek or a Tadzhic in a biological sense, to link "backwardness with biology" (Cavanaugh 2001). As D. Northrop points out, they lent support to the view that national-cultural distinctions in Central Asia were objectively real and empirically measurable (Northrop 2004, 52). He gives a peculiar example of a physician Iasevich, who in 1928 published a meticulous study "On the Question of the Constitutional and Anthropological Type of the Uzbek Woman of Khorezm" (Iasevich 1928, 35), proving that the women of then still imagined Uzbek community were to be identified with unique biological features that made them different from Kazakh or Turkmen women. The use of the photographs of naked women resembled the imperial voyeurism and collector's mentality, in the manner of the Victorian gentleman Arthur Munby, who was maniacally attracted to racial and gender ambiguity of the low class women, as analyzed by Ann McClintock (McClintock 1995, 75–131). These pictures also bring us back to the tradition of the zoo stories, freak shows, and human diversity shows, and particularly the infamous Sartjee Baartman's case (Holmes 2006). Iasevich's "models" presented on the photographs accompanying the article make us wonder how could Baartman feel as a live exhibit?

The girls studied by the Soviet scholar were supposed to present the six bodily types typical for Khorezm. Placed one after another, the pictures of embarrassed women reminded zoological comparative maps of subspecies. The sexualized orientalizing nature of such studies was obvious, but here the scientific authority was used to cover up the elaborate imperial violence: since women remained the most secluded and opaque stratum of Central Asian society, the imperial penetration into their life and violation of their privacy—peeping under the paranjee with a scientific excuse—turned out to be an effective form of oppression which presented itself as a liberation. There was also evidently a fear of a possible active resistance on the part of the colonized males which led to the choice of women as objects of Soviet propaganda and young girls and children, particularly boys, as objects of bio-medicinal and anthropological studies (Zezenkova 1953, Shyshov 1928).

The Bolsheviks turned out radical in this respect. Certain forms of the colonial Soviet women's resistance, for instance, their refusal to put children into the communal Soviet day care, resulted in campaigns of nationalization of the colonial children. Similar efforts in the metropolis remained just slogans, except for the real orphans and later the children of the enemies of the people. In some colonial spaces there emerged a phenomenon of artificial colonial orphans who had parents but were taken out of their families and put into the Soviet boarding houses where their ideological, social, and gender indoctrination was successfully performed (Tekuyeva 2006, 222–226).

In order to achieve a higher status in androcentric society, Russian and Spanish women often became the accomplices of the colonizing regime and started to express clearly male and colonialist views. In return the androcentric society allowed such women to become scientific authorities (as in the case of the Spanish in Morocco) or gave them some real and symbolic benefits such as the possibility of a socially important position which they could not hope to achieve in the metropolis (as in case of the Soviet modernity).

I have already touched upon the discourse on prostitution in various colonial contexts within the frame of coloniality of being and of gender. As demonstrated by Jiménez-Lucena, the Spanish faced a typical task of constructing a dichotomy of the decent Spanish woman, modeled on virgin Mary and a sexually loose Moroccan. The in-between space was occupied by the common local women and Spanish prostitutes. The latter were still considered higher than the Moroccans as in the view of the Spanish scientific authorities there was no one dirtier than Muslim women. The Spanish medical and hygienic discourses went as far as to erase the difference between Muslim women and prostitutes (Ovilo y Canales 1886, 192). In Central Asia in the 1920s the Russian activists of women's departments and the newly emerged local activists, struggling to demonstrate their loyalty to the Soviet power, created a similar discourse, linking local women with venereal diseases. Yet they usually blamed this on the local custom and the local males.

The next woman's image which Jiménez-Lucena analyzes in her article in connection with the redoubling of gender discourses in the metropolis and the colony is the woman as a care giver and nurturer. The case in question is women as nurses or doctors. This role was considered honorable for the Spanish woman, but the Moroccan women who practiced traditional medicine or midwifery, were regarded by the new Spanish power as harmful survivals. In spite of this demonization, her authority often continued to challenge the authority of Western doctors (both men and women).

In the colonies the ideal of the educated Spanish woman was propagated and opposed to the backward local ones—the victims who were in need of salvation from Islamic superstition. Here the naturalized imperial myth helped to sustain the mental colonization of the Spanish women, who experienced discrimination in androcentric metropolis, but were easily persuaded in their emancipation by the Western society when compared with uncivilized Muslim gender relations (Jiménez-Lucena 2008, 40, 44). A similar ambivalence was at work in the case of the Russian women in the colonial spaces. In the metropolis they would be actively struggling for their minimal rights, criticize the patriarchal nature of Russian society, the Czarist government's neglect of the women's needs, etc. But once they got into the colonies the same women immediately changed into racist and Eurocentric feminists. This logic continued in the Soviet Union as well. The Russian empire fashioned the familiar division into four main groups of the modern/colonial gender system, but it was complicated by a more active and resolute interference of the state into all areas, and also, in case of Central Asia and Tatar provinces, by Jadidism which questioned Muslim ideologies. Similarly to other aspects of the cultural and political imaginary of Russia, its gender sphere was characterized by a schizophrenic duality, more or less cynical, depending on how conscious it was.

The architects of gender order in the late Czarist empire did not want to allow for the women's emancipation in the metropolis. They were reluctant to change the patriarchal family, the voting, or educational laws. In this context it became tactically important to switch the attention to the presumably more downtrodden and backward Muslim women and to co-opt Russian gender activists into the struggle for the Muslim women's rights. Psychologically this step allowed the Russian women to feel that there is someone even more downtrodden and backward than them. The demagogic appeals for the defense of the poor Oriental women written by Russian bureaucrats and pseudo-scholars sounded almost feminist, attracting many Russian "emancipated" women who quickly forgot about their women's solidarity and turned to civilizing mission instead, which allowed them to enjoy their presumable racial, religious, ethnic, and gender superiority (Rorlich 2004, 50).

In the Soviet period the hierarchy of the colonized women and representatives of the metropolis was further polarized within the frame of the conscious construction of the secondary colonial gendered other, who received symbolic rights on paper which only made her subordinate status more obvious and painful. While the status of the representative of empire, the new Soviet woman as a champion of modernity, automatically elevated as soon as she moved to a colony, simply on the basis of her ethnic-racial belonging. This rule, rather universal for coloniality, was quickly naturalized in Russian minds, hiding for a while the imperial difference complex.

The discourse of salvation of the downtrodden women—Moroccan or Central Asian—is one more intersection zone between Jiménez-Lucena's work and the situation of Eurasian borderlands. The liberation soon stumbled against the necessity of keeping the difference between us and them. The woman's question was regarded as an insuperable impediment for Morocco's entering modernity and catching up with the enlightened Europe. It was assumed that the Spanish women would act in the role of ideal New Women while the Moroccan women would be vaccinated by the discourse of modernity and start transmitting it within their families and society. But this future agency of the Moroccan women, the possibility of which was indirectly admitted by the Spanish, did not match their own notions of the Muslim women's extreme backwardness. The discourse of liberation in the process of social changes in Morocco was fundamentally contradictory, as it negated its own goal by means of denying any importance of the Moroccan women or their ability to benevolent changes and conscious agency as such. As always in gender discourses of modernity formulated from above, what was crucial was to legitimize the forced liberation and not to make any real changes in women's lives.

This paradoxical logic of gender enslaving through the rhetoric of emancipation was best of all expressed in the two parallel campaigns in Caucasus and in Central Asia in the early Soviet period—the "Coat for the Mountain Woman" and *Hudzhum* (assault). In the center of both there stood efforts to bring women to the public space and get them involved in the collective mass production, making a real proletariat out of the "surrogate" one (Massel 1974), turning them into the conscientious and docile builders of the new society with minimal or erased gender differences. The simplest way to make these changes visible was through clothes and appearance. The 1920s "coat campaign" supplied a few local women with European style coats in order to make them socially active, unbound to their houses, to allow them to go to school, to work and, most importantly, to vote (Tekuyeva 2006, 227–232). *Hudzhum* used as its anti-fetish a special kind of Central Asian veil (paranjee and chachvon) and aimed at uncovering the woman's body and once again, dressing it in European style. In both cases the impetus behind was similar to Iasevich's photographs—based on interfering into the woman's most intimate world which was in itself a manifestation of imperial violence in the control of sexuality and subjectivity.

Behind the external changes however there hid the more fundamental differences which the authorities were not intending to erase either in Spain or in Russia. The Moroccan women were assigned their concrete limit of modernization. They were allowed to be no more than the low paid nurses working under the supervision of European medical stuff. In spite of the Soviet egalitarianism and show-cases of emancipated Oriental women, the same logic was at work here as well. An example is to be found in the oral history of Muborakkhanum Gaffarova, who spent half of her life in Xinjiang Uzbek Diaspora before coming back to Tashkent. She is free from Soviet mythology and sensitive to the problem of colonial zombification and the importance of cultivating resistance: "When I was appointed a senior nurse, one nurse told me directly, that I am a newcomer, I just arrived yesterday and already became a boss. I was very offended. I told her: 'Yedgar opa, if a Russian woman was appointed instead of me, this would not make you unhappy. I am from Tashkent the same way as you are. My parents were born here and I came back to my motherland, why are you so indignant? If there was a Russian instead of me you would be happy because you are used to being the slaves of Russians'. I was very upset. That is why later I would often send the Uzbek nurses to the qualification improvement courses, and also tried to teach them myself. There was one woman, Vera was her name. She used to do cardiograms and she ignored everyone. Then I took three or four of our girls and taught them how to do cardiograms. I told them, why cannot you do what this Vera does?" (Tokhtakhodzhaeva et al. 1995, 45). Similar to the configuration described by Jiménez-Lucena here too the local woman could act only as a simple instrument of colonial politics, her very inclusion as an "agent of modern health care" was allowed only if she was subordinate and dependent on the Western medicine professionals (Jiménez-Lucena 2008, 42).

4.3. A Diversion: The Soviet Empire's Contradictory Racial Discourses

In 2002 *Slavic Review* published a discussion on the understanding of race in the USSR. Eric Weitz drew a parallel between the Soviet and the Nazi discourses on race. He correctly pointed out that in the

Soviet Union the racial politics was implemented without any clearly formulated idea of race (Weitz 2002). It is true that the notion of race in Russia and the USSR was borrowed from Western modernity. Weitz contextualizes his theorizing of racial politics and the evolution of the concept of race in the Soviet Union within the wider rhetoric of modernity. The Soviet model was one of its manifestations. He correctly points out that along with official documents and rhetoric there was also the everyday practice, the private life of Soviet individuals, the (self)disciplining tactics, the prevalence of personal and group interests over an abstract state ideology. Weitz shows that behind the term "national" there stood, in fact, "racial."

His opponents (Hirsch 2002, Weiner 2002) refused to see Soviet racism as racism because they claim it was not biological. This argument is easy to contest if we remember that even during the flourishing of eugenics and pseudo-scientific racist discourses, the boundary between biology and culture was always blurred. What was more important was the tactic of assigning a permanent and inerasable identity of each group member, with a number of predictable and hereditary behavioral models. The latter was used as a basis for superiority and pride in case of Russians and led to deportations and forceful displacement, annihilation of the whole ethnicities, including the elderly, the infants, and even the graves of the ancestors—in many other cases. What was stressed here was the impossibility of reforming the enemy-nations. Besides, the understanding of the nation in the USSR was biological (Vyshnevsky 1998, 333–350), and replacing biology with culture did not really change much in real discriminatory practices. What difference does it make which arguments were used to explain the Russian superiority—their "development" or their correspondence to the socialist ideal or the discourse of the White man's burden? Racism remained racism. And this was intuitively grasped by the lumpenized *Homo Sovieticus*, who has kept proclaiming his superiority over the colonized.

The racial politics in the USSR were determined both by the historical evolution of the national form as such, and by the peculiarities of the Soviet system. The rhetoric and the tactics of the Soviet modernity were marked by a constant balancing between the light, egalitarian, inclusive and civil element and the dark, excluding, ethnic interpretation of the nation and nationality. The politics of strict regulation and construction of the population stood in the center of the Soviet ideologues' efforts and required specific attention to national which acted as racial. The pseudo-federative structure of the USSR served as an additional instrument of control but also as a time bomb for the future.

Soviet racializing and social engineering were a reflection of typical (for secular modernity) mechanisms of interpreting all negative characteristics and primarily class and morals through race. As a number of authors have persuasively demonstrated (McClintock 1995, 75–131; Davidoff 1983), in Great Britain the working classes, the prostitutes and the beggars were described in official and scientific discourses as the disseminators of degenerate genetic material and in visual representations were literally racialized, made to look similar to Africans and Amerindians. In the USSR the exclusion and the persecution of the unwanted groups also acquired a vaguely racist form. Certainly, one would not find here a commercial of a Black child washing himself with Pears soap until he got White (McClintock 1995, 213), but there were surely caricatures that depicted the bourgeoisie, the clergy and the aristocrats as racially degenerate elements. The Soviet posters advertising the friendship of the peoples were based on the hierarchy which was racial in its essence and stagist in its form: the central or higher place was always occupied by the Slavs (in the order of their closeness to Russians as an etalon), while the non-European peoples were put lower and farther from the center (Sahni 1997, 124–125). It is not a chance that the German-Russian Race Institute, which existed from 1927 to 1935 (Weindling 1992), concentrated mostly on the study of indigenous people and not on Russian or Ukrainian peasants. Their goal was to prove the full human value of the objects of these field studies—in opposition to the Nazis. However the very choice of material for such studies betrayed the Bolsheviks' own racist prejudice. They were against racism Western style and for racism Soviet way.

The racial politics and racial discourses in the Soviet Union graphically show that race is not biological, that it has little to do with the color of skin or the shape of the cranium. It has a symbolic meaning as an effective form of disciplining, exclusion, and constructing the human taxonomies. Weitz argues: "While racial distinctions have most often been based on phenotype, race is not essentially about skin color but about the assignment of indelible traits to particular groups. Hence, ethnic groups, nationalities, and even social classes can be 'racialized' in historically contingent moments and places" (Weitz 2002, 7). There was clearly such a danger in the Soviet Union. A biological interpretation of race by the 1930s had changed to the culturalist arguments, with the exception of the colonial spaces. In fact culture simply replaced biology but racism stayed intact. In E. Balibar's words, "this approach naturalizes not racial belonging but racial conduct" (Balibar 1991, 22).

The politics of *korenizatsija* (literally, "rooting") of the 1920–1930s, and later an anti-nationalism campaign, the forced deportations and the genocide of the whole ethnicities were the Soviet manifestation of the politics of creating, educating, and controlling nationalities from above. The very idea that some nationalities had to take a directed path of development until they got the right to become a part of the Soviet system of "national in its form and socialist in its essence" was a racist realization of modernity discourse. As Weitz points out, it is important how the social characteristic easily collapsed into biological (Weitz 2002, 11), the class enemies became the enemies of the people and enemy nations. The mid-1930s were a boundary after which the state began to limit the further proliferation of nationalities, pounding into the public opinion the cultural and political superiority of Russians. Even in relatively harmless cases when no repressions and deportation were involved, these politics led to the forced Russification and the erasing of cultural memory and history of the whole peoples in the country which successfully presented itself to the world as the "affirmative action empire" (Martin 2001). The rhetoric of the state as a family of brother nations easily masked the theatricality and simulacrum nature of Soviet multiculturalism. With the coming of Bolsheviks the positivist forms of othering became firmly linked with nation building and the unresolved contradictions of Soviet federalism, as well as with racial and gender hierarchies which were effectively masked under the slogan of proletarian internationalism.

The Soviet ideology contradicted itself in creating nationalities in the periphery, on the one hand (including the literacies and the sense of ethnic-territorial belonging), and on the other hand, regarding the national traditions and customs that came to be associated with this ethnicity only due to colonization—as a threat and something to be eventually erased.[7] The double-faceness of the Soviet discourses combined an external ideological lack of racism and its constant internal presence in the actions of the Soviet empire and its citizens.

To give the colonized equal rights in education, appearance or social status was dangerous in itself. Soon it became clear that the racial prejudice, according to which the Asiatics or the Mountain peoples were not ever capable of becoming equal to Russians, and were doomed to stay inferior due to their insuperable low place on the scale of humanity, collapsed with the first blows of Soviet modernization. The Soviet Empire thus got into a trap that it inadvertently put for itself. A modernized native not only threatened to become more accomplished than the Russian, even within the rules of distorted

Eurocentric Socialist progressivist logic, but also could destroy this logic from within using the instruments of colonial tricksterism including its gender version. The Soviet empire began to construct different principles of national policies based on chauvinism and the discourse of the "elder brother" to prevent the true equality and put invisible but effective stoppages which would not allow a real social, intellectual, or any other growth of the colonized. At the same time, new signs of ethnic-national identities were invented which were simultaneously ethnic and Socialist and kept the colonized within the limits of Soviet multiculturalism.

The Soviet "decades of national cultures," the promotion of ethnic dance and music festivals and other romanticized folkloristic simulacra were used to release the tension of the threat of a more serious opposition and resistance. All that worked for consolidating the perennialist tendencies in the Soviet rhetoric of the national according to which the non-Russian ethnic cultures were regarded as frozen, fallen out of time and never reaching the level of Soviet modernity, mainly associated with the Russian proletariat. Russians themselves were coded no less primordialistically but in this case it was not a negative feature. On the contrary, it worked as a role model for all the rest.

The rhetoric of Soviet modernity in the interpretation of the "great Russian people," the accentuating of particular, edited moments of its history as a heroic struggle for the liberation and independence from various enemies, as well as the racially coded positive features of Slavic character (the only officially allowed pan-ethnic ideology) went deep into the hearts and minds of Russians themselves and all other ethnicities in the USSR. Today this echoes in self-racializing of the ex-colonial zombified intelligentsia. The ideology of Slavic superiority flourished during the Great Patriotic War, when the Soviet Union coded its victory over Nazism in essentially primordialist terms of racial superiority of the Slavs and particularly the Russians. This was not openly said, but it was clear in the visual propaganda, in films and in paintings of the time. The growing racialization finally resulted in ethnic cleansings and the repressions based on ethnic national but in fact racial motifs.

Weitz's opponents argue that in the USSR there were no gas chambers and none of the deported nations were completely physically destroyed. This seems demagogical as the very idea of deportation clearly presupposed sending people to extreme conditions, starvation and eventual death. In the understanding of the Soviet empire these people were not fully human. They were dispensable lives and bad genetic material. The living conditions which the whole nationalities were forced into, their being divested of any civil and human rights made their position equal death, even if not immediately physical. What was at work in relation to such people was the ethics of modernity that justified the subhuman status of certain groups and allowed for any violence against them. The Soviet Union here acted in accordance with the all penetrating coloniality of being. Weitz grasps this when he mentions the problem of ontological difference: "In the period from 1937 to 1953 the Soviet state also defined certain nations as suspect and dangerous…and Soviet policies rested on the notion that ontology determined politics, that if one was born a Korean, a Crimean Tatar, a Chechen or, finally, a Jew one had to think and act in a particular manner" (Weitz 2002, 23). It was the ontological dimension of coloniality of being at work.

Yet Weitz's article does not quote the voices of the people who experienced the Soviet misanthropic skepticism. Such voices are still confined to oral histories, literature, art, essays, journalism, but they are so emotionally and psychologically dense that they can easily challenge the dry figures of the official documents or even some scholarly articles. A graphic example is a contemporary Balkar writer Boris Chipchikov's short story "A Pink Underground" (Chipchikov 2006, 119–123) based on a true account, where in just four pages he traces the life of an old man who went together with his suffering people through all the tortures of the twentieth century ironically referred to as nightmarish "fairytales." From the encirclement near Kharkov the man comes into a German concentration camp and later to GULAG. Having served his time there as a prisoner of war he is then sent—this time as a Balkar (an enemy nation), to Central Asia to where his people have been recently deported. Riding in a truck along the green countryside he sees "black people drifting in the field" and is explained by the Russian driver (obviously an ex-criminal) that these are the "Balkars grazing." When the old man protests that he is also a Balkar the driver does not believe him. The main character sees black faced and toothless people chewing the grass. They forgot about the simple human words and are surprised when he greets them. They start crying. He is shocked with slow, naked, sleepy, pot-bellied, and transparent children who have dark stains visible in the sun, where their heart, kidney and liver are. "But between the head and the heart, in the black house of ribs there is nothing" (Chipchikov 2006, 122).

The very choice of words demonstrates the Soviet racial hierarchy based on demonizing the other. In the mind of the driver who is a typical zombified Soviet/Russian, there rules not an ideological but precisely a racial superiority. He sees the Balkars as subhuman and he uses the word "graze" describing them as if they were cattle. A normal person in his view, such as the old man, cannot be a Balkar by definition. The Balkars are not destroyed physically. They are just taken to a subhuman status and firmly linked with famine. Then we look at the Balkars through the eyes of the old man who notices the same indications as in the concentration camp or in GULAG: the fallen out teeth, the transparent bodies of sick children whose souls are dormant and maybe will never wake up again. And this is more dangerous than a physical death.

Opposing Weitz, F. Hirsch disagrees with the analogy between the Holocaust and the Soviet ethnic cleansings. The skillful Soviet rhetoric, as it turns out, is still able to enchant. However, there is possibly another factor here at work. It is an intention to see the Holocaust and the Nazi racial discourses as unique and to disparage the importance of the Soviet racism by its partial justification. What is behind this move? Racism once again—a fundamental basis of modernity. It follows that the lives of Balkars and Koreans are not as important as Jewish lives. Taking Chechens or Crimean Tatars to a subhuman status even if without a declared physical annihilation based on racial difference, is presented in some works as not as horrible as the highly symbolic Holocaust experience. Yet the Soviet racial othering is not unique and in various degrees and guises it is typical of Stalinism, Nazism, and colonialism alike. In all cases there is the same operation at work—divesting the enemy of its human nature. He or she is associated with disease, infection, which the society needs to be cured from. Sometimes this zeal is milder, as it happened in the interpretation of the Oriental women in the USSR, who were seen as subject to (re)formation. In other cases it ends with genocide of the unreformable enemy nations and with erasing of even their names from all encyclopedias and dictionaries, as if they never existed. The final biologization of nationality and its primordialist interpretation took a racist form as the right to chose one's nationality even in the passport was granted to only selected citizens in the USSR and accompanied by discriminating policies.

Weitz points out the ambivalence of the Soviet national policies connected with both internal contradictions of nationalism and with the nature of particularly Soviet socialist project (Weitz 2002, 17). The Soviet policies were marked with blurred boundaries between the political and racial articulations of the nation and between the categories of nation and race as such. This was not a peculiarly Soviet trait either. Even in largely civil nations such as the United States the biological primordialist interpretation of the nation and national has always gone hand in hand with the democratic and civil one. According to F. Hirsch, S. Kotkin, J. Kotsonis, and others, the Soviet engineering of the population in this respect was a part of larger global tendencies of the time (Hirsch 1998, Kotsonis 2000, Kotkin 1995). They mean the strict taxonomies typical of many states and regimes—from communist to liberal and fascist (Weitz 2002, 18). In the Soviet variant the national primordialism was unreserved due to the totalization of scientific communism.

Genetics that was banned in the USSR as a bourgeois science, managed to stay in its negative variant of the specific Soviet racism, under which every individual representative of a nationality became a carrier of some stable and hereditary, usually negative, traits. This could be a nomadic way of life, a religious piety, individualism, a commercial talent, that is, qualities that are connected with the environment and bringing up, and not determined by blood. Weitz shows that due to the imperial multiethnic nature of Russia and the USSR, the rendering of nation and race, common to all modernity discourses, was further complicated. But the matter was not just the multiethnicity as such but also a specific subaltern nature of the Russian/Soviet empire in its intellectual subordination to Western modernity.

Weitz mainly speaks of the Russians and Russian nationalism forgetting the colonial peoples of the empire. They remain interesting for him only as objects. The association with the state is more important than with the nation. He mentions the Russian intelligentsia's reluctance to discuss the idea of race in the early twentieth century, contrary to the West, which painfully stressed these aspects at the time. Russian intelligentsia probably was not ready to discuss race openly, but it was ready to practice racism and it had been doing so for quite some time, at least from the beginning of the nineteenth century, as mentioned above. Colonialism then could not exist without racism. Social Darwinism, reductionism, and Eurocentrism with their claims at objectivity, the complex of anthropological superiority and the taxonomic drive permeated Russian linguistics, anthropology, economics, and philosophy.

Weitz, as well as other Slavists, speaks of race in Russia from the position of the metropolis, of the Russians themselves. This makes his analysis limited at times. Here in the center there stands the polemics on the official state and cultural interpretations of Russian-ness as a national characteristic. Then the racial discourses of criminal pathology, medicine, and eugenics are regarded separately from the colonialist rhetoric as such. As a result Weitz sees only one face of the Russian/Soviet empire.

In the 1920–30s in the USSR there were discussions on what could be the criteria of the national. Language, culture, geography, and biology were used one after another as a possible main criterion. At first, eugenics played an important part in these scientific endeavors. After 1931 eugenics was banned in the USSR and labeled a Nazi science. But as Hirsch points out, many scholars continued to practice it under the guise of medical genetics, even in the difficult times of Trofim Lysenko[8] (Hirsch 2002, 34). The Soviet criminology and ethnography were indirectly affected often by vaguely racist variants of German and French anthropology. This was accompanied by the class discourse that was changing the Western hierarchies in a Soviet Marxist way offering the evidence of the degeneracy of the upper classes and their biological deficiency. The situation in the colonies was different because here racism was expressed directly and openly, not in distorted and hidden forms.

In contrast with Nazi Germany, the USSR seemed to take after the lighter emancipatory side of modernity, but it reached its utopian goals by bloody means and liberated against the will. S. Kotkin is right when he points out that in the USSR a drive to fulfill the harmonious enlightenment utopia was dominant (Kotkin 1995, 364). But he does not mention the fact that this utopia itself included the seeds of violence and had a darker side, which was expressed much before and in equally cruel forms in the history of the colonized people. This logic was aptly analyzed by Franz Hinkelammert who criticizes J. Locke's formula according to which there are no rights for those who violate other peoples' rights no matter how they are defined in a historical period or context. "The inversion of human rights that Locke effects, can be summed up in a formula that he does not yet use, but which expresses his point of view well: no property for the enemies of property…It is the formula that legitimizes the terrorism of the bourgeois system. It already appears in the French Revolution in the following terms: no liberty for the enemies of liberty…Karl Popper assumes this same formula when he affirms that there is no tolerance for the enemies of tolerance…The same formula appears in the Stalinist purges in the discourses of the lawyer Wyschinski, adapted to that system. Thus, this is the formula in which modernity in all of its systems, as much as it sustains human rights, legitimates the violation of those rights, precisely in their own name" (Hinkelammert 2004). Before Locke this same system of annihilation was shaped in patriarchal society and used against women taken outside the humanity, and after Locke it was used in secular constructs of racism when a White male was regarded as a champion of rationality and the normative human being, while all others were not.

The discourses of the "new man" and the "new woman" in the early Soviet Union were particularly radical. They had to be created from the ideal genetic material. And there were nationalities who were not allowed to participate in the birth of the new entity—the Soviet people. Whether this or that nationality was good enough to become a part of the gigantic project of genetic engineering, was decided on racist grounds as a product of modernity, a part of which was the Soviet variant.

Weitz, F. Hirsch argues that in the USSR there was a certain idea of race. The Soviet anthropologists and physicians as well as their Western European colleagues, took part in the international dialogue on race and even did collaborative research (Hirsch 2002, 31). Race was regarded as a physiological and biological type within humanity, but the Soviet and Western European scientists disagreed on the question of racial features: if they were stable or dynamic and subject to development, if it was better to use the eugenic methods of controlling the heredity or the social hygiene and the human progress associated with the prevalence of the environment and, in the Soviet case—the socialist revolution as its factor. Along with biology there were clearly class and political issues behind these debates both in Europe and in the USSR.

By the mid-1930s when the German universities started to teach Nordic race biology instead of physical anthropology, it was decided in the USSR to condemn the German race studies as fascist and bourgeois. But the idea of race itself was still attractive to Soviet scientists. They only rejected its primordialist interpretation and the use of race as a direct scientific and ideological basis of politics. As with many other disciplines it was decided to create a Soviet Marxist-Leninist race studies based on historical materialism. In its basis there lied an idea of taking the physical, moral, and intellectual characteristics apart and the refusal to see race as a grounds for othering.

Backwardness and degeneration were linked by experts with the social and economic conditions and not with natural biological reasons. And the socialist reforms were regarded as an effective way of changing the human body and catalyzing the natural selection. So race was not denied altogether, it was historicized in accordance with the stagist theory which led to the idea of gradual erasing of racial features as the humankind marched toward the ideal society and the nationalities first developed fully and then mixed and disappeared.

However, Hirsch does not take into account that there as a gap between the official ideologies and rhetoric in the USSR, and the real practices (Hirsch 2002, 41). She ignores the fact that race and racism could mutate and acquire various forms and grounds depending on concrete formulation of particular ideologies. But the ontological misanthropic meaning of racism remained the same in the colonization of the Americas, in the USSR, or in Nazi Germany. There was an idea of race in the Soviet Union but it were masked as nationality or, in other words, the idea of nationality was racialized. For many historians of Russia in the West the people, whose lives they study, remain abstractions. They believe that the Soviet politics were turned to the goal of racial mixing in accordance with the "scientific" socialist theories of race. Yet the real practices were more complex and there was a clear gap between the official line and the concrete party activists, scientists, common people and victims of repressions. The Soviet anthropologists could write on the biological equality of all races and nationalities and the inevitable metisation of the Soviet Union. Yet, neither the scientists themselves, nor the ideological institutions that asked them to do this research, or the objects of their studies ever believed the official documents and scholarly articles, because the reality of every day existence was quite different. There race mixed with nation in a complex way and today's open racism in Russia is a result of naturalization of this view.

Hirsch points out an interesting gender asymmetry in the othering of the enemy nations in the USSR when she says that the deported women could get some of their rights back by marrying a representative of a different, not suspicious nationality. As Hirsch points out, this was connected with the culturalist and, I would add, sexist interpretation of nationality in accordance with which women could leave their previous national culture behind, by marrying and going through the Soviet remodeling in the family and the ethnic-cultural environment of their husbands (Hirsch 2002, 41).

Thus, the national was seen not exactly in biological but rather, in cultural and historical terms, yet it was largely assumed that the cultural features are inherited by all representatives of a given nationality no matter where they reside and how were they brought up. The culturalist interpretation still remained deeply xenophobic and put the Russians in a privileged position. Within the constant rivalry with the Western modernity it was necessary to invent more and more parallel discourses in all disciplines and social and political practices, which would answer the logic of modernity, yet would be Soviet and not Western. It was a difficult task due to the common origins of the discourses of Soviet and Western modernity.[9]

Hirsch defends the Soviet regime from any direct analogies with Nazis stating that the enemy nations were not physically destroyed. But she herself adds that instead of physical annihilation it was decided to destroy their language, culture, history, and group self-consciousness. Together with the horrible conditions of survival they were put in, such an effective program reached a result similar to the Holocaust. How else if not through racism can we explain the discourses of the "younger brother of the great Russian people," the trials of bourgeois nationalists which for some reason were never aimed against ethnic Russians, and the forced russification? Is there really a difference in how we call it—race, culture, or national character if in the end it still leads to deportation, death, and erasing from memory?

Another author who takes part in the polemics on Weitz's article is Amir Weiner. He stresses a purely political motivation of the Soviet ethnic cleansing (Weiner 2002). But to prove this he uses a notorious Soviet slogan that the son is not responsible for the father and the presence of Jews in power during the harshest anti-Semitic period. Eurocentrism once again creeps into these arguments. First, the reha-bilitation of the children of the repressed people was very selective, and again, based on racist principles. Thus Weiner gives an example of Ukrainian, that is, Slavic children. But in the case of the repressed Northern Caucasus nationalities the children, including the infants, were all packed into the cargo trains and taken to Central Asia to die. No one suggested taking them away from their enemy parents and reeducate and rehabilitate in Soviet orphanages and children colonies. This asymmetry can be explained only through biological racism.

Weiner's argument that the behavior of certain nationalities (for instance, their collaboration with the Nazis) and not their biology was the grounds for repressions sounds weak. If this were true, how would we explain the suspicion that the Chechen infants would inherit an essential feature of their people—a proneness to betray the Soviet power, that the betrayal gene was initially in them from the start, and they were unreformable in principle in contrast with some class ene-mies? This racist primordialism in actions was louder than the Bolsheviks verbal rhetoric and it was quickly internalized by the Soviet Russian majority.

The rhetoric of some Western slavists is built on a secret justification of empire and the repressive state as such, when they argue that it was necessary to strengthen the USSR borders in the conditions of the emi-nent Nazi attack by means of deporting the nonassimilated (and unre-formable) populations deep into the country. What is true though in Weiner's article is that it is crucial to take into account the Russian imperial traditions and the external and internal circumstances in any discussion of race and racism in the Soviet Union. At the same time there is no contradiction between this approach and Weitz's looking at the racial politics of the Soviet Union through the prism of modernity. Weiner demonstrates that even if there were an idea of race in both Czarist Russia and the USSR, it was never dominant in the social policies. For him the only clear example of racism remains that of anti-Semitism of the late Soviet époque (Weiner 2002, 50). The familiar birth marks of Sovietology come forward in these remnants of inadvertent racism and Eurocentrism. The Jewish experience is presented as a paradigmatic suffering, while all other sufferings are neglected because they refer, in this logic, to dispensable lives, not worth mentioning. Maybe for this reason Weiner completely ignores the relations with Islam, even if it were a crucial part of racial politics in Russia and the USSR, as well as the post-Soviet space today.

The presence of non-Russians in the Soviet government seems to Weiner a sufficient proof of the nonracist nature of the Soviet state and policies. But it is too simplified. Within the Soviet theatrical multiculturalism the presence of the assimilated and reformed aboriginals and colonials was an important external feature meant for the West and for deceiving their own citizens. But what was the price of this assimilation? The documents of the time are full of the panegyrics of the colonial communist leaders, glorifying the special leading role of the great Russians who contributed so much to the world civilization and culture (Sahni 1997, 160). Such a discourse was a necessary pass into the wonderful world of Soviet nomenclature for the colonial elites. But it could not save many of them from future repressions and accusations in nationalism and anti-soviet activities.

The very Soviet-ness as an ideal was very abstractly Soviet as it always slid into Russianness. The American scholars do not see a similarity in this logic between the USSR and the United States. The same way as the melting pot was melting the nations in order to create a new man—an American, but with recognizably WASPish norm in mind, in the Soviet Union they discussed the future birth of the new Soviet man who at a close inspection carried recognizably Russian features. The fate of those who did not melt has remained doomed everywhere. Weiner and Hirsch believe the Soviet rhetoric and take for granted its mythic goal of creating a new humankind. But a common Soviet philistine did not really want to change anything or anybody, particularly if he comfortably lived in a colony. He would nourish the age-old racist belief in his own eternal superiority, and erasing the difference was not what he was after.

Much more persuasive are the arguments of scholars who do not work in the paradigm of Western area studies but turn to subaltern studies or decolonial discourse, who are themselves representatives of Diasporic non-Western communities sensitive to the problem of othering and interested not just in official discourses of the Russian and Soviet empire but also in the voices of the others. One of the best books on the subject is the already mentioned Kalpana Sahni's *Crucifying the Orient. Russian Orientalism and the Colonization of Caucasus and Central Asia.* Sahni draws a colorful picture of Russian and Soviet Orientalism based on all-encompassing racism. A large part of her work is a demonstration of differences between the rhetoric of Soviet government and its real actions, and also the continuity between the Czarist regime and the politics of the Soviet state in the treatment of the other. She clearly demonstrates that both are results of the fundamental flaws of modernity. As it happened in the nineteenth century, any theories with unversalist claims had to wear a garment of objective scientific facts and truths, in order to justify the acts of violence and cruelty against the mythologized Orient. Sahni claims that "although the USSR accused the West of racism, predatoriness, and economic and cultural exploitation, the end results of the Soviet government's policies were identical. It could not have been any different: the case was not one of the Soviet Union's deviation from socialism" (Sahni 1997, 109). The matter was that socialism itself was a Eurocentric and racist theory and it reproduced the orientalistic tendencies of its time word for word, supporting it by the additional arguments of Marxist dialectics.

Sahni shows that already in the Czarist empire there was a tradition of systematic representation of the population of the East as primitive and retarded. It was hard to turn this quickly even into an ideology of the "elder brother" especially that the Bolsheviks did not see it as their goal. The Czarist government looked for justification of colonization in Orthodox Christian providentiality. The Socialist state changed this ideology to a distorted Marxism. But there was a similarity between them—they claimed their singular access to truth and salvation as well as the promise of paradise in the end of the path under the condition to agree with the dominant ideology. It was a taxonomically strictly organized "paradise" with first class seats for Russians of the correct social class, second class seats for the Slavs and the cultures which stood closer to European modernity, and third class for everyone else. The continuity between the Czarist and the Soviet modernity was expressed in eschatological messianism which carried different ideological discourses yet similarly discriminated against the other.

Sahni also stresses the obvious Eurocentrism and racism of the Bolshevik leaders that went parallel to their verbal declarations of brotherhood and equality of all nationalities. The scholar correctly points out that behind this Marxist Orientalism there were not just tendencies of romantization of savages and European messianism, but also dehumanizing and taking dignity away from the colonized people (Sahni 1997, 156). Take for example a quotation from Marx that Sahni gives to illustrate a typical Western opposition of Barbarian Russia and Civilized Europe: "Russians are Mongols and not Slavs, and therefore they do not belong to the Indo-Germanic race. They are intruders and must be thrown beyond the Dineper" (Sahni 1997, 157). In Lenin's devious efforts to adjust all this to October revolt there was always a refrain of proving that the underdeveloped Russia is still better and closer to civilization than the paradigmatically backward Orient. In this respect Lenin and his followers could not help being caught in the grip of the typical subaltern empire paradigm which compensates its inferiority complex in front of the West by discriminating its internal others.

If racism of Lenin's time was camouflaged under the guise of brotherhood rhetoric Stalin began to openly cultivate the familiar prejudice of the Russian empire. This task became particularly important during World War II when the new old heroic myths of Alexander Nevsky, Ivan the Terrible, Peter the Great, military commanders Suvorov and Kutuzov were (re)created in the mass consciousness in order to support the patriotism and the spirit of the Soviet people. No one asked a question why this corrected Russian history with a few mentionings of the demonized enemies (external and internal) started to be presented as a common history of all Soviet people while all non-Russians had to forget about their own genealogy and culture. For many peoples these very "heroes" stood for the Russian imperial cruelty and were the symbols of colonization, lack of freedom, and growing dependency (Sahni 1997, 161).

Sahni traces an evolution of racism in the Soviet Union, shedding light to some sources of unrestrained racial discrimination in today's Russia. It would not be possible if it were not prepared by the Soviet period. What is meant here is a gradual popularization and democratization of racism and Eurocentrism in the Soviet time linked with the erasing of difference between the elite and popular culture. If in Czarist Russia Eurocentrism arguably was confined to aristocracy and middle class strata, in the Soviet Union it became a common place discourse among the Soviet people (Sahni 1997, 162). Today we can trace remnants of the Brezhnev era myth interiorized by Russians and used as a justification of the colonization excesses and neocolonialism. First formulated in Lenin's time, this myth depicted the sacrifices of the "great Russian people" for the development of the backward nations. Soviet economists and ideologists of the 1970s revamped it by adding pseudo-scientific grounds. It was necessary in order to take the attention away from the deteriorating living standards of the rotting empire. The economic stagnation was then presented to the Russian majority as entirely a fault of Central Asia which presumably the heroic Russian people dragged to their own higher status risking their well being and prosperity. The sense of superiority and the lack of real interest in the other triggered xenophobic and chauvinistic outbreaks which are actively revamped today. In mass media, science, and public discourse of the 1970–80s similar arguments of redeeming the backward Orient by the "great" Russian people who taught the barbarians everything—from morals to carpentry, started to come forward again. In spite of the numerous evidence of the opposite and particularly, a thoughtless exploiting of non-European Soviet colonies as sources of raw materials, citadels of mono-economics, and places were local people were rendered subhuman, this myth continues to live today both in Russia and in Central Asia and Caucasus. Absurdly, the ex-colonies are zombified by the Soviet propaganda still generating many colonial complexes and psychologically unhealthy reactions.

The sanctioned discourse of imperial superiority is expressed in oral histories of Russian colonists from Tashkent who even having spent all their lives in Central Asia still clearly divide the world into us and them, see their ancestors as champions of civilization in backward Asia and readily reproduce the Soviet and sometimes Czarist mythology of colonial underdevelopment and imperial nostalgia. Many of such informants stress that their families have lived in Turkistan since the nineteenth century. But this antiquity has an obvious colonial aftertaste which neither the informants nor the interviewers are ready to see (Tokhtakhodzhaeva et al. 1995, 26). Such representatives of the colonizing culture remain blind to the ambiguous morality and manipulative nature of their positioning. A. Memmi formulated the imperative of the colonizer and the colonized though he ignored the gender dimension. Memmi's "colonialist" falsifies history and rewrites laws as he strives to erase from memory everything that prevents him from successful legitimating of usurpation of power (Memmi 1991, 52). A considerable part of Caucasus and Central Asian Russians are reluctant colonizers, who are offended today when the "aboriginals" seem unable to appreciate their noble civilizing efforts. They remain blind to the imperial-colonial problematic, and continue to call the bloody annexation a peaceful and voluntary reunion (Tokhtakhodzhaeva et al. 1995, 107).

This painful question has not yet received all the attention it deserves on the part of the local theorists. But it should not be ignored. The colonizers of both sexes share particular elements, such as the interpretation of russification as a civilizing norm, denigration of local languages and the idea of conservation of traditionalist culture as opposed to teaching the indigenous people the new and progressive ways. For Central Asian and Caucasus Russians it became natural to compare their ancestors with Northern American pioneers of the West and romantic adventurers. This allows them to elevate their own status and the status of their empire and erase the stigma of colonization and imperialism.

The official Soviet historiography was presented as the only norm and accompanied by the systematic silencing of alternative voices until they were completely erased. In the end a clear and simple image of the Oriental other was produced for the masses and opposed to the Russian sameness. A common Russian person remained ignorant about the history of his "younger brothers" and easily bought into the stereotypes promoted by the state in its mass-media, public rhetoric, and education system. The ignorance of common Russians as well as intellectuals pacified by the state generated a lack of interest in and despise for the other. The effective Soviet methods of silencing the alternative voices and nourishing of ignorance in relation to the East, an uncritical interiorizing of the official mythology by the majority of the population—have resulted in today's unrestrained racism. Contemporary Orientalism mostly takes anti-Muslim forms but Islam is interpreted ethnically and racially rather than religiously. In Russia tolerance is not seen as the norm. To be a racist is not shameful, but, on the contrary, honorable, as racism almost equals patriotism today. Hence the important difference between the liberal democrats in the global North and in Russia. The first would not allow themselves to be openly racist, Eurocentric or xenophobic, even if deep in their heart they could be. This would ruin their political and moral credit. The second speak of democracy, egalitarianism, and civil society, and at the same time, continue to express extremely xenophobic views, never risking their careers because of that.

Chapter Five

Dirt Fetish and Commodity Racism Soviet Way

By the time the Soviet modernizing efforts became intensified in
Caucasus and Central Asia, the Soviet ideology with respect to sexual
question had already changed from a scandalously famous glass of
water theory[1] to a much more traditionalist patriarchal interpretation
of sexual relations that allowed the Soviet state to control the subjectivity of builders of communism, including the sexual sphere. Vladimir
Lenin criticized the early Soviet "feminists" and the supervisors of the
zhenotdels Inez Armand and Alexandra Kollontai, stressing that free
love that both women defended in various ways, was a manifestation
of bourgeois immorality. The Bolsheviks fear in this case was a lack
of discipline in sexual relations and the insufficient control of this
sphere of human life on the part of the Soviet state. As F. Navailh
points out, in Lenin's metaphor of the filthy puddle out of which it is
not recommended to quench your thirst as out of a glass that was used
by others, we can detect his tendency to restore and maintain purity
(in various senses of the word) as an absolute value (Navailh
1994, 234). The Soviet wish to prescribe the strict roles and models of
behavior in sexual and gender sphere would flourish later in patriarchal Stalin's gender politics.

A Marxist psycho-neurologist Aaron Zalkind who translated
Freud into the language of proletarian science and called for the "revolutionary sublimation," wrote in his "Twelve sexual commandments
of revolutionary proletariat": "As the revolutionary class, saving the
whole humanity from its parish, has exclusively *eugenic tasks* in its
sexual life, that is the tasks of the *revolutionary communist improvement of the humankind through the off-springs* [Italics mine—M.T.],
it becomes obvious that the most powerful sexual attractions should
not be based on features of the class-sterile 'beauty,' 'femininity,' and
the brutal 'muscular' and "mustachioed" masculinity, which have
little place and which are of little use in the conditions of industrial-
ized, intellectualized socializing humankind" (Zalkind 1924). If we
substitute here "White/European" for "proletarian," we will be left

with a pure imperial racist discourse and the mission of maintaining the racial purity. However, because this article was written for the metropolis and stressed the class element, its racial side remained hidden. But if it could be ignored for some time in Moscow, in the national peripheries the Bolsheviks had to face the ethnic-racial side of modernity, and the opposition of cleanliness and dirt, interpreted through the prism of race and ethnicity, came forward.

In the early Soviet years the distorted forms of pseudo-scientific and commodity racism worked together. The control over subjectivity in the Soviet colonies was inseparable from dirt fetish as a peculiar imperial deviance which was expressed in the most graphic form in the Victorian British Empire but also in distorted forms in Russia/ Soviet Union. Dirt fetish and commodity racism come forward at the moment when the racial discourses mutate from romantic Orientalism and quasi-scientific racism to commercial forms in such areas as mass-media, advertisement, new kinds of art, such as photography. Ann McClintock calls this process a grandiose marketing of evolutionary racism and imperial power. She points out that the imperial spectacle now enfolded in the domestic sphere of the Victorian middle class. As a result the idea of race was reinterpreted. The colonies turned into a different theater where the spectacle of the Victorian cult of domesticity was rethought through gender (McClintock 1995, 100–112). The main correlation of McClintock's book then can be summarized as follows: the more racialized the domestic space of Victorian England became (class acquired racial features) the more domesticated and commercially appropriated became the colonial space.

Dirt fetish plays an important role in the shaping of the imperial and colonial subjectivity in modernity. Marry Douglas points out (Douglas 1966) that nothing is inherently dirty because dirt expresses a relation to social value and disorder. Dirt then transgresses the social boundaries. In such a strictly hierarchical society as the Victorian one the iconography of dirt, to use McClintock definition, is deeply rooted in the process of observing and transgressing of the social boundaries. Dirt is what is left after the exchange of commodities was completed. The bodily relation to dirt expresses the social relation to labor (McClintock 1995, 152–153). As all fetishes, dirt signalizes the crisis of values because it contradicts the liberal idea that the social wealth is created by abstract rational market principles and not by a concrete person's labor.

McClintock argues that "as the nineteenth century drew on, the iconography of dirt became a poetics of surveillance, deployed increasingly to police the boundaries between "normal" sexuality and "dirty" sexuality, "normal" work and "dirty" work, "normal" money and "dirty" money (McClintock 1995, 154). It is important that in the opposition clean/dirty deviance was coded through the economic-social-gender-racial complex, where dirtiness, disorder, illness, moral corruption, and racial degeneration were practically indivisible from each other, coming into a generalized simultaneously revolting and attractive image of a female (not quite human), where a maid, a prostitute, a Black woman, a miner woman, a circus woman all merged together.

The Victorian logic, as McClintock persuasively demonstrates, was looking for a medium, a third element through which it would become possible to fulfill an otherwise vague and weak connection between the normalized notion of the heterosexual family and the normalized notion of the circulation of capital. The only possible third element could be the negative image of deviation linked with the primitive and irrational. Money, work, sexuality turned to be connected by means of a negative analogy with the sphere of race and colonial difference.[2]

McClintock introduces two concepts or tropes which are relevant for the interpretation of the Russian and Soviet racial-gender complex: the panoptical time and the anachronistic space. Both are connected with the above mentioned modernity's defect—translation of geography into chronology and colonization of space by time. McClintock stresses the importance of social Darwinism in the emergence of panoptical time. It is connected with the translation of natural taxonomies into the social sphere and cultural history. Thus time turned into geography of social power, into a map on which one could read the global categories of natural social differences. And history became a spectacle (McClintock 1995, 32–33).

The anachronistic space in case of the Victorian British Empire was expressed in the colonies in a racial and gender sense, while in the metropolis it narrowed to a class dimension. As a result, the colonized and the low class women, both in the metropolis and in the colonies, were divested of their subjectivity. They were placed in the anachronistic space fallen out of modernity, or, in McClintock's words, in a prehistorical, atavistic, irrational realm. According to the colonial version of this trope the imperial march along the colonial spaces was regarded as a journey backward in time, to the anachronistic moment of prehistory, in a way, repeating again the evolutionary process itself. The colonial difference then was interpreted not in social or spatial but in temporal terms. This logic was further developed in metropolis where appealing to anachronistic space became central in racial and eugenic discourses on low class women. Quasi-scientific racism of the late nineteenth century regarded women as atavistic expressions of the primitive archaic. But there was also a class difference here at work which acquired racial dimensions, as there was a clear difference between the interpretation of the White Victorian lady and the White low class woman who was deliberately racialized and masculinized.

In Russia and the USSR dirt also expressed a relation to the social value and disorder while cleanliness was coded as a loyalty to the empire and connected with the imperial control and disciplining of the individual by means of ritual cleaning. But race itself was coded in Russia differently as it either collapsed into the racism of microscopic ethnic differences, or was interpreted in a transmuted way from the start, signifying belonging to European civilization, Christianity, Russian ethnicity instead of the color of skin. Coloniality of power was constituted through this altered form of racism, connected with a specific role of Russia in the global coloniality of power and marked by the Russian wish to purify their symbolically unclean status in the eyes of the West.

Racial narratives were present in the Soviet discourse in their clearest form in connection with cleanliness/versus dirt opposition and particularly, with their moral and hygienic reverberations. Even within the metropolis race it is always detectable in early Soviet hygienic campaigns. At first site it is strange to look for commodity racism in a socialist country. However it was in the Soviet Union and not in Czarist Russia that specific discourses were constructed for and applied to the colonial consumer. They were meant to shape a new Soviet colonial citizen. These practices also included turning of the colonial consumer himself or herself into a commodity. The process of domesticating the colonies by means of commodity racism began on any large scale only in the Soviet époque. The common sources of Marxism and Liberalism become obvious in the way the darker racial side of modernity and particularly the division of labor and the creation of the internal markets—real and virtual—were manifested in the USSR.

The Soviet imperial preoccupation with cleanliness had been mostly shaped by the mid 1920s. It signalized the presence of inferiority complexes and self justification by means of mostly invented connections with European civilization and progress. The polemics of the Russian futurists and a critic, translator and later children's poet Korney Chukovsky on cleanliness and dirt and the story of the "reformed" Vladimir Mayakovsky illustrate the imperial-colonial and transmuted racial dimension of the early twentieth-century literary struggle between avant-garde and traditionalists. In his notorious opposition to futurists Chukovsky demonstrated a peculiar obsession with cleanliness, similar to McClintock's Victorians whom he liked to translate.

Chukovsky's link with the imperial cult of cleanliness is expressed in his polemics with futurists on primitivism and stereotypical rendering of the image of Africa. The Russian futurists, as many other avant-gardists of the time, were enchanted with the non-European cultures, religions, and aesthetics, while Chukovsky was stuck in his worship of cleanliness as order, righteousness, hygiene, and beauty. He was a perfect example of the imperial difference gone mad. Whiteness was coded in his works in traditionally European terms as goodness, and blackness—as evil. It would be just banal and not worth mentioning, but in case of Chukovsky acquired an additional meaning in the context of his positioning as a Russian writer and his personal story, marked by constant efforts to prove his belonging to the "clean" society. Blackness as a racial category in Chukovsky's works easily turns into the blackness of dirt, malice, low class, and disorder. That is why his chimney-sweep is an evil character who cannot be a role model for children. This son of a laundress (as Mayakovsky rather cruelly called him in one of his poems) dislikes the dirty futurists. Chukovsky rejects the blackness of the futurists's black god borrowed from Africa, because his chosen god is the white Apollo—no less alien, but borrowed from a different and more legitimate (for Chukovsky) European source. He attempts to discipline the futurists and teach them to adopt modernity in the proper cultural meaning (Chukovsky 1969, 207).

It is not a chance that Chukovsky translated from English the *Mother Goose Rhymes* and created one of the favorite children didactic poetry series in the Soviet Union. It seems that directly from the Victorian mass culture Chukovsky borrowed the obsession with soap and sponges as symbols of civilization. From the same source but without the corresponding social and economic background, just based on intellectual and cultural mimicking of Europe, he reproduces in his children's poem the rendering of Africa as a dangerous uncivilized place. First of all this Africa is "wild." Tanechka and Vanechka who do not listen to their parents' warnings against going for a walk to Africa, express an unhealthy interest in this continent (as futurists did). Africa for Chukovsky is an anti-space where one can find only exotic beasts and "Barmaleys" (horrible monsters possibly prompted by Mayakovsky, as B. Gasparov attempted to prove (Gasparov 1992), not ordinary people.

The loyalty to the empire (not just British, but also Soviet) then is signified by cleanliness. The later Soviet V. Mayakovsky's hygienic obsession acquires a few additional overtones in dirt/versus cleanliness context. From an anarchic celebration of dirt the poet follows a quick course to hygienic and progressivist obsession of his Soviet industrial and social commercials of the 1920s, proving his loyalty to the USSR in yet another way. In his poem "Ivan Kozyrev's story of moving to his new apartment" we witness a radical change of the main character as a result of an almost ritual washing in the bath. Gasparov correctly points out that Mayakovsky thus coded his farewell to futurism (Gasparov 1992). But it is also the voice of empire that is ventriloquing (to use Michail Bakhtin's expression) through Mayakovsky, the voice of cleanliness and rationality. The panoptical eternal time of empire reaching an almost cosmic dimension, unexpectedly merges with the totality of the Soviet commodity paradise in Mayakovsky's GUM (State Department Store) commercial where he nonchalantly promises to "buy a dazzling and cheap Sun in GUM" (Mayakovsky 2009).[3]

In the poet's hygienic slogans there is a typical strive to cultivate the uncultured proletarian—yesterday's peasant, to make him/her fit modernity. A negative anti-image which grows out of these slogans resembles a negative coding of the lower classes in Victorian England. Hence his obsession with the concept of culture, which often simply equals physical cleanliness as a new Soviet fetish. The poet keeps teaching the future Soviet man to be "cultured," that is, wash his hands and spit into spittoons, to acquire "a cultured habit" (to visit the bath house weekly and wash with soap).

The racial element and the anachronistic space are hidden in most of these examples. They will come forward where the colonial difference would be obvious, for example, in Mayakovsky's slogans advertising different Soviet products targeted for colonial spaces. The difference is expressed in tea and galoshes commercials through familiar racial stereotypes and orientalistic local color. Yet Mayakovsky's racism is unconscious, and he never reaches the extreme of the Victorian metaphor of washing the Black baby with *Pears* soap until he becomes White.

A completely different rendering of the notorious galoshes as symbols of modernization and erasing of local culture is to be found in M. Gaffarova's oral history quoted above (Tokhtakhodzhaeva et al. 1995, 38–45): "My parents were crying and saying—oh, my people, my Uzbeks, with some regret,"—she says. "When we came, we used to wear shoes, boots, while here all the people then were barefoot or in galoshes. How did the Soviets change the Uzbek people? I was very upset with these changes. There was nothing Uzbek left" (Tokhtakhodzhaeva et al. 1995, 44).

The most graphic example of Mayakovsky's commercial slogans, encoding the racist logic of making the fallen out of modernity savage equal to animals and nature, is the Tea Headquarters commercial where he urges the Soviet consumer to warm himself with this wonderful tea as it is already done by everyone else "up to the very North Pole"—"the Eskimo, the bear and the reindeer," who for Mayakovsky apparently constitute a line of a similar species, not quite human, yet successfully used as a market for the new Soviet products. The Eskimo, who are certainly not the full fledged citizens of the empire, in the poet's rendering, stand closer to the deer and the bear. It is through their communion by the Soviet goods, through becoming a new market for them, the Eskimo can hope to raise later to the status of the real Soviet people. The "Oriental folks" (who of course are not aware of the fact that they are "oriental") become possible consumers for the wonderful tea produced by the "Tea Headquarters." They are depicted as clichéd primitives within the familiar entourage of camels, appearing in every slogan, tea houses, and exotic mountains, and yet, again, as possible customers for the galoshes of the "Rubber Trust." It is comparable to the British soap commercials depicting Native Americans and Africans discovering civilization in a piece of British soap (McClintock 1995, 224–225).

The process of shaping the second-rate colonial Soviet individual was expressed in the realm of fashion, everyday life, the culture of the quotidian. It could be yet another Soviet campaign of forcing European style furniture in the locales where people used to eat for centuries on the floor, of propagating European clothes corrected by Russian-Soviet influence, or the so called "rational eating," which often contradicted cultural, religious, and ethnic habits. But always, there were the two models at work. One was meant for the metropolis. It was the model of imperial difference with some abstract ideal of civilized life. It could be ideologically distinct, but essentially based on the same rhetoric of modernity as in the West. The early Soviet propaganda attempted to educate the new and not sufficiently civilized proletarians within this model. In the colonies there was a different logic within which the uncultured representative of the metropolis who had just learned to wash his hands, brush his teeth and spit into the spittoon (as Mayakovsky's slogans taught him to do), all of a sudden turned into a champion of modernity, civilization, and a new life for the backward nations of the East. This typical colonial metamorphosis attracted many Russian people as it promised compensating their complexes by projecting them onto the colonized (Tokhtakhodzhaeva et al. 1995, 20–24, 101–111).

In the first Soviet decades the opposition of backwardness and bright socialist modernity was coded primarily through dirt discourse. An army of Soviet experts who often had a vague impression of what they were studying, began to prove that the so called harmful survivals in the colonial spaces could be easily overcome by Soviet education. Dirt here was used in a symbolic sense. It was not real dirt as in reality the religious and cultural traditions of Turkistan were hardly less hygienic than those of Russian villages or dirty overpopulated cities with their tuberculosis, barracks, and communal apartments. The matter was that by definition the Muslim ritual washing before the prayer could not be regarded as a legitimate cleaning from the Soviet point of view. Religiousness had to be coded as a synonym of dirt, backwardness, and retardation. While cleanliness, as in the case of the British Empire, was not just a lack of microbes or dangerous infections but, once again, a system of values. Cleanliness was a synonym of the proper Soviet citizen's loyalty to the empire and its order, of the fundamental agreement with its power relations, suppression, and discipline. As Northrop points out, it would be nearsighted to see this early Soviet colonial public health campaign as a "disinterested, culturally neutral, altruistic enterprise. It was also deeply politically implicated in and contributing to the power relationships of colonial society" (Northrope 2004, 60).

Instead of the dirty chimney-sweep futurist who wishes to throw the previous authorities away from the ship of history and hence is potentially dangerous for the Soviet state in the future, there was an opaque woman in paranjee, and no one knew what exactly to expect from her. She was called backward, dirty, sick, and uneducated as the whole recently imagined Uzbek or Tadzhic nation. And her use as a negative model was needed to protect the Soviet authority that was far from being impervious at the time. Gradually to be an Uzbek or a Tadzhik became not simply equal to being dirty and backward, but also meant a moral and even biological deficiency. Cleanliness was equally symbolic. The Soviet experts co-opted for the construction of this mythology, they negated and castigated all national traditions—from the secluded life in the women's part of the house to the sanitary conditions of childbirth and folk holidays.

A Turkistan women movement activist Serafima Lyubimova profusely quoted by Western historians of Central Asia, was one of the few first representatives of the metropolis in the colony. She was typically uninterested in learning something about the local culture, language, or way of life before condemning them. She made no difference between the nomads and the sedentary local population. Lyubimova was not too far from one of the nineteenth-century Russian imperial ideologues exclaiming that a bunch of nomads could not be the object of the civilizing efforts of his great country (Danylevsky 1895, 63). Similarly to the interpretation of race and the color of skin, there was and is a peculiar aberration here at work: if the savage stands lower in the universal scale of humanity, he must be non-White, he cannot be fair-skinned. In Lyubimova's interpretation of dirt fetish this logic was slightly modified: the Uzbeks are lower than the Europeans, including the Russians, in their development, they are stuck in medieval ages, hence they must be dirty, even if in reality they are cleaner than the colonizers![4]

Little by little, as Northrop shows (Northrop 2004, 63), paranjee which at that point was already erroneously considered to be a medieval remnant of despotism and slavery, began to signify not merely backwardness but also moral and physical uncleanliness. For Lyubimova ignorance caused by paranjee acted (contrary to any logic) as a direct cause of various diseases—from weak lungs to sterility, from gonorrhea to flabby muscles and premature aging. What was at work here was the same Orientalist substitution—the phenomena that are not directly related to each other began to be regarded in a chain, as cause and consequence and, what is most important, led to particular actions, whose damaging effect became obvious only later.

A typical example of such hypocritical Bolshevik politics in the colonial gender question is M. Kalinin's 1928 speech that Northrop quotes at length. I do not entirely agree with his interpretation. The chairman of the All-union Central Executive Committee said: "I think that the time is not far off when the connection between the veil and the woman of the East will disappear, and when we speak of the Eastern woman, this will signify only the territorial presence of this woman in the Eastern countries, and no more. There will be no other particular connotations of the term…" (Northrop 2004, 68). Northrop argues that the Soviet Empire impersonated here by Kalinin aimed at erasing the differences between the colonized and the colonizers. The scholar uncritically reproduces the official Soviet discourse and the Orientalist idea of the homogenous impenetrable and frozen Orient signified by Oriental women who were not even considered women in Western/Russian eyes. But Northrop himself adds that for those who had just acquired their ethnic identity—Uzbekness, Tadzhikness, Kazakhness, even if it was invented and imposed from above—this was not a desirable way. What Northrop does not write about is even more important: the idea of ethnic-racial mixing with the goal of creating a future hybrid Soviet citizen and the erasing of differences between the colonizers and the colonized always clashed against the unquestioned racism and Eurocentrism. This erasing of differences for the colonial people meant assimilation to the imperial culture of Russia, but an assimilation which was decidedly incomplete. It determined a particular and not very high racial status for them within the Soviet human hierarchy in accordance with ontological racializing. In the coming years the Soviet colonials, were forced to study at high school history lessons, the Slavic princes' feudal wars, to memorize the *Tale of Igor's Campaign,* to read Pushkin's poems and L. Tolstoy's novels for literature classes, and to remain ignorant of their own culture and history. Kalinin's rhetoric cannot be bought at face value. And neither of the sides ever did.

The iconic image of the liberated Soviet Eastern or Mountain women, particularly those who became party activists or champions of the new Soviet life style (laying asphalt, jumping with a parachute, becoming a crane-operator or a scientist, etc.), answering the Soviet version of the brown-skinned Englishman type (Macaulay 1957), became one of the powerful myths of the Soviet gender discourses that have persisted until today both in the minds of the Soviet historians and local population and even some gender activists, who still believe that the liberated Soviet women were more emancipated than their non-Soviet equivalents. In reality the Soviet "liberation" often came to a nominal change of clothes and no less nominal Russian/ Soviet style primary education, that colonized rather than liberated the minds, left them ignorant about their own cultural tradition or history, epistemic or linguistic legacy, and effectively zombified both men and women, creating a specific self-orientalizing inferiority complex, compensated with heroic efforts to modernize as quickly as possible. The self-orientalizing of the local population has become one of the major successes of the Russian/Soviet colonization which made the colonial subjects internalize the once alien values and standards. A typical apprehensive attitude of non-White colonized people to the color of skin, based on their interiorization of Whiteness as a synonym of beauty and femininity has worked in the Soviet Empire as well, which fashioned itself as racially unprejudiced. Today in Caucasus (and less so in Central Asia) we find a peculiar interiorization of Orientalist and racist discourses in desperate efforts to prove their own Aryan or European roots.

Chapter Six

Colonial Gender Tricksterism in Central Asia and Caucasus

Women of the similar cultural and religious background who did not go through a forced Soviet modernization, while maintaining a memory of a never implemented ideal of a different modernity, often turned out freer in their thinking and subjectivity than the forcefully emancipated Soviet colonial subjects. This was connected with alternative pluritopic ways of reconciling modernization with local ethnic-cultural, epistemic, and religious models, such as Jadidism (Tokhtakhodzhaeva at al. 1995, 38–46). Thus, the above mentioned M. Gaffarova is clearly a border dweller, open to other ways of being in the world. From her testimony we find out about a different image of Muslim culture, than the one presented by Western feminists and some of their local pupils. Although she never discusses gender specifically, her oral history indirectly testifies an obvious respect for women and children, a lack of gender inequality in the questions of education and career and a certain parity between men and women which was maintained in Xinjiang Uzbek Diaspora in contrast with the Soviet Uzbekistan where the ugly excesses of patriarchal practices prevailed. Gaffarova is the only informant who is sensitive to the imperial-colonial side of this problem, while people shaped within the Soviet system, even if they are critical of the regime, are thinking entirely in progressivist paradigm, demonizing any traditional and religious culture, and remaining ignorant of any alternative models. Gaffarova, by contrast, openly speaks of the reasons for the degeneration of her people, calling the Russian colonization a direct source of their slave psychology (Tokhtakhodzhaeva at al. 1995, 45), which she was shocked with after her return from China. As an outsider she clearly sees the typical colonizing tactics and the darker side of the modern colonial gender system which is not accessible to other informants belonging to both the colonized and the colonizers. She is one of the very few people, able to grasp the importance of ethical, epistemic, and existential dimensions of coloniality. In this respect she resembles the Zapatistas with their key concept of human dignity and respect, poorly theorized in traditional leftist discourses. These concepts do not find easy correlations in the Western notions of cultural or human rights and we cannot understand them without attempting to look at indigenous cosmology in its own terms. Human dignity and the task of its restoration is not a new abstract universal. It is a necessary link of often quite different colonial experiences allowing for pluriversality as a universal project.

Both in Caucasus as early as in the nineteenth century and in Central Asia from the early twentieth century onward there have been active transcultural exchanges going on. However the Bolsheviks did not expect that the cultural contacts with the local population might take a reciprocal form. They were trying to impose the unidirectional acculturation and exercise their right to define the vector and the nature of cultural borrowings. It was not a mere conversion into Leninism, but the acculturation of the local population to European norms and morals edited by Soviet Russians. In the end, life itself corrected their ambitions. When we look at contemporary culture of Central Asia or Caucasus we see that transcultural processes indeed went in both directions effecting the locals and the local Russians, Ukrainians or Jews—the voluntary and involuntary colonists. These people slowly developed their own subjectivity, different from the Russians in Russia—from the way of life to language, from cuisine to the system of values, which makes their assimilation back into the Russian society quite problematic today when and if they decide to go back (Tlostanova 2004).

In the iconography of the early Soviet metropolis there was a change from the masculinized working class or peasant Amazon with erased gender differences, to the more conventionally feminine (and bourgeois) identity of the New Economic Policy and even later (the Soviet ladies in squirrel fur coats and hats in the Fur Trading commercials and the old style delicate and capricious young ladies advertising *Chlorodont* tooth paste (Savelyeva 2006). The situation in the colonial Soviet spaces was more complex. Here fashion had to embrace a link between the old, presumably ethnic-national cultures and the new Soviet culture with ultimately erased (or replaced with Russian/European) ethnic features. However what had to be maintained was the visual difference. If the wives of the new party activists could afford upon rejecting a paranjee to buy expensive stockings and European shoes, to make dresses according to European fashion, the low and middle class women complained that they had nothing to put on instead of the paranjee to cover the clothes and the shoes which were considered improper for the public space. The Soviet state did not have enough money to dress the liberated women in European clothes, but it also did not intend to make them look identical to Russians. As a reaction to these complex interactions a new version of the modernized national dress emerged in Central Asia. A transcultural balancing marked the Soviet multicultural discourse which was further corrected by the colonial gendered subjectivities themselves. The invented new national dress demonstrated a commodification of colonial difference in a striking way and, at the same time, inadvertently gave a chance of negotiating a new and more dynamic identity to colonial women.

Thus a new Soviet Uzbek national dress was a compromise between the European urban style clothes and the invented ethnic tradition. Within the Soviet temporal matrix it was further on juxtaposed to a negative emblem of the medieval survival—the old national dress. The ethnic fashion in the USSR incorporated the contradictory play on the rethought orientalist stereotypes and modernity discourses, which were often unconsciously accepted or contested by the local people. The new Uzbek dress was more modern/European in its style, yet it retained some elements of previous traditional fashions. It was also made of the Uzbek pure silk hand-made fabric, which later began to be mass-produced in a cheaper artificial acetate version. This dress was an ideologically marketable symbol of the Soviet cultural diversity sold to the world (see figure 6.1). The final goal seemed to be the complete visual erasing of the colonial status—the neutral Europeanized clothes of the Soviet emancipated educated women.[1] But proclaiming the goal of making everyone look identical and erasing the colonial status was not the same as actually allowing the colonial to claim her equality in the sphere of education, job opportunities, or self-realization in general. It remains questionable if the empire was ready to accept the erased differences (see figure 6.2). As it also remains questionable how passive were the colonial women themselves in this process. It seems that we should rather speak of the flexible change of identities, of a play on them, which the Soviet educated gendered colonials used with various goals—from mimicry to strategic positioning at the border, giving a double vision and a multidimensional understanding and perception of oneself in the world, a possibility of remaining within the rigid Soviet multiculturalism yet practicing a difference in the forms which would be impervious to imperial censorship.

This is another face of the Soviet colonial tricksterism where the Soviet and the colonial merge in a peculiar way and where a balancing on the verge of resistance and acting around the power structures

Figure 6.1 The "modern" version of the Uzbek dress (1960).

Figure 6.2 An Uzbek member of the Soviet Ministry of Education delegation among the Indian teachers (1959).

to avoid their policing becomes possible. For example, the all-encompassing lying and lack of trust in the official discourses is an overall Soviet feature, but lying particularly to Russians and readiness and skill in outsmarting them—is clearly a colonial one. What did colonial Soviet women want and could do in this case? In order to understand this we should pay attention not just to the well advertised success stories of the young colonial women from peasant families who became opera singers and pilots in the Soviet Union thus escaping the traditional arranged marriages. We should also attempt to reconstruct the background of more complex transcultural, trans-value, and trans-epistemic identities, which have indeed become more frequent in the Soviet time and today.

One such example is a testimony of R.K.[2] who has found her own way of reexistence around, beyond and at the crossing of several models—the early and late Soviet Orientalism and multiculturalism, the Muslim culture, the ethno-cultural patterns of Uzbek people, the Western modernity and today's internal neocolonialism. Her story and voice crash the existing gender taxonomies based on vector temporal schemes. She is a colonial gendered intellectual who does not slide either to the paranjee or to the parachutist with the young communist league batch on her chest. She attempts instead to negotiate her identity between these binaries and eventually beyond them. She loses the freedom of thinking in her native language. The crucial link with a local value system and knowledge is seriously damaged, but never completely replaced with a different system. The necessity of corresponding to the Soviet values is negotiated by means of often unexpected gender forms and images. This becomes obvious in fashion, hobbies, intersexual relations, and leisure activities. In D. Northrop's book we find mostly the photographs of veiled enigmatic Tashkent women, even as late as the 1940s (Northrop 2004, 319, 322, 236). M. Kamp offers just a handful of mostly encyclopedia derived stories of selected new women, usually the Jadids. But the majority of gender identities which exist between these extremes skip the attention of the Western scholars. A different and more nuanced impression arises from R.K.'s testimony and corresponding photographs.[3]

In a 1951 picture which corresponds timewise to some of Northrop's photographs we see a young girl in an inexpensive cotton dress, yet tailored according to European fashion, copied from the trophy movies, wearing a pair of worn-out-after-the-war shoes but with a tennis racket in her hands (see figure 6.3). In another picture she has a stack of library books on which one can make out the authors: Somerset

Figure 6.3   An Uzbek girl from Tashkent after playing tennis (1951).

Maugham, Romen Rolland, John Galsworthy, but certainly not the forbidden and forgotten Khalikdod, Anbar Otin or Abdurauf Fitrat.[4] In one of the pictures she is surrounded by a group of six male class-mates (see figure 6.4) and smiling into the eye of an old camera thus rejecting the mythic gender roles usually prescribed to colonial women. It is hard to reconcile these images, objects, and environment

Figure 6.4   An Uzbek woman student of Central Asian State University among the men class mates (1951).

with the pictures drawn by the majority of Western historians of Central Asia.

R.K. was born in 1932 in Tashkent, in the late 1950 she went to do her graduate studies in Moscow, from 1964 to 1994 she lived in Caucasus and afterward moved to Moscow. There are two leitmotifs in her life—one is obviously migration, lack of roots, a paradigmatic unhomeleness, loneliness, and otherness in any place, yet at the same time, an ability to flexibly adjust to any space, acutely reacting to its signals and resonating in response. She always keeps her core, which remains intact under any change of identity. The second leitmotif is that of education and avid learning and reading which in the end contributes to the sense of otherness.

This paradigmatic otherness is expressed repeatedly in her testimony—on existential, social, ethnic-cultural, linguistic, and other levels. R. K. links it with her developed imagination and stresses a crucial role of reading fiction already as a young child in the shaping of her future identity. From early on she somehow rejected this world and wanted to escape from it to some different realm. It could be flipping over while on a swing to look at everything upside down and sink into a strange, unusual reality. Or it could be getting engrossed in a historical novel from medieval times. Or still later, it could be choosing Urdu as her university major instead of more practical School of medicine, engineering or chemistry as her siblings did. It could be also a love for traveling and learning about other people's worlds. She formulates it in a psychologically distilled way when she says: "All children were equally loved in our family. Yet I could feel from early on that I was somehow different from others. Sometimes it was bad for me because I felt lonely" (Tlostanova 2009, 281). An underside of this proneness to changing worlds and escaping reality was a constant sense of fear and humiliation that the Soviet 1930s and 1940s were filled with. It was not always conscious, particularly in a small child, yet this fear and humiliation constantly break through her testimony: "I was little but I remember that my father[5] was burning photographs at night, in a big bowl in our veranda. In those pictures he was together with the secretary, they were hunting. It was dangerous to keep the pictures because the massive arrests were starting at the time. And we were not told anything, of course, because it was safer that way" (Tlostanova 2009, 283). It was also safer for the children (see figure 6.5) not to know who their ancestors were, but was it better for them in the long run? R.K.'s testimony is a painful effort of a most sensitive of such children to create a complex identity practically out

Figure 6.5   Uzbek children from Tashkent on a Sunday trip to the park (1937).

of nothing or very little—not going back to the past, but building a future which would be marked by bits and pieces of this past or rather, real and imagined pasts, even if half erased.

For me she is a good example of a colonial gendered trickster. Several times in her life she had to start from the beginning, from scratch, changing cultures, people around her, her profession, in a way, remaking herself. For example, she had to change from an Orientalist studying India to a university professor of modern European and American literature. But this metamorphosis proved to be good. Of course, India stepped back, but she "discovered" Europe and America for herself. This was appreciated by her students, not only in Caucasus colonial province but later in Moscow. She is a real worldly person, though she could not develop her cosmopolitanism fully, due to the time and the locale where she was born. However the roots of this cosmopolitanism are not always entirely happy or willingly chosen. She repeatedly mentions her "handicap"—a lack of knowledge of her own culture and her native language and therefore a lack of link with her community. Explaining her lacking sense of belonging through a lacking knowledge of Uzbek R.K. mentions that at home they spoke Russian because in their communal yard in the center of Tashkent they were the only Uzbek family: "If I had known Uzbek well, probably it would have been easier for me to live in Uzbekistan. I would not have had a feeling that I was not at home. And I had this feeling…Among the Uzbeks who speak their native language easily, beautifully and naturally I have always felt myself a cripple and I still do. I am certainly a cripple because of this incorrect national policy…an imperial policy at work" (Tlostanova 2009, 284).

She touches upon the typical colonial asymmetry that makes a colonial intellectual forget his/her culture, history, language in order to succeed, always leaving an aftertaste of guilt: "Really there was no way I could learn my language. First I studied and in order to be equal or better than those who I was compared with I always worked a lot, precisely to be better than others. And then I worked in three or four places at once" (Tlostanova 2009, 285). In high school she had to be better than the Russian students and painfully felt the social and race discrimination always having to prove her intellectual solvency due to colonial status: "I noticed this racial discrimination and disdain, particularly on the part of the teachers. We had a teacher of Russian…who once told to one of the pupils in my presence: 'You are from an intelligentsia family, this kind of behavior does not suit you!' And it was very painful for me because no one thought that I was from intelligentsia family. The girl was Russian of course…and this probably was not a conscious racism, because there were only three Uzbeks in class…and one would have to be very biased to humiliate us, because we were all good students. But of course that teacher would die but never put me an 'A' in Russian language" (Tlostanova 2009, 282). What is hidden in this passage is that the girl in fact did belong to the old local intelligentsia which the family had to hide fearing repressions, and her offense was not connected with jealousy but rather with a sense of justice that did not correspond to the imperial-colonial social code.

R.K. chose to study India at the university as this was her roundabout (and the only allowed) way of coming back to another "Orient" whose history was erased from the minds of the local people. Through India she was hoping to collect bits and pieces of a different history of her own land and her people. She firmly links her interest in India with an instinctive dissatisfaction with the imperial-colonial asymmetry that she witnessed every day: "Why did I choose the School of Oriental Studies? I was always attracted to the East. I always felt deep in my heart, that maybe this would allow me to come closer to my people. This pain and this dissatisfaction with myself have lived in me from the time I was five. Very early I started to pose various questions. For example, during Easter one would come to a bakery and one would see the *kulich* there, the Russian Easter bread. At the same time, during our holidays, for example, *Kurban Hait* or the end of *Uraza*,[6] there were never any special dishes typical for these holidays on sale in the stores, never. We always cooked it all at home. But we made sure we did. It was our mother's merit" (Tlostanova 2009, 285).

A different side of her identity was that she was very close with her deeply religious yet independent grandmother who was not trying to control or police the girl's behavior, praised her granddaughter's feminine image, good (and modern) taste in clothes, and at the same time, secretly taught her to pray in Arabic. This flexible positioning could reconcile the seeming opposites and was marked by an ironic questioning of imposed norms and laws that she refused to accept at face value: "Our grandmother used to read *namaz*[7] and no one ever forbade her to do so. Of course those who wanted to show their loyalty to the Russian elite behaved accordingly. For example, once uncle M. saw that grandmother bought herself a new and very beautiful paranjee, because she veiled herself, so he cut it into pieces. She was a strong woman and very beautiful, delicate. She had six sons and women who have many sons have a higher status in society…When uncle M. said, let us all have one last name, he registered my grandmother as K. She had a good sense of humor and we got along very well, she loved me. And she told me: 'Can you imagine he registered me under my husband's name as if my husband was my father!'" (Tlostanova 2009, 288) In Uzbek tradition as in other locales women used to keep their clan and family names when they got married. This started to change with Russian and Soviet modernity. Therefore R.K.'s own refusal to change her last name when she got married is a peculiar mixture of her emancipated feminist stance and a vague memory of this once existing gender code which gave women more chances to keep their independence and dignity intact. It is mainly the people from the pre-Soviet generation that are presented in her testimony in a favorable way and often linked with bits and pieces of Muslim and ethnic-cultural traditions and/or a different way of life and a system of values (her grandmother, the grandmother's uncle who owned a vineyard, later the old Russian and Jewish professors-Orientalists at the university). When this young woman who lived in the European part of Tashkent started to teach Urdu and Hindi in a secondary school in the so called Old City (see figure 6.6),[8] where her well off and educated family had resided before, often the unknown elders would see her and comment that she belonged to a particular clan. This fleeting, transient sense of belonging to a clan that she did not know anything about, she would later treasure and attempt to reinvent from scratch.

Yet, the question of racism keeps surfacing in R.K.'s testimony at different turns. She reflects on the infamous Soviet passport policies which attempted on the one hand, to fix the biological ethnicity (nationality) in an ID form, and on the other hand, to forcefully impose such a biological ethnicity, which often had nothing to do with the individual's sensibility, in accordance with what was needed to Soviet propaganda at a particular moment: "When I was sixteen I came to our local police station and took the passport form to fill it out and I wrote there my last name and my first name and my patronymic. There was a man there who asked me: 'Why did you put a patronymic? Uzbeks never had patronymics. If you want a patronymic, I will write that you are Russian'. I said that I did not want to be Russian, that my mother and father were Uzbeks and I will be Uzbek too. Then he crossed my patronymic out. So from sixteen and until twenty five I had a passport with no patronymic...I do not know if this was a result of some campaign. I thought I was just unlucky to bump into this disgusting person. But it could have been some campaign. They could have wanted to have more people with Uzbek names registered as Russians" (Tlostanova 2009, 286).

Her lack of Uzbek command indirectly links with her inability to restore justice in imperal-colonial contexts and perform the role of the defender of the weak. She blames herself in failing to act in this

Figure 6.6   An Uzbek instructor teaching Hindi to Tashkent local children (1957).

role, to be with her people and one of them. A graphic example here is a tram story in which one finds a constellation of many imperial-colonial motives—from a persistent (secondary) Eurocentrism to a rejection of non-European knowledge, literacy, language, a reversed class dimension and the imperial remapping and renaming of reality. This complex mixture is presented through a clearly border in-between perspective: "Most often such conflicts took place in a tram, where you would find Russians of a particular social status. An Uzbek elderly man with the whitest beard and portly bearing would climb into a tram and give money to the [Russian—M.T.] conductress. He could not explain what kind of ticket he needed. So he would just say where he went, for example, *'Beshagoch'*[9] But it did not mean anything to her. She needed to be told that he wanted to go to some kind of 'Budyeny Avenue'[10] And this vulgar woman would start yelling at him: 'Thirty years of Soviet power have passed and you, idiot, still cannot speak Russian', as if the Soviet power was a manna and Russian language was a God's language which would bring him to paradise. I was furious when I saw that…But again, my bad command of Uzbek prevented me from interfering. Otherwise I would have come up to the old man and say: 'I am sorry that you have to endure all that'. But I was afraid that I would find myself in a ridiculous situation" (Tlostanova 2009, 288).

In R.K.'s testimony there is a peculiar interplay of different identities as a gendered colonial in various contexts: first in the colony itself dealing mostly with imperial authorities (in her case, intellectual and academic) and discovering their fake nature. She stresses her naïve readiness to erase the differences with Russian and Jewish older colleagues and their suspicious and hostile reaction in which ethnic prejudice mixed with professional insecurity. When she comes back to Tashkent after finishing her graduate studies in Moscow the hostility grows into an open hatred: "They gave me only a part time job, because they were afraid that I might want to become a chair of the department. You see, neither of them had a degree except for the chair, but he was already senile and besides, he got a degree at the Institute of military interpreters for making an Urdu-Russian dictionary. This was not really a scholarly work. So they were afraid" (Tlostanova 2009, 292). Here we see one face of the Soviet multiculturalism at work. The colonial gendered individuals had to act as symbols of themselves as liberated Oriental women, but always remember not to become better than the Russian originals, keeping a safe distance and remaining their weak copies. R.K.'s feeling insecure in Uzbekistan was linked precisely with her early refusal to accept this role and her becoming a threatening and not a theatrical and predictable other in the eyes of the same.

A different configuration was at work in Moscow when representatives of metropolis coded or miscoded her in accordance with their own degree of self-sufficiency, intellect, internal culture, and indoctrination with racism and orientalism. R.K. is careful to never slide into the simplified mode of stereotyping that both sides (the imperial and the colonial) often applied. Instead she sees people, rather than Russians, Uzbeks, or Jews, whereas the muscovite treatment of the colonial gendered other stretches from an open jealousy, humiliation and efforts to explain her success through personal connections or the Soviet policy of promoting the nationals, to treating her as a real human being whose opinion matters, and even to an erotic yet detached fascination and respect for an Oriental woman on the part of the Russian male Orientalists.

R.K. constantly comes back to her leitmotif of escaping to a different world and never coming back to what she left behind. Yet her many travels are not really voluntary, acting as a substitute of this unattainable ideal: "Most often I wanted to go away to a different country, a different world really. Sometimes I would even feel sorry that I did not stay in India when I was proposed by an Indian" (Tlostanova 2009, 292). Instead of India she moved to Caucasus—"to cut something and start a new life." Going from one Russian/Soviet colony to another was a unique experience marked by a peculiar secondary racism and an unhealthy rivalry between different others on who is closer to Europe or in this case, Russia, who is more modernized and civilized: "For a few years I experienced a terrible racism... There were some totally tactless things: 'Can you imagine, some Uzbek and she looks like a human being'. It reached that point. And I had another problem—I changed my profession and I did not want to be average. So I would work at night and teach at the university in the day time" (Tlostanova 2009, 292).

Several times R.K. repeats that there was a cult of education and knowledge in her family as opposed to material values. This happened thanks to her mother and was and is far from being typical for Central Asia, or rather, this is a strangled line linked with Jadidism which translated either into the allowed Soviet forms, or into the hidden private sphere. R.K. elaborates on this, linking the prerogative of education and self-improvement, that were always more important for her and her sisters than a convenient marriage, to a still deeper level of her mother's bringing up which she links with decency and a special kind of humanness—a sense of responsibility for being a human and for doing properly everything you promised.

All in all this testimony is a good example of a double critique of Uzbek, Russian, Caucasus and several other models in none of which she belongs completely to sameness or otherness. Due to her peculiar life trajectory of voluntary and involuntary migrations marked with imperial-colonial divisions and narratives, she became extremely sensitive to multiple otherness and difference and what is most important, she learned to make her hidden and often suppressed resistance into a sad and ironic trickster reexistence. This is obviously a much more complex picture than the veiled women from Northrop's book, the party activists, and Turkmen women-crane-operators of the Soviet ersatz multiculturalism or the emancipated colonials simply turned Russians.

Part III

Trans-Epistemic Dialogues and Contemporary Gender Discourses in Caucasus and Central Asia

Chapter Seven

Eurasian Borderlands in Dialogue with Mesoamerica

The previous chapter helps to easily move to the next part of the book where it becomes necessary to go back to Mesoamerica, yet do it on a different level, connected with the quest for trans-epistemic and trans-value grounds for a possible global dialogue between Eurasian and Mesoamerican borderlands. My attempt to analyze R.K.'s testimony was also an attempt to practice decolonial gender anthropology a fascinating example of which is to be found in Sylvia Marcos's book *Taken from the Lips: Gender and Eros in Mesoamerican Religions* (Marcos 2006). What follows is a virtual dialogue with its author. I attempt to interpret and at the same time rethink her method in relation to Central Asian and Caucasus subjectivities and local histories. This method is not a merely participatory anthropology. As a Bolivian scholar Silvia Rivera Cusicanqui (Cusicanqui 1990) pointed out, participatory anthropology may still remain within the traditional anthropological agenda. A decolonial anthropology would mean epistemic and political projects with indigenous agendas working with anthropologists, such as THOA (Taller Historia Oral Andina) or the Zapatistas. In such a radical anthropology the very object in the traditional understanding is gone and the ethnographer is a part of the world she or he describes, establishing close inter-personal relations with subjects of her/his research, in order to avoid sliding back into othering as a methodological basis of traditional anthropology, betraying its historical links with missionary or civilizing discourses. The subject of such decolonial anthropology, as I see it, takes an active and conscious part in "research," for lack of a better word. She/he can and does direct this research and change its course, pose and refine questions, softly making the anthropologist learn the same way as he or she is learning himself or herself as a result of being inquired. Both the anthropologist and the subject are always self-reflective in the process of this research turning into dialogue, always ready to question not merely the other but also oneself. The subject then is not an object any more in the fixed understanding of area studies and Western disciplines. While the researcher is freed from the enchantment with principles of objectivity, according to which an anthropologist has to be maximally detached from the world he or she describes and make a point out of hiding his or her own subjectivity while doing the analysis. The decolonial anthropologist does not aim at grasping and fixing one particular frozen image of the subject's self, arriving at a singular result of the analysis. Rather he or she is after constant tracing of the fluid and changeable multiple and complex selves of transcultural tricksters. Yet, the researcher necessarily shares with those whom he or she dialogues with, a common or at least intersecting horizon of understanding—in this case, initially pluritopic.

I will try to compare Sylvia Marcos's insights with a few elements of Caucasus and Central Asian epistemologies and demonstrate, how exactly she rethinks Western anthropology turning it into a decolonial knowledge. This would allow us to bring together several problems around which this book has been evolving: the emergence of decolonial humanities and social sciences, the trajectory of non-Western gender studies, the crossing points and dialogues between the Amerindian and Caucasus and Central Asian border epistemologies, which make future coalitions possible.

Marcos's book is both a wonderful anthropological investigation, a contemplation on the future of anthropology as a discipline, and a model of a new type of anthropological research likely to emerge in the twenty-first century as part of a major decolonial rethinking of humanities and social sciences. The author reworks the very mode of cognition at the base of her discipline. This refers not just to the methods and strategies but, more importantly, to the changing paradigm of thinking, of interpreting the world, the interpersonal communications and the very being in this world. Marcos's subject stretches from the first sixteenth century attempts at "casting the oral tradition into the alphabetic mode," to the models of the "past" constructed by the Spanish intelligentsia of the seventeenth–eighteenth centuries, and finally, to the ethnography of the oral traditions of the twentieth century, rethinking the past in order to make it usable for the present (Marcos 2006, xv). But no less important is her own interpretative method—that of "adaptive and creative resistance," which is embodied in the project of "re-appropriation of a spirituality rooted in their soil" (Marcos 2006, xv). Marcos makes her personal intellectual history a part of her research, so that both the subject, the mode of her research and the subjectivity of the author who looks at the material not as a detached and objective scientist, but regards it as a "part of her own ancestral past," form a unity, leading away from typical assonances, silences and voids of subject-object relations, marking traditional anthropology, and going toward a powerful and persuasive, truly dia-logic result.

No less important was the kind of education offered at Ivan Illich's *Centro Intercultural de Documentation* where Marcos first got acquainted with Mesoamerican cosmology. It is a model of education that can counterbalance the corporate university on a global scale. This education is based on the students' direct access to primary sources of all kinds and sometimes, as Marcos says, to their authors as well. It is a model of a "two-way learning-teaching" (Marcos 2006, xv), marked with horizontal, not vertical and nonhierarchic connections, where Roberto Rosselini stands in the same row with Che Guevara and Boaventura de Sousa Santos, but also with the painter and shaman Chanta from the state of Guerrero, who for Marcos is probably the most important of all, as she first introduced the author to the ethnology of healing and allowed her to catch the glimpse of indigenous cosmovision. There is a specific community of learning here, where "community" reacquires its true meaning of spiritual bonding based on real dialogue and coalitions with the intellectuals, activists, and politicians—both on regional and global levels.[1]

The most attractive element in this new model of thinking is the attitude to indigenous tradition as to a living, changing, variable within itself, slipping out of the Western logic of either/or. This element Marcos acquires from the subject she writes about although in her case there is no strict division into subject and object, legitimating anthropologists in the eyes of their discipline. It is from this source that the familiar accusations in romanticizing the past usually come and are used against intellectuals like Marcos. Marcos stresses the lack of romanticizing or objectification of nature in Mesoamerican civilization, which is connected with the specific indigenous interpretation of the world and the people as an integral part of it. The Amerindians did not see themselves as the dominating species divided from nature and cosmos by their superior, outside point of view. Rather they saw themselves as an equal element along with the myriads of others, coexisting in the complex spiritual and physical continuum with other people, gods, ancestors, nature, and the world. In this sense Marcos's own book also lacks romanticizing of Indians, but is marked instead with a sincere intention to understand and share their world vision, at least temporarily, and not just rationally, but also by means of indigenous instruments of spiritual and supernatural connections.

The mode of the book destabilizes anthropology as a discipline as this work is spiral in the temporal sense, not because of its link with Hegelian dialectic of synthesis, but due to its connection with and a conscious recreation of the specific mode of cyclical motion with a variation, characteristic of Mesoamerican culture, which is multilogic by definition. Marcos revisits in her spiral mode the many versions of the past which are unstable, changeable and yet retain certain recurrent and always recognizable and reconstructable elements. Marcos's work becomes a dialogue of the synchronous and diachronous analysis, as it combines historical ethnography and the unique ethnography of contemporary field studies. The concept of homeorrhesis, that is, "the balance of conjunctions in flux" (Marcos 2006, 25) refers not only to the equilibrium of Mesoamerican cosmology, but also to her own book in which there are several points of confluence or major nerves holding together the non-linear structure of this work which rejects the vector logic of the written discourse and attempts to reconstruct on paper a completely different logic of the oral tradition.

Marcos's book is also a comparative book, yet she refuses to compare exclusively from the position of the Western imperial subject. In fact the author is juxtaposing not merely the two worlds, but rather the two equal ways of formulating theory, thus shifting the geography of reason from its absolute Western position. Such a shift leads Marcos to serious changes in her scholarly approach—from descriptive and monologic, typical of traditional anthropology, to dialogic and epistemic, striving to engage with the way of thinking and cognition, the very perception of the world by indigenous people. This is a key to understanding of often disjointed details, as it unites them together and makes sense of them, allowing to see the design of the carpet as a whole, not only its separate ornaments. This method is based on understanding of the universe as a complex interaction of similarities and differences in which there is no longer one correct point of reference, where all elements are on equal terms and their study is not biased by Western categories of analysis anymore.

A crucial difference between Marcos's position in the interpretation of the border and that of Yuri Lotman or M. Foucault is that she deals from the start with tremendously asymmetric power relations between the two cultures, based on racial, religious, gender, social, economic and other aspects of imperial and colonial difference and coloniality of power. Both Foucault and Lotman—for different reasons—remained blind to this element. Marcos's project of archeology of knowledge turns out particularly complex and hard to fulfill, as it is non-linear and often based on association, because today the

Mesoamerican oecumena is known mainly through archeological data and the descriptions of Spanish missionaries (with the important exception of the continuing oral tradition). Marcos manages to tear through the layers and layers of official discourses and gather bits and pieces of occasional subversions, resistance and challenging of the imposed models, reconstructing the Mesoamerican system of gender relations and the dual interpretation of gender, which she persuasively presents as a key to understanding of duality as a basis of the whole indigenous cosmology. She is equally careful with both indigenous sources and their Spanish interpretations, never trying to just reject or criticize the latter, but rather attempting to understand their internal logic and the nature of their limitations, paying attention to how the confrontation between the two worlds was enacted, to the dynamics of their transcultural interaction.

This way presupposes a self-reflection on the part of the author who has to voluntarily get rid of the tenets of Western epistemology, scholarly analysis, and philosophic thinking. It is a difficult task but Marcos successfully copes with it. She stands with one foot in the Amerindian world and this allows her to be attentive enough to the material she analyzes, while the material gives her an adequate method of its understanding in return. This is clearly expressed in the chapters devoted to corporality, completely different from that of the West and later distorted by the Spanish missionaries, the essentially open orality, which in the Western tradition has been condescendingly regarded within the scope of the primitive archaic pre-literate culture, and in the chapter on the "precious jade stones"—the pearls of Mesoamerican wisdom and poetry, based on a complex metaphoric, which the Spanish missionaries were not able to understand because of its fluidity, changeability, and associative nature, far from the fixed allegorism of European literary and theological thinking of the time. Marcos aptly compares the oral tradition with a river, which may change its path, but always remains the same river. Orality then becomes a key to recreating the unity of Mesoamerican universe. Implementing the archeology of knowledge Marcos questions both the Western condescending dismissal of orality (putting forward the task of reconstructing the immediate evidences not distorted by the rules of the written discourse and shaking the Western notion of alphabetic writing and literacy as a sanction of a text's validity), and a typical approach when only the Western episteme itself is given a status of true epistemology and the monopoly of truth.

Marcos's approach to the interpretation of the past and the present of the Amerindian cosmology is a trans-epistemic interpenetration and dialogue. An additional difficulty in this case was that the voices of these people were pushed aside and buried in the Spanish chronicles and those of their local disciples. The reconstruction of the buried became Marcos's project. She managed to restore the symmetry of multilogic interaction, impossible in reality until now, but existing in her book. Deconstructing the Spanish texts she sets free the "third voice" of indigenous cosmology and epistemology, distorted and muted by the official monologism of the Catholic texts but continuing to "ventriloquize" from under the burden of these restrictions.

In the first chapter Marcos lays out the conceptual frames underlying the therapeutic practices of healing, and consequently, questions the Western interpretation of syncretism as assimilation, and votes for "interpenetration of civilizations" (quoting R. Bastid's work) instead (Marcos 2006, 2). However, later on, she questions this definition as well, claiming that rather it was a switching of images and invocations aimed at eluding punishments by the agents of the conquering faith (Marcos 2006, 59). This is clearly a position of a trickster fooling more powerful forces by cunning and wisdom.

In this respect not only Mesoamerican cosmology in a historical sense, but also Marcos's book is an example of a constant double or multiple translation, between the indigenous and Western epistemology, of a dynamic interaction of various undercurrents in the river of Mesoamerican cosmology—from pre-Hispanic through Spanish colonial to modern elements. Such a layering of various influences is true not only of Mesoamerica but of many other regions, and particularly those which were caught in between various imperial traditions. Even a brief analysis demonstrates the presence of important intersections and similar reactions in the treatment of the interpenetration of cultures, as well as significant differences due to different local histories. A good example would be the indigenous epistemologies of Eurasian borderlands, such as Caucasus and Central Asia where the newer layers never completely pushed out the previous ones, but rather counterimposed upon them, coexisting as layers of the skin in an onion-bulb. This phenomenon of similarity in difference, according to Marcos's metaphor, can also be likened to the river of indigenous epistemologies in a wider sense, the river which manifests itself differently, yet always remains the same river.

In case of Mesoamerica on top of indigenous religion there is a layer of Catholicism and, as a result, there emerges not a syncretism in some homogenous melted form, but a much more complex structure of attraction and repulsion. A more powerful and wiser tradition (not Christianity) ultimately wins in the sense that it makes the process of transculturation more symmetrical, not allowing the Western modernity to perform a complete subjugation and annihilation of indigenous culture. In Central Asia and Caucasus the religious genealogy was even longer and more complex. As it was pointed out above, in the first centuries A.D. a part of Caucasus was Christianized by the Greeks but the other part remained under the indigenous polytheistic religion and cosmology. The contacts with the Ottoman Sultanate brought Islam much later (late seventeenth through early nineteenth century). This religion of the book attempted to replace the local religions, which took several centuries and never came to a real success.[2] Up to now the Muslim Cherkess, when they want to intensify the effect of their actions and words, do not call for Allah, but rather for *Tkha*—a pre-Islamic deity, which was divided into two interconnected, not exclusionary to each other but complementary aspects— the benevolent (linked to the sky) and the judgmental (linked to storms and lightening that were considered sacred). This deity was not seen as above the world or outside it. On the contrary, it was its integral part along with people, nature and other supreme beings.

In Central Asia Islam was established earlier, although the process of pushing out the indigenous cosmologies also took several centuries and was accompanied by bloody excesses and later, by the same mechanism of choosing a lesser evil of the two—the external Islamization under a partial preservation of indigenous cosmology. In the Czarist period the same logic was expressed in the external Russification (adopting of Orthodox Christianity, Russian education, serving in the Russian army, etc.), balanced by a quick readiness to chose another ally (for instance, the Ottoman Turkey) in the struggle for independence. In the Soviet period it was expressed once again, in an external loyalty to the empire by infiltrating the Soviet institutions with representatives of anti-colonial movements attempting to weaken the Soviet power from within, and in the survival tactic between the more powerful enemies.

Under all these historical perturbations the cosmovision of Caucasus and Central Asia was based on the grounds in many ways similar to those of other indigenous peoples, including the Mesoamericans. The fluidity and flexibility of non-exclusive dualities mentioned above is present in Caucasus cosmology, based on the idea of dynamic equilibrium which the humans as well as the gods are responsible for. An evil act of a single human being can no less than ruin the balance of cosmic processes. This element is expressed in a particular ethical code, in the system of rules and etiquette, including the gender sphere, based on parity. It demonstrates the one-ness and unity of religious and social spheres and the importance of keeping the cosmic balance at all levels. It is also expressed in Narts epic tradition which laments the lost wholism and communitarian harmony. The characters of this epic—the giants Narts—kill their hero Sosruko themselves—out of spite and envy. By this act they destroy the cosmic balance and are subsequently punished by the universe for their foolish forgetting of the law of mutual interconnections and the moral dimension of nature: they turn into ordinary people with no supernatural abilities and with the lost connection with cosmos. And the mission of restoring this equilibrium is performed at least partially by the traditional healers.

Both in Caucasus and in Central Asia there emerged a specific duality of faith comparable to the one described by Marcos. Under many differences between the local histories of Eurasia and Mesoamerica, there is a similar inner logic that runs through them all. That is why today Islam acts for many traditional healers from Caucasus and Central Asia in the same capacity as Christianity for Marcos's curanderas. It is just a certain semiotic system which adds separate elements, counter-pointing the core of pre-Islamic indigenous cosmology, and considerably transforming the tenets of classical Islamic monotheism and written tradition, to which these healers often do not have a direct access (due to their unfamiliarity with Arabic). Thus, a Kyrgyz healer L.K.[3] stressed her firm grounding in the oral tradition, in specific spiritual legacies that have been transferred orally from grandmother to granddaughter for many generations and the decidedly pre-Islamic, in her case—nomadic Mongol nature of these healing practices. Both in the Islamic part of Caucasus and particularly in Central Asia there is a well developed system of border forms of popular Sufism with their well preserved often pre-Islamic Saints who were frequently women, and with a no less heterogeneous (in their genealogy and functioning) system of rituals. The latter are of a complex, non-assimilated, open, and unstable nature, hard to define within the Western logic.

In Caucasus cosmology the female element has been always very strong and remains important even today. It refers, for instance, to its central female character—Sataney, the great mother of all Narts and the mother of Sosruko. Sataney is connected in the oral and poetic tradition with Mazitkhe—a forest deity representing the crucial link with the forest as a symbol of life (this can be compared with sanctification of earth in Mesoamerican cosmology). Mazitkhe acts both in its male and female forms and only in the later written distorted versions made by the local variants of Spanish missionaries—the Western travelers, the Russian explorers and the Russified locals—it acquires a distinctly masculine image. Sataney's only child is a solar deity (the mother-son relations in this case indicate the hierarchy of natural phenomena in Narts ancient cosmology: the Forest is the mother of the Sun), while his father is unimportant and defined in the myth only by his professional belonging: he is a shepherd. Sosruko is born as a result of extra-corporal conception and gestating inside a stone-womb, which Sataney later brings to the black-smith asking him to make a steel boy out of it. Thus she acts as a cultural hero herself, bringing to the people the knowledge of how to make metal out of stones. All the important events in Narts life and the heroic male deeds take place under a direct participation and supervision of the wise, eternally beautiful, young, and immortal Sataney. The women in Narts epic (not only Sataney but also Adiyukh, the old Warsar, whom the Narts consult each time they need a wise advice and the maiden variant of the feminine—the small Malechiph in whose description intellect, cunning and wisdom are more important than her beauty) are presented as carriers of the prophetic and magical qualities and also as warriors who often use their exceptional physical and spiritual power.

In order to understand Central Asian and Caucasus cosmology it is necessary to take into account the pre-Islamic elements, the marginal and syncretic nature of this Islam and the influence of Russian and Soviet modernity. The difficult work of reconstruction of this legacy with the focus on gender is just starting today and Marcos's book can be a model for indigenous anthropologists from Eurasian borderlands.

Interviews with *curanderas* are a unique part of Marcos's work which really make this tradition alive and bring it close to the reader. They also made me think of my own experience of interacting with such people in Caucasus where, as in Central Asia, the indigenous cosmologies also have been better preserved in the rituals of the healers, closely connected with the oral tradition. As in the case of Marcos's book these were mostly women, while the sphere of healing remains one of the very few areas where women are able to overcome their lack of basic rights.

I am offering this comparison not for the sake of Western comparative studies but to demonstrate that the indigenous oral traditions in many locales of the world are a reservoir of not merely wisdom which the so called modern man rediscovers for himself today with much delay, but also of political and social activism and reexistence. Establishing dialogues between representatives of these often only partly alive traditions all over the world is a necessary step for the future, if we want to survive as a species. However, in contrast with Zapatistas, in peripheral Eurasia such movements have not yet acquired a political force and influence, have not yet become a part of the emerging political society. One of the reasons for this is obviously the powerful vertical state controlling everything and everyone, which is the case of both Russia and Central Asian newly independent states. Other reasons include the deeply rooted Soviet aggressive atheism and mundane materialism, the rejection of everything spiritual, combined with the age-old servility in relation to the regime, all of which together deny the possibility of an other thinking. Today they are also accompanied by the poisonous effect of neo-liberal values and cultural homogenizing. Yet, there are at least sporadic attempts at specific tricksterism negotiating various forms of modernity and indigenous spiritual legacies. Thus, L.K. works in an NGO most of the time traveling to distant Northern and cold parts of the country to aid the poorest and socially vulnerable people. She told me that her NGO colleagues do not understand her heroism (she could stay in the warm and comfortable center) but for her it is a hidden or altered form of healing which allows her to keep the shell of her modern identity yet fill it with her deeper vocation to help people as she feels that they need her.

I had a chance to closely communicate with several healers in Caucasus. Some of them corresponded completely to the model described by Marcos. They were women uneducated in the Western sense who had an enormous power inherited and learnt from their ancestors. Their rituals combined the use of amulets with seemingly Arabic (but in fact only looking as Arabic) scriptures, the specially prepared pieces of wood, wrapped in leather, herbs. Fighting a bad eye or a "bewitching" they acted as receptacles for these emanations, literally taking the illness off the patients. Others were adapted to the modern life. There was even a university professor among them (as Soviet modernization and "emancipation" can be responsible for even stranger happenings), but after the tragic or dramatic events in their lives they usually went through a revelation and started curing people. It was interesting to follow their peculiar evolution in the religious sense. First one of them coded everything in Muslim terms demonstrating intolerance to any other religions and symbols. As her mastery grew she started performing the role close to what Marcos calls mediumism, and gradually lost her intolerance and began to interpret representatives of all religions and even atheists on equal terms. Finally she formed a completely different idea of the world, the human being and the godly presence as parts of it, existing in and through each other. Her method of diagnostic and treatment consisted in drawing on paper the *spiritualo-grams* of her patients which conveyed their condition, somehow materialized it and by doing it made these people free of their ailments—spiritual more often than physical. L.K. mentions very similar practices although she belongs to a different local tradition. Describing the use of herbs such as *archa* (a kind of juniper), she combines her identity as a healer and as a modern individual. L.K. says that *Archa* is a sacred plant in Central Asia, but then she adds that it is a natural source of phytoncides, that in *archa* ritual she pronounces the ancient chants asking to take the illness away and that *archa* is brought to her from far away woods where it is (ecologically) the purest. The scientific explanation thus always comes after the indigenous one.

An even more interesting configuration is to be found in the case of the modern Uzbek "saint" Habiba (Allione 1997) who after a revelation that came to her in a dream, made a connection with Bahauddin Nakshbandi, a fourteenth-century saint and a founder of the Sufi order of the same name with over forty million followers all over the world. Nakshbandi was born near Bukhara where now stands his mausoleum to which thousands of people have been paying homage for six centuries. Nakshbandi Sufism was one of the main versions of Islam in this locale for a long time, and was predictably banned in Soviet years. This Sufi order did not stress the ascetic life and turning from the real world to the transcendent one, but rather spoke for the equality of both worlds—the real and the mystical, their existence in each other and through each other. This philosophy was marked by a special tolerance and rejection of orthodoxy. It regarded women as equal to men and even allowed them into the main parts of the mosques.

The interpretation of Nakshbandi philosophy by *tabiba*[4] Habiba is a subject of a separate study. Suffice it to say here that there are a few elements that allow us to glimpse into the core of this cosmology and also put it into an imaginary dialogue with the voices of Marcos's curanderas. In this philosophy the mystical and the transcendental are a part of everyday life of every person, but he or she must learn to understand and feel these dimensions of being. Like in *espiritualismo*, here there comes forward a peculiar cultural mixing of a region where none of the religions is rejected in favor of any other. Egypt, Persia, India, China, Buddhism, Christianity—all of it, according to Nakshbandi, coexists and correlates in the explosive and fruitful interaction giving birth to a special kind of Islam he prophets. Habiba believes that there is one God but many religions. And it is not a statement of monotheism. Rather it is an effort to describe the cosmic power of the universe that monitors our lives no matter which language we speak when we pray. It is not a chance that Habiba says that she receives information from the universe, while various gods and saints only help her in that. Reading Quran, she also speaks of the energy of the woman-snake sending the "yellow light" to help Habiba's patients. Praying to Allah, she regards him not as some abstract power which exists outside of human lives, but as a concrete—and not a sole—helper in her mission of saving people by sharing her spiritual energy with them. A similar dynamic symbiosis of Muslim, pre-Islamic (nomadic), Christian and Buddhist (Tibetan) traditions is to be found in the practices of the Kyrgyz healer L.K.

Habiba follows Nakshbandi's advice of speaking with every person "according to his understanding" (Allione 1997). The teacher should be fluid and flexible, and exist beyond the binary oppositions, above the time and space. The teacher must be careful not to disturb the world's equilibrium and "remain silent when it is needed and talk when it is necessary, act when the action is called for and always listen to the rhythms not just of this world, but also of the other worlds, surrendering to God's love and compassion" (Allione 1997). Habiba points out another crucial Nakshbandi's metaphor which aptly describes the difference between the Western perception of the world and the Central Asian cosmology, resonating with the Mesoamerican model, as described by Marcos. It is connected with the idea of all-encompassing interrelation and interconnection of the people, the nature, the cosmos, where each of us represents the other. "Take a hand—we can concentrate on the differences between each of the fingers, marveling how different they are, but then we risk not noticing the movement of the hand as a whole" (Allione 1997).

Habiba's appeal to the woman-snake, who as she claims initiated her into healing, and to Allah, as well as to the great mother Anahita (an Avestan Indo-Iranian cosmological figure associated with water who is responsible for fertility, wisdom and healing), the Christian Saint Nicholas and to Jenny Abdrahman, and her healing methods (herbs, balms, blowing at and patting the patient, repeating specific chants, a symbolic use of the knife imitating a surgical operation, massage, hypnosis, etc.) are all concordant with what Marcos describes when referring to Mesoamerican curanderas. It makes us wonder if all of them are remnants of an other knowledge and understanding of the world that the humankind had lost everywhere. Yet they survived in many regions and remain alive and fruitful models, constant yet changing.

Marcos points out a specific interpretation of gender in Mesoamerican cosmology completely different from Western fixed dichotomous division into sex and gender, which often lies in the basis of mainstream variants of feminism and is connected with Western and Christian dichotomous juxtaposition of the body and the soul, the material and the spiritual. Through the whole book Marcos weaves the link between gender and a specific understanding of all-penetrating duality in Mesoamerican culture, based on fluidity, openness and non-hierarchical structure. She demonstrates that in Mesoamerican civilization gender relations were not based on biology, but rather connected with social status, seniority, profession, and so forth. Most importantly, they were not fixed, but changeable. Therefore it is important to avoid artificially imposing the categories, assumptions, and fixed gender roles of Western feminist analysis onto these locales thus distorting the meaning of their cosmologies.

Marcos's concept of "homeorrheic" describing the relations between masculinity and femininity and the cosmic equilibrium, overcomes the limitations of Western thinking, based on exclusionary oppositions, and reaches instead for the concept of dual unity, based on fusion and blending of the masculine and feminine and on the possibility of defining both biological sex and gender through changeable social relations and roles and spiritual supernatural characteristics. Crucial in this context is a chapter devoted to corporality closely connected with the duality of gender and its organizing part in the understanding and sustaining of equilibrium and fluidity, penetrability and interconnection between all the elements of the universe—in this case, between the body and the world, or the body and the spirit.

Marcos argues for the interconnection of the sacredness of the earth and the sacralization of sex and earthly manifestations of Eros in Mesoamerican cosmology. Sex is presented as a ritual, expressing the unity with earth. In Caucasus as in many other locales there was also a custom of the ritual sex on the grave as a means of restating life. The sexual actions, often collective, could be also linked to the calling of the rain as the necessary condition of a good harvest in a ritual devoted to thunder god Shible. Sanctified sex, as Marcos points out, is typical for many indigenous cultures where the earth is linked with sexuality, on the one hand, and with morality on the other. This shifting and complex connection of sexuality and morality through earth has nothing to do with Christian and Western notions and is not repressive in its nature.

This is why a certain gender liberty of indigenous peoples of Caucasus and their refusal to regard sex as a sin and woman as its source, was perceived by the European travelers from Renaissance onward (Giovanni da Lucca, prefect of the Dominican mission in Kaffa in the seventeenth century, a German scholar and traveler Adam Olearius and others), and later, by Russian officers in the Caucasus war, as a manifestation of moral degradation and savagery of indigenous women. Similarly to Spanish missionaries they saw only what their eyes were trained to see not noticing that indigenous cultures gave women more rights and guarantees than modernity. The relations between the sexes were regulated, as in the case with Mesoamerica, by an intricate system of didactic oral teachings and presupposed both a lack of bigotry, and a lack of sexual looseness, trusting each other and respecting each other's rights, freedom in family relations and sexual practices at every age. In other words, the erotic and the bodily were not suppressed or regarded through fear and shame.

As it was pointed out above, demonization of others—be they Indians, Blacks, peoples of Caucasus, Muslims, homosexuals—has always been based in the logic of Western modernity on the mechanism of blaming the victim for the crime which was committed against it, for the sake of self-justification. When Marcos speaks of the Spanish distortions of the indigenous tradition, I think of other ideological distortions that took place in both Caucasus and Central Asia. Through them the whole histories of peoples were erased and rewritten depraving of any links with the past and methodically eliminating any subversive sources linked with passive and active resistance to colonization and reexistence, and being in spite of everything. This is how the indigenous peoples were brainwashed with the idea of their own presumable backwardness and the false belief that only the Bolsheviks (Russians) allowed them to make a leap from medieval times into socialist modernity, or even from the cavemen to the communist future, as it happened with many ethnicities in the Far North and Siberia.

Marcos also dwells on the spiritual colonization brought by the missionaries to Mesoamerica which turned out worse than economic exploitation and even genocide. Unfortunately this process of zombification appeared to be very successful in many parts of the world including Eurasian borderlands, particularly in the Soviet period. Today's lack in these regions of the models similar to interculturalism and plurinational state is linked with the "success" of the Soviet empire's modernization, with its carefully elaborated strategies of brainwashing of indigenous peoples, with the Jesuitical nature of Soviet ideology, that surpassed in this respect the clumsy and under-reflected double faceness of the Czarist empire. Cynicism, resourcefulness and many-faced pattern of the Soviet ethnic-national ideologies is hard to match, the same way as the repressive mechanisms of the accelerated and cruel Soviet modernization, as a result of which even the smallest traces of indigenous cosmologies and ethics were irreparably erased from the collective memory and replaced with either Soviet Eurocentric progressivist discourse or today—with ersatz ethnic nationalism. Yet, the Russian and Soviet colonizing efforts were never one-way streets. The same way as in Mesoamerica, they always generated various forms of resistance and reexistence.

In "Beyond Mesoamerica: the Hermeneutics of Orality" Marcos comes back in a spiral way to the question of rethinking the humanities and particularly, to the necessity of dialogic anthropology. It is connected with deconstruction of Western hierarchy according to which the oral traditions are inferior to written ones, and with the new approach to the analysis of these traditions in their own terms, not based on the Western model of the fixed written tradition and canon as the norm. Besides, the oral traditions cannot be regarded as historically fixed and archaic because they continue today, incorporating and creatively reworking the colonizing models but always retaining their own core at that. It is necessary to study synchronously this contemporary phenomenon or rather a *process* of orality within the frame of ethnography of the present which would have to be social and even political, as well as focused on revamped field studies. Marcos stresses the necessity of questioning the concepts of God and deity, the binary opposition of the sacred and profane, the interpretation of nature and gender relations in the analysis of oral traditions (Marcos 2006, 110). Then a hermeneutics of orality would emerge based on rethinking of rhetorical devices of the oral traditions, of their symbolism and metaphors—in their own terms, based not on the canonical written/alphabetic tradition, but on the collective memory instead.

Radical and dialogical participatory anthropology advocated by Marcos develops today all over the world, although it faces many impediments on the part of the orthodox Western anthropologists. Such anthropology thrives particularly in the ex-third world and second-world countries. I will give just two examples illustrating this tendency: a collection of articles co-edited by Seteney Shami *Women in Arab Society: Work Patterns and Gender Relations in Egypt, Jordan, and Sudan* (Shami et al. 1990), where the young Arabic women-anthropologists reflect on the necessity of rehabilitation of participatory anthropology in which the scholar herself is a part of the analyzed world or stands at the border between the Western and local systems. The second example is more ambiguous but very telling because it shows the continuing power asymmetry at work. It is a book by the director of the Institute of Anthropology and Ethnography (Russian Academy of Sciences) Valery Tishkov about the Chechen war (Tishkov 2004), an example of the ethnography of the present. As the author admitted himself, while writing this book he used the help of his former student—an indigenous Chechen woman who was the one doing the field study and interviews. Without her being a part of the world described in this book it would have been impossible to write it.

The epilogue of Marcos's book is in fact a beginning of a new spiral, not an end. Her work is based on the principle of openness, unfinished nature and fluidity—the very principle she strives to analyze. Behind the concepts that Marcos introduces in her work, such as "sexual spirituality," "embodied thought," "homeorrheic equilibrium," "gender fluidity," there lies a bottomless universe of meanings and possibilities of research which the scholars not only from Mesoamerica, but also from the rest of the world, will now have a chance to understand and start creatively working with.

Chapter Eight

Two Dialogues

8.1. A Dialogue with a Caucasus Healer

A Caucasus healer F. Zh.[1] has a peculiar aphoristic and lapidary style of formulating her ideas, leaving many unverbalizable things in the sub-text. Her answers are an example of mediumism, as there is an other voice prophesying through her in these simple yet overloaded sentences. Similarly to Habiba she is eclectic in her sources and the leitmotifs of her cosmovision are clearly Yoga, theosophy in its various forms as a translation and adaptation of Eastern cosmologies by Western interpreters, further reconceptualized by F. Zh., and the written higher versions of Sufism as opposed to its popular forms. She does not appeal to Christianity (the only direct link to Western models for her being that of astrology—a decidedly marginalized tradition) or to pre-Islamic Caucasus indigenous systems a link with which was lost in her case. There is an indirect and not entirely conscious resisting element and a higher learning preference in her choice. She often uses the word "synthesis" understanding it in a specific (not Hegelian) way as a marriage of rational and intuitive, bookish and oral, soul and body, based on parity but never blended or completely fused. In contrast with Mesoamerica F. Zh. observes a hierarchy where the spiritual and the soul as its container stand higher than the bodily and the material.

This dialogue continues a line of trans-epistemic gendered border thinking and being, intersecting with Marcos's model in several ways, for example, in its ecumenist stance, in a specific interpretation of gender relations, in accentuating the links between the individual and the Cosmos. But it also signalizes the important difference between the Eurasian borderlands and Mesoamerica. This difference mainly lies in a much more pronounced individuation, an accent on the spiritual and esoteric individual growth which has nothing to do with Western individualism yet in F. Zh.'s as in other Eurasian border people's cases is a result of a clash with modernity which forcefully made colonial others into Western style individuals, pushed them into the abyss of existential problematic, but robbed them of Western rights and instruments of coping and survival, at the same time preventing them from any community support or links with other healers as a result of Soviet modernity that radically erased this continuity. A colonial other devoid of these links and made into a subhuman, can buy into Western modernity or start looking for other ways of individuation which F. Zh. found in Buddhism and Sufism.

For me she is a trickster and a border person in an utmost trans-epistemic sense even if she does not realize it herself. Her resistance functions in a channel completely inaccessible to (and thus uncontrollable by) modernity, as she is translating agency into the esoteric spiritual sphere rather than material world. Due to the (post)Soviet void in the realm of communal spirituality F. Zh. does not yet see a need in collective agency. This is one of the crucial differences with Mesoamerica. The Caucasus healer rejects any attempts to translate healing into political agency stressing the importance of individual spiritual growth and praxis at the expense of any material conditions and everyday circumstances. She prefers to ignore the material side, transferring the evolution (understood in the Yoga sense rather than usual Western rendering) completely into the spiritual sphere thus attempting to escape the bondage of modernity. In this respect her position is close to delinking as articulated by Walter Mignolo. Instead of fighting modernity she goes around it, she in a way transcends it. But in her case this border being vacillates around the self-perfecting way of constant looking for the sources (not some primordial going back to archaic frozen tradition) that would be uncontaminated by the material world of modernity. It is a learned and learning way of spiritual *satori* and ascending.

Translating the spiritual links with non-Western cosmologies into praxis in case of Eurasian borderlands is difficult precisely because of the conditions of this world such as the repressive social, cultural, religious, and linguistic environment. The links with ancestors including the healing legacy are lacking or extremely complicated in the post-soviet space (although the Kyrgyz healer L.K. is one such example). So in F. Zh.'s case the way to healing is an individual and lonely way of spiritual growth and learning from books and extrasensuous experience rather than learning from a teacher or an ancestor. Outwardly her position looks like nonresistance. Yet it is a form of resistance which transcends the irreparable conditions of the material world of colonial modernity refusing to play by its rules. This stance has a painful personal dimension of essential splitness and constant code-switching which F.Zh. does not openly acknowledge but obviously practices. Certainly she cannot escape the modern material world where she is not a very successful or happy person. But her real self and her real destination of helping people to find their way can be expressed only in this specific other-than-modern/material realm.

> *M. T.*: What events in your life, what reflections and landmarks of your inner evolvement have brought you to healing? Would you say that you are a healer, a person with paranormal abilities, a spiritual teacher helping people to cope with their problems?
>
> *F. Zh.*: It is important to live in high tension on the level of the soul, seeing all difficulties as working off the fruits of your Karma, as cleansing your soul. It is crucial to learn to know oneself as an individual, as a soul. I am a contacter, a medium by birth. People born on January 13 are born mediums. My work is grounded in three "I"s—instinct, intellect, and intuition.
>
> *M. T.*: What elements are most important in your identity, what layers juxtapose and interact in your idea of the world (Muslim, Pre-Islamic, secular, Christian, ethnic-cultural, mono- and polytheistic)?
>
> *F. Zh.*: The key aspect of my "self" is the link with conscience, a synthesis of all layers. Aquarius is a sign of synthesis, of going from particular to general that is, to the Heavenly source.
>
> *M. T.*: What is the recipe of your healing combination of rational knowledge, a self-conscious understanding of your praxis, controlling your ability and the unconscious, spontaneous, irrational linked to revelation? When helping people do you ground yourself in some "traditional" methods, cosmologies, religious and ethnic-cultural models? What was your path to them?
>
> *F. Zh.*: It is self-reflection, spontaneity, the unconscious element linked to revelation. I apply cosmology and religion. My path is grounded in collective ancestral memory, as well as reading books and above all, in an independent spiritual development. I refer to extra-sensual experience and I fear the God as a source of Wisdom.
>
> *M. T.*: Is there any written tradition which you use in your healing? For example, do you know Arabic or do you have an access to Muslim "texts?" How important is it for you?
>
> *F. Zh.*: Yes, there is a written tradition. It is the language of Sufism. Sufism is an inner gist of religion, to quote Idries Shah.[2] An access to Muslim "texts" is crucial for me, as they are a touchstone to check if I am following the right, the pious path and this gives me assuredness.
>
> *M. T.*: It seems that most of the healers are women. Why is it so in your view?
>
> *F. Zh.*: Women are more sensitive. Their nervous system is more subtly organized. Hence mediums are always women.

M. T.: What concrete practices and rituals do you use in your healing? What is their meaning? Have you come to them intuitively or learnt from someone or something?

F. Zh.: My practice consists in cleansing the bio-field from the intrusion of the lower vibration energetic forces which destroy the human being. I came to this practice intuitively, yet I also was influenced immensely by the God's word (prayers) from various Holy Books, starting from Sanskrit and to Sufism and many others. An important aid for me was esoteric literature, such as Helena Blavatsky's *The Secret Doctrine,* Jual Khul's *Letters to Healers, Psychologists and Teachers, Ascended Master Teachings, A treatise on Cosmic Fire* as rendered by Alice Bailey, and also *Treatise of Seven Rays.*[3]

M. T.: How important for you is to remain within the limits of one particular healing tradition? Do you find it possible and necessary to refer to different cosmologies and experiences, religious and cultural grounds and are there any limits for you in this respect? Who or what determines the trajectory of your movement?

F. Zh.: I use a synthesis of different cosmologies and postulates of Holly Scriptures. It is necessary to compare and choose what you feel and what your soul selects. The soul is a Monad—the Sunny Angel, that is, your Essence.

M. T.: Since you started your healing practices have you noticed any changes in your religious views, your ideas of the way the world functions, and the way you relate to people?

F. Zh.: I follow the postulate: Know yourself and you will know the whole world. And I know what it means that all people are equal in front of the God. I constantly ask myself questions like: Who I am? Where am I going? What am I doing in this world? I know that I woke up and I strive to go upward!

M. T.: Do you help all people regardless of their nationality, religious, social and gender belonging or you have preferences in this respect? Do you agree that there is one god and many religions?

F. Zh.: I help all people no matter what is their nationality, religion, social, or gender belonging. This process takes place on an intuitive level. I think that there is one God while religions are paths of the human spiritual growth on the evolution scale.

M. T.: What is more important, to heal the body or the soul and can we divide them at all?

F. Zh.: The source of all ailments is the suppressed life of the Soul. A conflict of the Soul and the body is manifested in the form of various ailments—this is the second heavenly punishment, plus Karma. Having cured the Soul we can cure the body as the body is the Temple of the Soul.

M. T.: How do you see the relations between human being, nature and cosmos? Is there any ethical dimension of the natural? If so, what is it?

F. Zh.: The world is a single whole. The Spirit in its lowest form is matter while matter in its highest form is Spirit.

M. T.: How do you see the ideal or desirable form of gender relations, the masculine and the feminine? Should it be based on equality, dynamic balance, interaction, antagonism or something else?

F. Zh.: As long as there is no understanding and no realization of the fact that men see things in general which women cannot do, while women percept the details which men are not capable of, the so called psychological incompatibility would persist, or if you wish, a lack of coincidence between the thoughtform and the world-feeling, leading to conflicts.

M. T.: Is it possible to sustain the continuity of spiritual traditions of your people in the conditions of modernity which erases the uncomfortable history and destroys the genealogy of other knowledges?

F. Zh.: Spiritual traditions that help to widen one's conscience are the postulates of the Pious Path of those who are aspiring. One needs to keep them no matter what are the conditions of modernity in any guise.

M. T.: There is an opinion that the mission of the healers in many regions of the world is to liberate the spiritually colonized consciousness of their people, to protect and take back their rights to "spirituality rooted in their soil." Do you agree with this stance and is this an important question for you?

F. Zh.: Everything depends on the point in evolution at which a human being or an ethnos stand. It is important how they interpret evolution, as a punishment or as a Noble Truth. Therefore I am not interested in assisting people in their fight for their rights, it is not an issue for me as I work on a different level. I know from my own experience that people connected with God through conscience ascend higher and higher on the evolution scale thus widening their consciousness. Can we explain to an ant that his ant hill was destroyed by a tractor driver?!

M. T.: How do you see the opposition of tradition and modernization? Can it be overcome?

F. Zh.: There are three ways of going back to the source: (1) the pragmatic way (for instance, studying the human legacy using books); (2) the religious way (following the commandments of the sacred texts); (3) the way of the chosen (by means of self control, self-perfection). I use all three ways in synthesis.

M. T.: How do you manage to combine your existence in contemporary world and the esoteric, spiritual, mystic and transcendental level? Does not it lead to a certain splitness of your self? Do you have to make a choice in favor of the former or the latter? Does healing give you a chance of additional self-realization as a human being and as a woman?

F. Zh.: It is a difficult question as I have to always struggle for survival. This is where the tension lies. The more tension the higher is the vibration which allows asking questions (esoteric, spiritual, mystical). It is not a matter of choice, because the Heavenly Gift cannot be sold in this world (in this material, thickest world). In this world we have to make a living according to the laws of this world, by means of a profession fit for this world, as money and gold are concentrated energy.

M. T.: Is there a subculture of healers in your ethnic, religious, cultural environment? How does it correlate with similar systems of other people and would you be interested in having a dialogue with similar subcultures in different parts of the world?

F. Zh.: The inner gist of religion is the same everywhere no matter in what form it is expressed outwardly (ethnically, culturally, linguistically, in points of official religion). What is at work here is the law of going from the general to the particular. Yes, I would be interested in a dialogue with other healers in various regions of the world (particularly, Tibet, Arabia, and India). After all the Caucasus mountains are the continuation of the Himalayas.

M. T.: Have you ever experienced discrimination as a woman, as a representative of non-European ethnicity, as a Muslim, as a healer or in a complex intersection of various elements? What strategies of resistance did you use in this case? Have you ever used the trickster way of outwitting the more powerful opponent?

F. Zh.: I have always felt discrimination in Moscow as a representative of a non-European ethnicity. As a healer I am in a certain trap of circumstances of this world. The life of any healer is an opposition and a struggle with the negative side, with the eternal antagonist, with people who are generators of bad energy. Any trickery can be used by the opposite side and any thought is written down in the cosmic book. So one has to be extremely careful, honest, and responsible in one's thoughts and deeds.

8.2. A Dialogue with a Central-Asian Gender Activist

The following dialogue[4] is a border text, as, on the one hand, it presents a certain contrast with trans-epistemic gendered border consciousness, theorized by Marcos and partly illustrated by the dialogue with the Caucasus healer. And on the other hand, it makes a link with the conclusion, where I am going to elaborate on what could be the future decolonial gender discourses in Eurasian borderlands. My interlocutor is Svetlana Shakirova—the director of gender studies center in Almaty and one of the central figures in contemporary Central Asian gender activism. In this respect her discourse is highly symptomatic of the whole gender studies in the region. She is a border subject in a different sense from what has been discussed so far. On the one hand, she is extremely acute in her criticism of many non-Western feminism problems. On the other hand, due to her personal feminist trajectory grounded mainly in Western and Russian sources and to her institutionalization within the state, the NGO system and most importantly, within the academic feminist community, which has managed to rebuild in the post-Soviet and wider, post-Socialist space a rigid and, in my view, quite imperial-colonial hierarchy, Shakirova is often evasive when discussing issues that may be dangerous for her reputation within this complex and hierarchical feminist community. Yet every once in a while her sincere attitude or sensibility, oozes in a stray word or an unfinished utterance. Svetlana's discourse is publicly oriented rather than existential or spiritual as it was the case with the healers. She operates easier with measurable categories of designed courses, organized conferences and summer schools, and enumerating concrete events representing the development of Central Asian gender studies. I am far from trying to discredit Svetlana's position here or present it as inferior. Yet I think that this interview demonstrated to both of us the far reaching and grave consequences of institutionalization on any level which can effectively disempower gender and other contesting discourses and their activists by imposing an invisible set of rules which they are not allowed to transcend. It is clear that we need other forms and ways of coalition and dialogues that would not be co-opted and minced by the dominant structures.

> *M. T.*: How and why you entered the gender movement? What events in your life were the most important for triggering an interest in gender problematic?
>
> *S. Sh.*: I have been always a serious and calm girl—a good pupil, a good daughter, a straight "A" student. In high school I decided to read Marx's *Capital*. I read one chapter from the beginning to the end and the rest of it I just skimmed. I used to read carefully the so called thick journals, like all other representatives of Soviet intelligentsia. My mother is a librarian and she taught us all in the family to read a lot and to love reading. Out of this interest in serious literature there emerged an interest in philosophy. I enrolled at the School of philosophy of Kazakh University, I was an enthusiastic student, a diligent one and at the same time, it all came easy to me. I remember quite well the Perestroika years. I was a third year student. It was the peak of the student life. The social life was storming, there was so much happening. I asked myself a question: "Why

there were no women among the great philosophers? Why half of our professors are women and half of the students as well, but only men ever gain a real recognition?" I was perplexed: am I also going to become just a good lecturer of philosophy and nothing else? It was a sad discovery. I began to think. Then I wrote a BA thesis "The Male and Female Element in Philosophy." In the fifth issue of *Philosophic Review* in 1998 I found articles by Olga Voronina, Tatyana Klimenkova and Nina Yulina, devoted to feminism, feminist epistemology and philosophy. These texts were the detonators of my then dormant woman's identity. Feminism acquired one more champion in Almaty, Kazakhstan.

After graduating I worked as a sociologist at the Ministry of education. I found myself in the all women collective, where people would drink tea all day, chat, put makeup on, slowly do their simple work. Is this how I am going to spend my life?! I was doing a sociological study of different stages of the system of education. Then I got married and soon got a maternity leave. When my daughter turned two, I got enrolled in a PhD program and my dissertation was called "Feminist epistemology and the cognition theory." In the beginning of the 90s there was almost no feminist literature and the concept of gender had not yet entered the scholarly language. I felt myself isolated, with no referent group and with no consultants—a fish with no water. I had no access to English-language sources and I had already read everything with the word "feminism" on it that I could find in Almaty. But in the summer of 1993 I heard on the radio that in Almaty House of Scientists there would be an international conference *Woman and Society*. I went there and got acquainted with Yu. Zaitsev, the editor of *Malvina*—a newspaper for girls with a feminist stance. He and his friends had an idea of founding a feminist organization and I could take part in it. At the constituent meting of the Feminist League I was asked to write the program for this organization. I wrote it using the collection of articles published in Moscow *Feminism: East. West. Russia* (1993). This book was the first brick in the foundation of my feminist consciousness.

For the first time in Central Asia we positioned ourselves openly as feminists. The words "feminism," "gender," "gender egalitarianism," "sexism" began to appear in our articles and interviews. Our organization at first had no resources except for enthusiasm. My colleagues had a decent library and contacts at the Moscow Center for Gender Studies. My traveling life began in the summer of 1995. I went to Moscow to the seminar *Women in ethnic-political conflicts* organized by the Soros Foundation. Then I went to Bishkek to the Central Asian conference on *Gender and Mass-Media*. All July long I was writing my thesis. It was a hot summer. I would work from morning to night while my four year old daughter would walk in the yard by herself. Periodically I would look from the balcony to make sure she was fine. Normal mothers walked with their children and wondered how I could let the child go by herself.

In August the Peace Train came to Almaty. It was coming from Europe to the Global Women's Forum in Beijing and there were many women's movement activists from various countries on board. It was a hot day and we were standing at the train station, the official delegation of *akimat*,[5] with orchestra and everything. I was astonished with the way the guests looked, how different they were from our women. Europeans, Americans, feminists, which also marks one's phenotype. They were so special, passionary, unusual, and there were so many of them!

The preparation for the arrival of the *Peace Train* made the women's NGOs unite. In 1995 there were not too many of them, the *Feminist League* was one of the leading. All of the participants were brought to the House of Scientists where three papers were presented. Gulsara Tlenchieva said that Kazakhstan has been always known by its emancipated women, that the idea of equality is connected here with Tengrism, where the main god *Tengri* and the goddess *Umai* are the archetypes for the equality of the sexes. Consequently, in Kazakhstan there is a potential for women's activism.

My paper was called "Feminism in Kazakhstan." I explained our goals, mentioned how the Soviet achievements worked for the feminist tasks and what features of feminism would hardly find support in our society. There was a question from the audience: "What feminist extremes would you like to avoid?" I said that we would probably never be so radical as to set the society and the state against us, we would never get involved in some scandalous behavior and most probably we would never have lesbian feminism, I saw it as one of the extremes of radical feminism. An elderly American approached me in the lobby: "You said that you will never have lesbian feminism, I am interested to know why. I am a lesbian and I have been in women's movement since the early 1970s, and believe me, you will have this too." I told her "Maybe, but now it is highly unlikely." Even today (fourteen years since the Beijing train) radical and lesbian feminism in Kazakhstan have not been shaped institutionally or ideologically. But it does not mean that they are impossible here.

And then we went to Beijing—the nongovernmental delegation of twelve Kazakhstan women. It was a powerful feminist action, forty thousand women from all over the world and two weeks of constant meetings, performances, and actions. One of the feminist legends Betty Friedan, was present in a wheel chair, everyone wanted to see the author of the *Feminine Mystique*. Beijing was the next point in crystallizing of my feminist ideas. There was this enthusiasm of the pioneers, the joy of communicating with the colleagues from the Commonwealth of Independent States and everything seemed so fascinating. Then came the first project, the first grants from the Americans, different seminars, conferences, journeys.

The Gender Studies Center was founded rather spontaneously. In 1998 a colleague from the bureau *Gender and Development* offered me to take part in the project "Introducing gender disciplines into the college curricula." We prepared and launched a pilot interdisciplinary course on gender theory at Almaty State University. Along with teaching we would prepare projects, seminars for professors, trying to create an environment for the development of gender discourse, a community of like-minded people who would speak the same scholarly language. But it is difficult to create such an environment because you have to start from the existing material and human resources. In our circles we started to use an expression "to earth up." Before you expect any results from a person you must earth him or her up, feed with information, motivate with a particular idea. Yet it does not always give desirable results.

When you try to create a new environment there are always some structures or human boundaries which you cannot change, particularly, it refers to consciousness, to the way people think. As pregnancy, this process can not be accelerated: everything has to go step by step. In the early 1990s it was difficult to imagine that there would be gender university courses and gender studies as a scholarly sphere and research projects would be financed. Then it turned out that everything is possible provided there is a drive and the motivated people and of course, resources. In the summer of 1998 I went for a short training at Rutgers University, New Jersey, to Charlotte Bunch's Center of Women's Global Leadership. The 1998–2000 were an intensive time of self-education when I and my colleagues read a lot on gender studies, translated texts, published collections. Maybe never again would I have such a thirst for knowledge and intellectual drive as in those years. My interest in and my devotion to gender problematic had shaped by the time I was around thirty. The following years were the years of development, deepening and disappointment with this sphere.

M. T.: How do you see your own identity? What are its dominant elements?

S. Sh.: I have lived in Kazakhstan for twenty five years, I feel myself at home in this country, but I never forget that I belong to an ethnic minority. I have a prestigious (for my place and time) education but I deal with nontraditional new scholarly sphere—gender studies. I speak Russian and English, but not Tatar or Kazakh (which would have been logical). I have visited twenty seven countries but often I hear that I do not know anything about real life. I like to go abroad, but I prefer to live and work here. There are things which I dislike in this country but I do not like it when people scold Kazakhstan. I am a very calm woman but in an argument with men I can become sharp and straight-forward.

M. T.: After having worked for many years in Central Asian gender movement can you say that there is a real dialogue and relevant coalitions among Central Asian gender scholars and activists?

S. Sh.: Yes and no. In 2002 our center held the first regional educational program in gender studies—a Summer School for university professors from five Central Asian countries. It was called *Gender Studies: from the West to the East*, that is, we clearly showed the direction of gender indoctrination. There we initiated the Central Asian Gender Network which nominally exists even today. There were four Summer Schools in Kirgizia, which considerably supported the potential of Kyrgyz colleagues. We also used to train Tadzhik professors and review their syllabi on gender studies, as well as conducted a training of activists, journalists and university professors of Uzbekistan. Gender scholarly community in Central Asia is small and comes, in my estimate, to a maximum of one hundred people.

M. T.: What is the situation with understanding or lack of it (ability and willingness to understand) of the specificity of Central Asian gender movement on the part of Western European, American and Russian colleagues? With whom do you have more points of confluence and dialoguing and why?

S. Sh.: Before answering this question I would like to reflect myself on what is the "specificity of Central Asian gender movement," does it exist at all? First we were afraid of becoming the last car in the gender studies train in CIS countries. Then later came an understanding that in scholarship as in other spheres of human creativity, the most important thing is individuals, the authors of ideas and approaches. I judge the development of gender studies in a country by its leading scholars. Thus, gender studies in Tadzhikistan for me mean mostly S. Kasymova, in Uzbekistan—M.Tokhtakhodzhaeva, in Kirgizia—G. Ibraeva, A.Tabyshalieva, A. Moldosheva, M. Karybaeva, A.Dzhumabaeva, B.Kydyrmysheva. What is the gender studies specificity in our region? We can discuss it in points of subject, methodology, conceptual approaches and a degree of methodological authenticity in relation to primary sources—American and European gender studies. I do not think that American or Western European colleagues (except for those connected with the program on gender studies of Central-European University in Budapest) are really concerned with the qualitative or quantitative growth of gender studies in Central Asia.

We must remember that gender studies have not emerged spontaneously in the post-soviet space. They were not a result of internal needs of society or scholarly community. They were imported together with the new social sciences and humanities from the West.

Gender Studies are a part of a larger modernizing political project which was offered to us and other transit and third world countries. From the Western part the task of supporting the growth of gender studies in Central and Eastern Europe, in CIS countries and in Central Asia is successfully performed by the Open Society Institute in Budapest. As for the Russian colleagues, here a lot depends on personal contacts and sympathies. There are certainly more points of confluence and dialoging with them. I could mention such Russian and CIS colleagues whose approaches to the study of our region I find relevant as Olga Zubkovskaya, Anna Tyomkina, Yelena Zdravomyslova, Irina Tartakovskaya, Sergei Ushakin, Sergei Abashin.

M. *T.*: I have an impression that there is not much interest in Central Asian and wider post-soviet gender studies in any dialogue with third world and women of color feminism in comparison with Western variants. If yes, then what are the reasons?

S. *Sh.*: It is connected with the direction of indoctrination (from the West to the East). There are not too many possibilities for cooperation or mutual interest and holding mutual research projects with gender studies centers in the third world. Among my personal contacts I would mention scholars from the universities of Lahore, Delhi, Jakarta, Beijing, Manila. I have some acquaintances in the gender movement of the South African Republic, Suriname, Argentina, New Zealand (a Samoa woman). Recently I was disappointed after talking with an American and I had a very positive impression and felt that I was ready to cooperate with a gender scholar from India.

M. *T.*: The development of women's movement in the post-soviet space seems to be a part of the wider global political project in which the old logic of relations between the first, second and third world is reproduced once again. In terms of decolonial thinking it is the coloniality of power and coloniality of gender here at work. Is it possible for Central Asian gender activism to practice a certain degree of independence and alternative choices within this opposition, and if yes, than how is it possible?

S. *Sh.*: I am afraid that before the collective gender subject of Central Asia starts practicing independence and alternative views, it would have to think over and define itself in terms of decoloniality or postcoloniality. In my opinion, postcolonial theory has not yet become generally accepted in our gender studies. Probably it has to do with the post-soviet inertia of thinking. Ideological frames set by official ideology in Kazakhstan avoid any clear interpretation of the Soviet period as a colonial past. Bitter invectives on Russian colonialism in Kazakh steppe remain the prerogative of Kazakh historians, but not sociologists or scholars of gender. Hence the lack of any discursive "decolonial resistance" in our gender studies. There is of course a desire to be no worse than the Russian authors, but there is no wish to show them a fist, figuratively speaking. On the other hand, I notice more and more an intention to speak, on the part of the women's subject of a particular country and with one's own voice (for example, in Sofia Kasymova's works). And this is gratifying.

M. T.: In several of you works you speak of (neo)Orientalism and an unconscious or deliberate self-orientalizing which the women's movement in Central Asia is subject to in order to have the right to exist in international gender movement. What is the reason for this constant reproduction of Orientalism? What can be opposed to it?

S. Sh.: This was a result of grant politics of international donors. There was competition for projects and advocacy in the areas of kidnapping of brides, polygamy, women's sexual traffic, women's self-immolation, the worst forms of children labor. This stimulated the NGOs and the researchers. Demand created supply. And if the West wanted to see Kirgizia as a country of bride-kidnapping it would receive the desired picture, a cheap stereotype. If the International Organization for Migration created a national network for fighting against women's traffic, trained the NGOs and supported the orphanages, want it or not, we had to support the opinion that this is an important problem for Kazakhstan. It is irrelevant that every year they would bring back home just two or three women and put one souteneur in the hands of the police. The foundations created a number of NGOs, which were ready to present and PR any problem. The best remedy against self-orientalizing is criticism on the part of local intellectuals, scholars, NGOs and the civil society at large.

M. T.: In connection with Orientalism another question arises: Nawal el Saadawi once observed that there is a specific class of contemporary "colored" orientalists who see their own world as tourists or experts, who turn into public intellectuals and academic stars which are indistinguishable from the old (Western) Orientalism. They have also become a commodity and got used to producing and consuming dissidence as a profession which is very far from real struggle. Is there a similar problem in Central Asian gender movement?

S. Sh.: In Central Asian women's movement there are such tendencies as well. There is such a thing as feminist tourism and there are champions of this sport and naturally they are scorned by colleagues. Yet without feminist and gender tourism it is impossible to build coalitions and networks. Without them there is no global women's movement. The phenotype, the way of life and thinking of such "dissidents" are recognizable in any country or region. They are similar in their wish to live using the resources of the richer part of the world and escalating the problems of that part they come from. The more I visit foreign countries the less I want to practice self-disparagement. It is good that Kazakhstan has objective factors for maintaining its public dignity (oil, a stable political regime, an acceptable standard of life and, last but not least, a sensible gender politics).

M. *T.*: How the crisis of identity is expressed in Central Asian gender movements? Have there emerged in the last years any new models, particularly grass-roots, grounded in the local historical and bodily conditions of inter-subjectivity? If yes, then what are the grounds for this and how do you see the role of such movements in the future?

S. *Sh.*: There is no rapid growth in women's movement. There is a stable cohort of activists which was formed by the mid 1990s. They communicate from conference to conference and from project to project. Starting from the 2000s the women's movement in Central Asia has been stagnant. This is connected with the lack of any visible results and a wave of disappointments, with a psychological fatigue of the leaders and the change in donor's policies. The problem in Kazakhstan is also that the governmental structures try to take the financial resources away. It is difficult to bring to life the wish to have some inter-state projects. It is difficult even to do a comparative research project between Kazakhstan and Kirgizia. Informational networks still work, but they also experience fatigue. The emergence in 2005 in Kirgizia of the fundamentalist Muslim women's movement and also the Lesbian-Bisexual-Gay-Transsexual organizations are regarded as linked with the new historical and bodily conditions. These are really the new bodily practices institutionalized with the help of Western foundations. As far as I know there are no such tendencies in Kazakhstan.

Conclusion

Why Cut the Feet in Order to Fit the Western Shoes?

Let us take a look at contemporary gender discourses in Central Asia and Caucasus, briefly trace their links and differences, and point at possible parallels and future intersections with non-Western and particularly decolonial gender discourses. Central here will be the phenomenon of the colonial gender tricksterism touched upon in the second part of this book. But this time it will be regarded as a possible ground for decolonial gender discourses and activism in Eurasian borderlands. (De)colonial gendered tricksters try to restore and construct their multiple identities, resistance, and reexistence as an other way of being, around the Russian, the Soviet, and today, the post-Soviet (national) and global gender discourses, all of which invariably retain a simplified set of social roles for these subjects, based on a stereotypical interpretation of the non-West through assimilation or negation.

If in the Soviet period theorizing on gender had to be masked because the official discourse proclaimed that the women's question was solved and forgotten long ago, the post-Soviet period generated a fashion for gender studies, particularly in the Soviet ex-colonies. The colonial gendered tricksters whose legacy was never interrupted even in the harshest Soviet times, be it in the form of *Otin* institute in Central Asia, traditional healers in Caucasus or intellectual post-Jadid models, that survived the Soviet materialistic atheist Sahara and monotopic gnoseology, have begun to produce new knowledges for these locales. These knowledges are far from being always accepted by the scholarly community or even known to a wider audience. Moreover, they do not always exist in generally accepted disciplinary forms, often heading in the direction of nonrational and esoteric knowledges and/or arts.

In my view, accentuating these forms of colonial gender tricksterism can help Central Asian and Caucasus gender discourses avoid the limbo they frequently find themselves in today due to the necessity of corresponding to Western feminist theory and wider, the philosophy of science (including the social sciences), and to act as exotic native informants or suppliers of raw knowledge to the Western theorists and historians, who later process and package it for everyone to consume, thus sanctifying it with the authority of coloniality of knowledge. For Central Asian and Caucasus gender discourses decolonization of thinking remains a central task. Within it the most important thing is to delink from the enchantment of modernity with its myth of progress and development, as a result of which any alternative women's roles and identities were erased, forgotten, and taken outside of the legitimate. The majority of gender interpretations of the history of Central Asia and Caucasus remain blind to imperial and colonial differences and to particular understanding of sex and gender in colonial spaces.

Gender studies that have emerged in the last decade and been written by both ex-colonized gendered subjects who received a Western style education for lack of any other, and Western feminists and activists and their Russian clones (Vigmann 2005, Tyomkina 2005, Harris 2000, Solovyeva 2006, Abasov 2006, Kamp 2006, Northrop 2004, Sahadeo et al. 2007, Adams 2005, Kandiyoti 2002) have been built on a progressivist model of development, and based on a simple juxtaposition of archaic gender discourses (here conceptualized as Muslim ones) and modernized Western patterns of women's liberation from the patriarchal system. What remains unaddressed then is a complex juxtaposition of several levels and forms of modernization in these locales that frequently led to conflicting subjectivites and fluid gender models. As pointed out above, the Russian imperial model worked in parallel with the Afghan, Turkish, Persian, and Arabic modernization influences. The Soviet radical modernity strangled all alternatives, and allowed for only trickster forms of passive resistance. Today it is replaced with the prevailing neoliberal version, which is projected directly (without the Russian/Soviet mediation anymore) together with the possibility of yet another borrowing from the Muslim secularized pattern. In most cases however, the epistemic premises remain the same—it is the Western European categories, value systems and paradigms, while the cosmology, ethics and epistemology of the inhabitants of Eurasian borderlands are largely ignored, and the stable binary opposition of modernity/versus tradition is never questioned.

In 2007 *Ab Imperio* published Olga Zubkovskaya's survey article (Zubkovskaya 2007) which attempted to do one of the first Russian scholarly investigations/appropriations of theoretical concepts elaborated by Central Asian gender studies, by means of appealing to postcolonial discourse and criticizing the local models for their desire to keep their difference. The voices and opinions of the ex-colonial others were then put into the procrustean bed of alien theoretical models, formulated for different local histories, discrediting the right and ability of these subjects to produce knowledge. Zubkovskaya certainly does this unconsciously, simply following the epistemic logic of Western scholarly discourse, based on objectification of the studied and the willingness to take a zero view point. Yet the text condescendingly dismisses the subalterns for their wish to speak and their lack of interest in fashionable hybridity theories. Remaining enchanted with postmodernist reflections on ludic identity, Zubkovskaya preferred to ultimately forget G. Spivak's idea of the necessity of strategic essentialism in the conditions of the continuing asymmetry of knowledge and power.

This article at least makes an effort to step away from the previous black-and-white opposition of modernity/versus tradition or Western/versus local to look at gender discourses in Central Asia through the prism of more flexible postcolonial studies. Yet, Central Asian local histories, imperial/colonial relations, geopolitics, and body-politics of knowledge do not allow for the mechanical interpretation within the postcolonial frame. Behind the fence of mutually contradicting and de-contextualized quotations, by the middle of the article any connection with Central Asia is lost. This is symptomatic. Indeed I would prefer to read a meticulous and detailed historical work of an American scholar who does not really feel the reality of Central Asia, yet comes to his or her task with a "good faith" than such an analysis written by someone marked with secondary Eurocentric fundamentalism, whose unconscious hidden task is to prove that she is not worse than the Western colleagues and that she can also maternalistically rebuke the native informants for deciding to have their voice, never really showing any interest in their opinion.

I am not calling for going back to some initial primordialist pure source, criticizing the negative interpretations of tradition within the Western scholarly disciplines. That is why I feel close to Sylvia Marcos's position. The aboriginal gendered model is variable within itself, and not fixed. It is not something that one has to go back to. This cosmology falls out of the Western logic of either/or, assuaging what Western culture would interpret as contradictions in the all-penetrating act of balancing the change and the continuity. That is why we need not to go back to tradition but to liberate it from the grip of Western disciplinary divisions, concepts, and categories of thought and action. It is necessary to stop condescendingly negating its ways of expression, resistance and reexistence which would not necessarily be academically sanctioned by the West.

Such categories and scholarly pigeon holes are products of Western feminism distorting gender relations and discourses in other locales. Thus, women's activism in the Soviet colonial period is still measured by their participation in demonstrations and protests or their enrollment and involvement in the Soviet education and ideological institutions as if they cannot be regarded as full subjects before they started to use the accepted Western forms of political and civil activity. This approach is expressed in Marianne Kamp's *The New Woman in Uzbekistan* mentioned above, which incorporates many interesting facts but in the end provides a biased picture, as it always happens when a foreign scholar comes to study the impenetrable other relying too much and uncritically on his/her disciplinary approaches, political and moral ideals, universalized liberal feminism and naively believing that surrounding oneself with archival documents (in Soviet cases mostly falsified) can facilitate the difficult task of pluritopic hermeneutics. The majority of Kamp's elaborations can be found in earlier books and articles by an Uzbek gender activist M. Tokhtakhodzhayeva and her colleagues published in Uzbek and in Russian (Tokhtakhodzhayeva 1996, 1999, 2001). However her name and her works are only briefly mentioned in Kamp's book, mostly in references. This testifies again to the asymmetry of knowledge production and distribution: anything that Kamp would write will be by definition more reliable in the academic world than Tokhtakhodzhayeva's or Shakirova's works who are assigned the role of native informants and diligent pupils of Western gender theorists. Their knowledge is appropriated by the West and reproduced under a sanctified Western name, or sometimes non-western but still sanctified by Western education or tenure at a Western university. Kamp's orientalism is also inadvertent and unconscious. It is connected with disciplinary rules in the humanities at large. In other words, it is the coloniality of knowledge enunciating itself through such scholars.

The situation is further complicated by the fact that the Western and Western-oriented scholars are still divided between the two extremes in the interpretation of Soviet modernity—the passing extreme of demonization of everything Soviet and the younger generation of scholars who were shaped after the collapse of the Soviet Union. Their problem is often that they trust the Soviet propaganda too much and do not see the gap between propaganda and reality, remaining also blind to the psychological realm, to the way the objects of their study see and feel the world and themselves in this world.

Many Western intellectuals have stepped into this trap before. Today the younger generation of Western scholars of Central Asia and Caucasus often repeats this mistake. They sentimentalize gender slogans of the Soviet empire. A number of local women intellectuals also tend to interpret the Russian/Soviet modernization positively by contrasting the Soviet modernizing projects in the colonies, including the gender ones, and those of the Muslim developing and third world countries. A symbolic rising to the status of the second world (instead of the third) together with the Soviet empire is still regarded by them as a positive step.

Any possible parallels and intersections with women of color or third world gender discourses are automatically erased as threatening or irrelevant. Kamp in her analysis of nationalism in Central Asia quotes Benedict Anderson more often than Partha Chatterjee whose work would have been much more relevant in the case of Uzbekistan. The same refers to the virtual lack of any categories of third world feminism in the Western or local interpretations of gender problematic except sporadically in postcolonial and Marxist forms. In this context Kalpana Sahni's works are much more rewarding because of their additional dimension of the colonial difference and even colonial crack which is lacking in Western works and hidden and suppressed in local ones.

A number of post-soviet gender theorists tend to deny the previous Soviet forms of state feminism in its Amazon versions of physical equity or in its gender forms of inefficient and double-standard quotas, and promote Western feminist models as a novelty without seeing the common sources of Western and Soviet gender discourses. In the Soviet Union feminism began to be regarded as a harmful bourgeois influence as early as in the 1920s. That is why gender studies indeed were able to reemerge in their critical form only after the collapse of the Soviet Union and the flooding of different Western NGOs, grants and scholars. But the newly emerged gender studies in Eurasian borderlands have remained blind to the geopolitics and body-politics of the colonized, racialized and gendered knowledges. In these new works, created in and about Central Asia and Caucasus, gender as a myth, a contextually determined construct, turns into some absolute universal given, while the scholars fall into the well known heresy of absolutist Western gender ideas and their automatic application to the rest of the world.

The majority of gender discourses in post-soviet Central Asia and Caucasus are grounded in applying Western feminism to local material. Many collections of articles, field studies, and oral histories, betray a developmentalist paradigm even in their titles and structures. Thus in 2006 in Nalchik a Northern Caucasus scholar Madina Tekuyeva published an interesting book *Man and Woman in Adyghean Culture: Tradition and Modernity* (Tekuyeva 2006), where behind the rigid grid of western ethnographic constructions one finds a fascinating and unique argument. This is one of the very few critical works on gender, published in post-Soviet Russia by a representative of the present colony. In 2005 a Dushanbe (Tadzhikistan) collection *Gender: Traditions and Modernity* (Kasymova 2005) used the same old cliché in its title. Yet, some field studies in this collection contradicted the simple scheme juxtaposing the emancipated Soviet and repatriarchalized post-soviet social relations (Vigmann 2005) signalizing the emergence of a new women's identity in Tadzhikistan—the poorest and the least modernized women are pushed towards a forced and unwanted gender equality or economic supremacy over males which goes hand in hand with women's oppositional and independent thinking. This signalizes parallels with radical colonized groups fighting for independence in other regions of the world.

The opposition of modernity/versus traditions has marked an earlier Tashkent collection of oral histories *Destinies and Time* (Tokhtakhodzhaeva at al. 1995). In the introduction the editors demonstrate a peculiar mixture of un-reflected upon Soviet and Western modernization ideologies, a developmentalist theory of social-economic stages, and universalist notions of patriarchal nature of traditionalist societies as the main impediment for women as such. The legitimacy of modernization for any woman is never questioned except in the oral histories themselves, because it drags a number of values and features, that were naturalized in the collective unconscious and are singularly associated with modernity/modernization. I mean an access to Russian (and colonizing) education, to decision making, career, social security—exclusively in the variants prescribed by Soviet or/and Western modernity. An enchantment with the rhetoric of modernity is obvious in the texts, written by non-Western feminists of Central Asia and Caucasus who are stubbornly clinging to the Western feminist thought and Eurocentric stereotypes in the analysis of their own culture, which is a clear sign of the coloniality of gender. But between the lines the informants would tell us something that they were not even aware of and the interviewers were certainly not asking them about. And this other reality emerging through, around and beyond—is the most valuable part of these oral histories.

In one work after another we find familiar mutually exclusive extremes of emancipation and backwardness, neo-Orientalism and religious extremism, paranjee and mini skirt. Svetlana Shakirova and other Central Asian gender activists attempted a nuancing of this simplified model of gender relations and stressed a lack of negative or positive emotional characteristics in the interpretation of traditional and emancipated women (Shakirova 2005). But if we continue to use the opposition of the modern/versus traditional we would not be able to avoid the Eurocentric bias. In spite of the author's good intentions the binary model is inevitably grounded in vector teleology—from tradition through the Soviet half-tradition and half modernity to today's Western emancipation. A deconstruction of this model is a necessary condition for decolonizing of gender and of being. The most promising gender discourses go beyond the frame of this tripartite model and are based on difference, mixing and delinking from vector teleology. They must be regarded precisely as particular full-fledged models instead of dismissing them as abnormalities. These border gender patterns are based on a double critique of different variants of modernity, and various half forgotten ethnic-cultural-religious models.

The Soviet empire was racist, Eurocentric and patriarchal in spite of its rhetoric. But it does not mean that the women themselves were simply passive victims. They created various ways out of the imposed binarity and conscious paths of flexible (re)construction of their identities in different social contexts. These models offer mediation and an ironic trickster play on stereotypes, as a way of coping with them. They are seldom discussed by gender scholars both in the West and in Eurasian borderlands themselves. Some local anthropologists and sociologists still tend to idealize the Western models of emancipation and seriously consider the change in body care in their locales to a presumably more Western one as a way of unproblematic emancipation (Beknazarova 2005). It has long become a common place for gender theorists that gluing artificial nails or being scared to death of gaining half a pound and losing one's similarity to a Barbie doll are not really signs of emancipation. Isn't the so called "traditional" woman who calmly understands that each of her life stages is associated with a particular body, with a certain appearance, who flexibly changes her social identities in different contexts and pays more attention to parameters other than primitive erotic appeal in the way she looks or behaves, fundamentally much more free than the presumably "emancipated" one? Would not it be more fruitful instead of condescendingly dismissing the principle of seniority and praising Central Asian or Caucasus women for finally learning to understand their physical bodies as social entities, thus erasing the difference between sex and gender altogether, to remember that in many precolonial societies, the body was not a basis for social roles, inclusion or exclusion, it was not a foundation of social thought or identity, and it does not have to be frozen in that role today either.

In any attempt to problematize a simple tripartite scheme of traditional-Soviet-Western woman a crucial and understudied phenomenon would be that of the (post)colonial gender tricksterism where the (post)Soviet and the (post)colonial merge and it becomes possible to balance on the verge of resistance and act around and beyond the power structures to avoid censorship and policing. This model does not answer the Western gender stereotypes which often rob the women of the richness of their worlds and creative possibilities of their potential multidimensionality, always enhanced at the borders of cultures, languages, religions, and epistemologies. Here even the initial set of gender roles may be different from the Western dichotomy and generate more complex models. (Post)colonial gender tricksterism exists today both in the ex-metropolis and the ex-colonies. What needs to be stressed in this pattern is the multiplicity and the constant movement, the tension and the changeability, within which coloniality of gender is questioned again and again by specific relational forms of resistance connected with human memory (Lugones 2008).

It would be unfair to fail to mention that a number of Central Asian gender studies in the last few years have started to demonstrate an interest in in-between transmodels that act as an alternative for many women of the region (Kasymova 2005). This alternative is still conceptualized predominantly in terms of Western interpretation of border as a deficiency, as a state of being stuck in time, which requires synthesizing or negation in one or the other direction. Understanding of the border not only in temporal sense (between tradition and modernity), but also in spatial-cultural one is not typical of Western thinking. It is crucial to pay more attention to geopolitical and body-political understanding of the border and the first steps in this direction are already taking place. I mean a 2006 Summer School on *Postcolonialism and the Prospects of Central Asian Gender Studies* at Issyk-Kul Lake, or the same year conference on *Contemporary Women's Movement: Ideologies, Practices and Prospects* organized in Byshkek (Kyrgyzstan). A summary of this conference is provided by Svetlana Shakirova who similarly to a number of non-Western feminists, is dissatisfied with the state of affairs in international gender movement and a lack of real dialogue or influence in gender sphere in the social, political or economic sense: "I am persuaded that in the last years the enchantment of conferences and seminars has considerably faded. In spite of the deficit of studies and theoretical conceptualizing of current processes, the applied studies remain effort consuming, and do not bring visible dividends. No one reasonable in Kazakhstan would go to any mass actions (for or against). What is left? Trainings, networking, virtual activities, analytical work ordered by international organizations, conducting seminars, representative functions on a regional, local and global level. Interaction through networking seems to be the most effective form of work for the women's movement" (Shakirova 2006).

Shakirova grasps the most painful problems of women's movement in the ex-Soviet colonies—from the lack of theoretical element (I would add, sometimes, a fear of it) to an inevitable shrinking into the networking and virtual forms, which answers a general tendency of alter-discourses today: such effective forms of globalization as internet are used not only by the champions of neoliberalism, but also by its opponents, aiming at creating flexible and fluid global alter-communities. Shakirova's and her colleagues' own child—the Central Asian Gender Net is a good example, as well as the net project *CaucAsia* created by Galina Petriashvili, uniting the post-Soviet journalists writing on gender problematic (CaucAsia 2006).

One of the painful questions discussed at this forum and other gender conferences in Eurasian borderlands, is the lingering necessity of corresponding to Western gender theories and assumptions, to hidden Orientalist stereotypes, which leads to secondary self-reorientalizing by playing the role of the eternal Other, or studying our own ex-colonial space, using the Western area studies tools (the cold war disciplines) and Western feminism. Identity then is not being de-essentialized, but quite the opposite, it is being reessentialized again and again. Shakirova shrewdly points out in one of her talks: "The proliferation of such themes as the kidnapping of brides in Kirgizia, the sexual women traffic in Central Asia, the self-immolation of women in Uzbekistan, the arranged marriages in Tadzhikistan and prostitution in Kazakhstan—what is this all if not following the Orientalist clichés ?" (Shakirova 2006)

Gender discourses of Eurasian borderlands seldom venture into epistemic sphere, leaving this privilege to Western feminism and thus agreeing with their own dependency. Such a positioning was described by Chinese feminists who managed to overcome a fascination with Western modernity and claim that there is no need to repeat the Western way, that they already went a long way along their own road (Li Xiaojiang 1993, 104). Gender discourses of Caucasus and Central Asia have not yet reached this conclusion, silently agreeing to cut their feet to fit the Western shoes of an outdated mode, stuck at some early feminist stage, with no questioning of social and biological gender or fragmentation of identity, a persistent juxtaposition of modernity and tradition, and a homogenizing of all women as discriminated by all men.

This continuing dependency on Western feminism is not surprising, as the majority of Eurasian feminists' works are paid by Western grants and supported by Western NGOs. In case of the remaining colonies (such as the Northern Caucasus), they are paid by Russian pro-government foundations. What is at work here is what Obioma Nnaemeka called "the politics of poverty" and the politics of the belly" (Shu-mei Shih at al. 2005, 159) which makes the work for NGOs the only safe harbor and often the only material means of existence for many local women. It would be unethical to blame them for their positioning. But it proves one more time the vitality of naturalized universalist Western notions, scholarly categories, forms of thinking and subjectivity. This is not just a post-Soviet problem. Oyěwùmi points out similar tendencies in her African colleagues (Oyěwùmi 1997, xv). I. Wu (Wu 2005, 41) and S. Marcos are even harsher in their criticism. Marcos claims that she refused the role of Western feminism's mirror and a "local instrument of feminist imperialism" (Shu-mei Shih et al. 2005, 145). This role is associated with a number of advantages, not entirely material but also symbolic—the exoticized non-Western women are accepted only if they translate word for word the ideas of Western feminism. Then they are immediately given a chance to travel around the world, speak at international congresses, and act as legitimate representatives of their cultures and women movements in academic and political spheres. This is in fact a problem of ethical choice which is often harder on non-Western feminists than on Western ones because of the persistent epistemic and economic asymmetry.

Shakirova is right when she states that we have neither cultural feminism nor radical anarchism present both in the West and the non-West, as an ideological ground of gender studies. She correctly links the skidding of feminism and gender studies in the post-Soviet space with this condition. Svetlana's conclusion is rather cheerless: "In the end the goal of feminism in both variants—a strive for equality with men, and a stress on women's difference—prove to be hard to fulfill" (Shakirova 2006). In my view this correct diagnosis should not be interpreted as final. Feminism indeed continues to be regarded as a radical and suspicious project in the post-Soviet largely patriarchal space, while women's movement almost instinctively puts itself apart from feminism as an undesirable association which would cause mainstream's rejection and is opposite to the values of social and professional "success." But these categories and values of personal achievement, competition, success, and respectability are in fact values of Western modernity which we would have to question in case we really want to deal with gender problems, at least with a minimum degree of independence. This difficult step has been taken by such scholars and activists as Sylvia Marcos, Maria Lugones, Chela Sandoval, Shu-mei Shih and many others. It is definitely connected with an existential choice. To become a border individual voluntarily, thus erasing for oneself the easy way of decent feminism, to join the movement of epistemic disobedience (Mignolo 2007), is a hard step. So far this way has been leading to isolation and impossibility to take any part in decision making. But the situation does not have to stay like that forever. On a global scale there emerges a large number of those who practice epistemological disobedience and an important task is to build connections and solidarity with them, even at the price of the loss of Western legitimation and popularity or the seeming influence and visibility at a local level.

In this sense I cannot entirely agree with Shakirova's position. In the positive part of her scenario she offers the following solution: communication with elements of institutional mechanism and first of all, with the national commission for the family and gender politics, a mutual understanding and cooperation of women's movement with international organizations and a strive to build partner relations with them instead of the present vassal-patron ones. Gender discourses on a state level do not give any hope for a possible communication with power. In my view, we should rather speak of resistance to and criticism of the state and not of co-opting. Shakirova speaks of the necessity of straightening the biases in relations with international organizations (meaning the Western NGOs). Here again, a deep dependence on the logic of modernity comes forward. The scholar realizes that the vassal-patron type of relations and Orientalism are unacceptable, yet she does not see any other international or local organizations of the political society with which Central Asian women could definitely have more in common than with Western feminism.[1] It also remains questionable if we can really hope to persuade or make the Western international organizations change the power asymmetry to something more dialogic.

Expert community today not only defines the leading scholarly discourses but also controls the accessibility and dominance of particular positions and points of view in the academic world. Therefore the "sanctioned ignorance" of the non-Western paradigms is promoted in

the global academic community. While the works which go beyond
the generally accepted mainstream notions, including gender ones, are
not ever translated, published or introduced, remaining known and
interesting merely to selected enthusiasts. Decolonial feminists and
border thinkers are shaping today the new trans-modern gender discourses, rethinking both Western feminism and traditional (for lack
of a better term) cultures. They are based on the principle of dialogic
knowledges and traveling between the West and the non-West, opening points of crossing between the Western philosophy (usually of a
contesting kind) and the cosmologies, subjectivities and social justice
systems of indigenous people. Such is Oyěwùmi's attempt to question
the category of woman as a Western construct imposed upon Yoruba
culture (Oyěwùmi 1997). She argues that we cannot apply Western
gender notions automatically to the rest of the world, when we attempt
to analyze the presumable humiliation of women in traditional cultures and other religions (Oyěwùmi 1997, 137). Something similar
happened in Central Asian and Caucasus cultures where women were
also far from being constantly and always discriminated. Their roles
changed dynamically through their lives—from a relative condition
without rights typical for the young wife to a respected mother of the
family with grown-up children and grandchildren who took an active
part in decision making. In Adyghean cosmology one can find many
well preserved traces of previous gender parity, women's active participation in politics, their property rights, a specific gender labor
division never based on coding one (female) labor as less prestigious
than the other, in some cases and spheres, even the predominance of
female over male, which were a result of a longer retaining of feminocratic system in this region (Tekuyeva 2006).

Many local histories manifested feminocratic or gynecentric traditions and/or gender egalitarianism and lack of fixed gender divisions.
Traces of these alternative relations and models are still to be found in
Amerindian and African cultures, but were almost erased in the collective memory of Eurasian borderlands and hard to restore. In contrast with Mesoamerican cosmology, which has always remained a
living tradition, in Eurasia, as stated above, there were too many layers and radical forms of colonization which interacted with each
other. Each of them added a new wall between the aboriginal cosmology and the people, preventing them from making a link with their
own precolonial history and epistemic models.

Traces of such links are to be found today mostly in mythology and
folklore and seldom in everyday modern culture. But even these
remaining sources were considerably distorted first under Islamization,

and then under the Russian and Soviet imperial power, when they were divested of all contesting elements—from heroism and love for freedom to the strong women's element and gender parity. The latter is clearly seen in such a specific genre of Turkic heroic oral history as *dastan* linked among other things with pre-Islamic ethical, epistemic and cultural systems (Shamanism, Buddhism, Zoroastrianism, Tengrism) (Paksoy 1995). A small number of *dastans* was published in distorted forms in the USSR, while most of them were simply hidden in inaccessible archives while their reciters (shamans, azans) were eliminated or co-opted into socialism. This refers to heroic dastans on decolonial indigenous movements, such as the well known *Koroglu*, and also the dastans where the main part was played by women warriors—the Amazons of Central Asia.

In Caucasus-Iberian mythology and cosmology the oldest layers tend to be feminocratic, and even a later social structure reflected in the Narts Epic still carries traces of gender egalitarianism. It seems that women in Caucasus had remained for a long time outside the patriarchal law, while in the social life of Adyghean community there was a guiding principle of fluidity and flexible contextuality of gender roles, and also the principle of seniority: the older wise women were often more respected than men and also connected with a number of sacred acts and rituals that only they could perform. This included healing, the control of rain and thunder, particular rituals performed at the building of a new house, rituals connected with the initiation of the younger generation into adulthood and marriage, and family law (Tekuyeva 2006, 106–137).

In the oral poetry and songs of Adyghe people, particularly of the time when they fought for their independence from Russia, we find "texts" that were created by women themselves and from their perspective. These songs did not describe them from outside but concentrated on women's feelings and emotions, on their willingness to be active and to make decisions in all spheres, including the erotic one. These poems and songs, as was the case with Mesoamerican culture, were later erased or edited by the indigenous colonized culture itself as it was becoming more and more patriarchal, and also by the no less patriarchal interpretations of Western and pro-Western and Russian ethnographers and anthropologists, who misinterpreted the majority of symbols, images, metaphors, connected with women's world and their vision of this world (Tekuyeva 2006a).

Anticolonial gendered resistance and reexistence luckily have survived in various oral forms. Such is Khanifa Kazi series of epic poems from Northern Caucasus. The main character Khanifa had a real historical prototype and combined the woman-warrior faculties with the healing ones. Her story was closely connected with the Caucasus war, that is, an outstanding situation of colonization of the whole ethnicity in which a woman was allowed to cross the usual gender boundaries. As M. Tekuyeva points out, for Khanifa, there was a priority of patriotic motifs over the personal feelings which served as a role model of the selfless devotion to the idea of liberation and a stimulus for the continuation of the struggle (Tekuyeva 2006, 142).

The idea that the dichotomous structure of gender roles is mostly a Western phenomenon, naturalized thanks to modernity all over the world, is proven by many practices of marginal Muslim cultures in Caucasus and Central Asia. I have already mentioned above the *bacha* cult which could take a male and less frequently, a female form with a clear trans-sexual element. A milder example which does not cross sexual boundaries is connected with medieval Eastern poetry with its much more nuanced gender system. Along with the Sharia ideal of woman and its opposite it has a powerful image of a beautiful and sly coquette—the treacherous *Afet* (translated literally as disaster). This beautiful dame of the Muslim poetry, in N. Mekhti's words (Mekhti 2005, 137), takes an in-between position. It is a good example of non-Western culture's sensitivity and intuition in grasping of such intermediary transvalue and at times transgender models which do not fit the Western binary opposition of Madonna and a whore.

If in case of Mexican Zapatistas the main task is to decolonize from the Eurocentered racist epistemologies in their White Creole rendering, the women of Caucasus and Central Asia face a more difficult task due to the multiplicity of the modernizing and colonizing agents in their case. (Re)making of women's identities between and beyond neoliberalism, Islam and ethnic-national cultures becomes a true challenge. What is meant here is not just a simple and direct negation of one tradition for the sake of the other, but a dynamic interpenetration and mutual transculturation.

Soviet modernity destroyed the complex and nuanced models of interaction between the indigenous thinking and Islam which had been refined in these locales in the centuries of Muslim influence. The religious turn of border thinking in today's independent ex-colonies, including its gender overtones, is connected to the fact that Islam in contrast with Christianity, is associated with the banner of global anti-colonial movement against the West and, consequently, its own expansionistic nature is symbolically forgotten and even forgiven in the larger dimension where it lost to Christianity and Western Modernity and turned into a religion and ideology of the "damnés."

Today's attempts to go back to hijab in Central Asia and Caucasus are a way of appealing to what is interpreted in the collective unconsciousness as "traditional" (though is not always so) in the form of a protest against westernization in its Soviet, national, or global variant. In Turkey, Central Asia or Caucasus this consciously chosen ludic hijab identity is usually accepted by young and middle aged urban educated and professional women, mobile enough in the social sense, and attempting to legitimize the social, political, and cultural changes and the shaping of alternative normative values. In Turkey, according to Göle (Göle 1996), it is expressed in a generational conflict of Kemalist parents and Islamist daughters. In the post-Soviet space it is a conflict of Soviet mothers and "traditionalist" daughters. However, in Turkey the process of radical Islamic revival and shaping of the new Muslim identity took several decades and intensified towards the end of the twentieth century. In the case of ex-Soviet colonies which became independent suddenly and unwillingly, the situation was more graphic and required an immediate and often intuitive choice on the part of the women.

It is important to realize that Islam is not an essentially misogynist or women liberating religion the same way as pre-Islamic traditions could carry various often conflicting elements. On the one hand, some features of women's cults and a reverence for women survived, on the other hand, according to *Adats*[2] the woman was losing almost all of her previous rights. Patriarchal society and clergy distorted Islam as it happened in case of Christianity as well, making it more and more sexist. As it was stated above, in a number of Arabic countries there emerged a whole tradition of Muslim women theologists who reinterpret Quran from a gendered perspective (Ali 2003). In Caucasus and Central Asia this impulse has not been yet expressed in academic forms (although as an intention it was present already in Jadidism), but emerges in the continuing traditions of rethought Sufism with its often pre-Islamic (women) saints, in the practices of modern healers and shamans. By contrast, the male forms of new Islamism in Northern Caucasus make the value of women's life a zero as in the case of the so called "black widows" that are used as dispensable lives by the colonized males themselves. This attitude to women as dispensable lives is not an ancient "tradition" but rather a new custom, closely linked with the violence of modernity and colonization. As a result of the Soviet modernization and post-Soviet period, which made the majority of women to become bread winners and to support their families, there started a rapid process of the final suppressing of all elements of local cultures, mentalities and societies, which used to protect women before.

In the end she has not gained anything, because the external emancipation turned into a considerable growth of women's responsibilities and resulted in yet another loss of rights.

Gender sphere along with art, non rational and other rejected knowledges, is one of the very few remaining realms of (post)colonial subjectivity in Eurasian borderlands where the process of attuning to trans-modern epistemologies and building other trajectories for the future is still possible. Here we find the border sensibility and the trickster subjectivity. Both in Caucasus and particularly in Central Asia this meditative nomadic identity is not new. Yet today it acquires a global dimension in the phenomenon of border trans-identity. It is connected with the shift to geo- and body-politics of the racialized and gendered subject, who exists in Anzaldúa's "open wound" which gives him/her the epistemic advantage of the border. This colonial wound as a new space of knowledge production, does not heal not just in South America, but also in Central Asia and Caucasus which continue to experience even today the internal colonialism and the imperial dependency.

Attuning to trans-modern dialogue is linked with a constant questioning, with the unfinished nature of any ideas and models, with a striving to walk while asking questions and carefully listen to answers, in Zapatistas's rhetoric. Such an approach is far from simple and static going back to the archaic past, without leaving the Western vector of history and cosmology. It presupposes that we constantly keep in mind both the diachronous dimension linked with the revival of the erased histories and silenced resistance voices of the colonized people, and a synchronous perpendicular dimension of critical trans-modern dialogue of many groups of the "damnés" around the world. As a result there emerges and reemerges again in a forever changing mode, a pluriversal and open agenda based on the principle of sustaining an epistemic diversity of many coexisting and interacting worlds. An acquaintance and a dialogue of Central Asian and Caucasus activists and theorists of gender with decolonial feminists would be a fruitful step as it would add additional points of reference and allow to finally stop catching up with the West.

On the one hand, Caucasus and Central Asia have always carried within themselves the ideal of a transcultural world of harmonious and just social relations, including the gender sphere. On the other hand, it proves to be difficult to delink from the mutant paradigm of the secondary colonial difference, the double standards in the sphere of coloniality of gender with one ideal for the Western (or Russian in case of the Soviet modernity) gendered subject and an opposite ideal

for the colonial and ex-colonial spaces whose women remain the subjects of redemption by means of various discourses and tactics—from
Christianity to civilizing mission, from socialism to overall consumerism today. There is a specific variant of colonial modernity which is
still being sold today. It has been promoted in the Socialist colonies,
in the third world, and in the ex-second world now. This colonial
modernity is a cheap throw-back of the culture of Western modernity
which is giving the colonial groups a pacifying feeling of their belonging to a Grand Modernity, incarcerating them into the triumphant
vector pointed towards emancipation in accordance with typical heresy of stagism.

Delinking from this point of view requires a self-reflexive and critical stance and a readiness to fight on different levels. In the conditions of the continuing zombification, extreme poverty, and often
lack of even minimal human rights and informational isolation it is
hard to imagine that Caucasus and Central Asia would consciously
reject the rhetoric of salvation and attempt to offer viable alternative
decisions in any near future.

In order to come to an understanding and global interaction and
coalitions at the points of difference with other colonized, racialized
and gendered subjects, the women of Central Asia and Caucasus
need first to decolonize their own minds. This would lead to a feminism which would not be a simple clone of the Western (or Russian)
one and would not simply repeat the Soviet official gender discourse
either. It has to be an independent and critical feminism, based on
careful differentiating and empathic grasping of particular values
and sensibilities born in particular historical and cultural contexts
of Eurasian borderlands. There is a danger that having gotten rid of
the hijab as a result of Soviet gender emancipation, women often
find themselves today in the clasp of a much more hierarchical
regime—not of veiling, but of silencing and leveling of their opinions and selves, promoted by Western epistemology and Western
mainstream feminism as its integral part. In the concept of coloniality of gender it is particularly important to stress the oppositional,
fragmented, and coalitional gendered subjectivity and activism,
pointed to the future. Coloniality of gender generates a counteraction, a virus of negation in terms and from the cracks of the colonial difference.

Conducting a dialogue under the preservation of difference is a
difficult task—money and power remain in the hands of the feminist mainstream, and if they get into the hands of freely thinking
and acting female heretics, this can change even their nature. As

S. Marcos pointed out, institualization is a dangerous thing because having access to financial resources and power, immediately makes the relations between gender activists fixed and inflexible, while their dialogue often becomes false (Shu-mei Shih et al. 2005, 150). Unexpectedly this idea is echoed by Beatriz Preciado—one of the most interesting European representatives of radical trans-feminism and transgender studies and the author of *Manifesto Contra-Sexual* (Preciado 2000). Preciado is tired of feminist politics and craves invisibility, a micro-level which she regards as a necessary condition for real political work and not a fake identity politics in the sense of representation and visibility in mass-media. For her the main political arena is our body, because body is not necessarily individual, it is already a community. Preciado believes that desire is not a source of subjectivity, but much more a result of political regimes. That is why she invents rituals for programming desire and its changing with the goal of avoiding the reproduction of normalcy or perversion within the frame of the existing logic. This is a political therapy of a sort which has to do with a radical understanding of situated knowledges as described by Haraway (Haraway 1998), questioning knowledge itself, its context, and the place where it is produced, as well as the micro-levels which generate other knowledges and the position of an expert. Therefore it is necessary to create new institutions instead of the discredited old ones that turned into political regimes. These new types of institutes may turn out to be merely events, floating changeable nets which are created for an hour or a day. Yet they generate a specific space, they stitch reality through, they pierce it but necessarily on a micro-level, to avoid becoming a pray for mass-media and normative stable institutions (Herbst 2006). From different positions Marcos, Preciado, Lugones and many others speak essentially of the same thing—of the social erotics of difference, of the creation of the critical border epistemology in gender sphere, an example of which is the concept of "nepantilism" as it was used by Gloria Anzaldúa (Anzaldúa 1999, 100).

Even if we cannot escape the dependence on Western grants and NGOs, we can still maintain and cultivate a certain degree of freedom and self-reflection, a conscious rejection of the dominant ego-politics of knowledge and an attempt to build a geo- and body-politics of an other gendered border thinking. This can help elaborate an other dynamic of action, a specific transcultural language which would be linked with more symmetrical and dialogic relations between Western and non-Western cultures and epistemologies. This does not mean that we need to reject the influence of Western feminism altogether, or take the position of aggressive and rigid nativism and nationalism. But having shaped the multiple vision of critical border thinking, which can hope to see and adequately reflect the diversality and contradictoriness of various existential experiences of our variegated world, we exercise our right not to knock any more on the Western door waiting to be accepted, and stop limping behind the so called civilized world in the shoes that are chronically rubbing our feet sore.

Notes

One Between Third World/Women of Color Feminism and Decolonial Feminism

1. By alter-modern here I mean other than modern or a demodern stance as a way of delinking from modernity and its discourses (Mignolo 2007). For more details see chapter two.
2. One of the new grounds for uniting the women of color discourses is the decolonial option discussed in detail in chapter two.
3. Jayawardena's later works such as *The White Woman's Other Burden* (1995) and *Nobodies to Somebodies* (2000) reconsider and problematize some of her initial Marxist interpretations concentrating on transcultural and trans-epistemic encounters between Asian and Western women.
4. Sandoval's critical dialogue with modernity and postmodernity is more flexible and open than many male heterosexual variants of non-Western emancipating discourses. Instead of the intellectual operation of denouncing modernity in all its manifestations she attempts to find certain impulses, ideas, and drives in critical modern philosophy that would echo the decolonial agendas and thus be used as a ground for dialogue.

Two Decolonial Feminism and the Decolonial Turn

1. For more details see Mignolo and Tlostanova 2006.
2. The first or Christian phase of modernity in decolonial option stretches from the sixteenth century and until the enlightenment while the second secular modernity is a post-enlightenment phase.
3. For the argument on intersections and differences between the decolonial option and postcolonial studies see Mignolo and Tlostanova 2007.
4. Race is fundamental in the shaping of the modern/colonial imaginary and its reverberations can be felt in distorted forms even in such countries as Russia and its former and present colonies. However, the complex European history and the critical view of European scholars, linked with a not always conscious guilt in their reflections on the legacy of racism and slavery, imbues their understanding of decoloniality with additional overtones seldom felt in the Americas where the picture of modernity/coloniality is drawn with wide strokes and is more straightforward.

5. For a detailed analysis of the views of these authors see 2.3 and 2.4.
6. The possible ways of decolonial rethinking of humanities in such locales I will try to demonstrate in part III.
7. A Nigerian scholar Oyèrónke Oyĕwùmi shows that an obsession with gender is an entirely Western phenomenon which was forced onto Yoruba culture together with colonization and destroyed all previous social, gender, linguistic and cultural discourses based on different principles (Oyĕwùmi 1997). In her view it is the Western society that is patriarchal, body-centric, highly visualized and based on the ideology of biologic determinism while gender as a category is read into reality by scholars, relying on Western values.
8. Western cultural feminism has recently started to question the absolute nature of egalitarian claims, symbolically creating an advantage out of deficiency, and postulating the specificity of women's way precisely as an advantage. In this sense cultural as well as ecological feminism stand close to non-European colonized and gendered subjectivities.
9. An African American gender theorist K. Crenshaw analyzes this paradox in its modern manifestation in the lives of African Americans demonstrating that particular gender models and stereotypes are interiorized by them as role models or negative examples. However, they are immediately negated by racism: a Black man is never regarded as a manifestation of power or a defender, and a Black woman does not correspond in the eyes of the society to the White female stereotype of passivity and purity (Crenshaw 1989, 155).
10. For a detailed analysis of this essay see Tlostanova, 2000.
11. One of the interesting examples of the interpenetration of decolonial and gender discourses of trans-epistemic nature is to be found in the philosophy of the Caribbean thinker, poet, historian Sylvia Wynter, who reconsiders western humanism and the meaning of the human in order to shift from the concept of Man (White European) to the concept of Human and Humanity, uncontaminated by previous limitations. Similarly to Lugones, Wynter is not after totalizing gender. She wants to regard it in a dynamics with other elements of coloniality of being and of knowledge. She understands gender as a function of genre (kind) of man (male). Wynter uses the world "genre" in a specific sense, stressing its mutual origins with the world "gender." Both for her mean a kind. Gender, in her idea, has been always a function of the "instituting of kind" (Thomas 2006). Another point of crossing with Lugones is that Wynter questions the bases of Western knowledge and feminism as one of its disciplines. She argues that the struggle of non-White women lies in the rejection of the very genre of man as a European male. Its negation would be expressed in and by the non-White population—men, women and children. For Wynter gender becomes a part of the more fundamental task of setting oneself free from the narrow and closed systems of thought which the humanity has been confined to for many centuries. In this respect she is neither in the position of Marxist feminism, nor in the

liberal Western feminist stance, but rather within the decolonial discourse.
12. The Soviet modernity brought colonial women forcefully into the public sphere as I will show in part II.

Three   Race/Body/Gender and Coloniality in the Russian/Soviet Empire and Its Colonies

1. Although the position of Caucasus within the cultural imaginary of the West was more complex as I will show later in this chapter.
2. For more details on Russia as a Janus-faced empire see Tlostanova 2003.
3. Thus, only an intersection of racism and gender discrimination can explain the fact that in Central Asia it was the local women and children (and not the Russians) who worked at the cotton and tobacco fields in the worst possible conditions and mostly for free.
4. In 1819 a land-owner Anna Strelkova was vacationing in Caucasus when someone introduced her to Shora Nogmov—one of the first "enlightened Circassians." She was offered to look at Nogmov's bride. Later Strelkova depicted this encounter in Eurocentric terms, though in the social sense the situation was different: Nogmov's bride was not a captive and stood on top of the Circassian society. Strelkova finished her ethnographic description of the dress and the house of the bride with a stereotype: "The Asiatic princess greeted us with just one small nod and did not even attempt to get up" (Tekuyeva 2006).
5. Maxim Maximych first describes Bela in conventional terms as a beautiful girl, tall and slender, with black eyes "as those of a mountain chamois," which "fairly looked into your soul." Later he takes a resolutely negative position on Bela's kidnapping calling it a rotten business, but gets Pechorin's rebuke that a "wild Circassian girl" ought to be happy with such a charming husband as himself (Lermontov 2001).
6. Translation is mine—M.T.
7. As a Northern Caucasus ethnographer M. Tekuyeva points out, they "did not shun from giving their favors to local males who were loyal to Russians. It is then that the first cases of venereal diseases came to be known in Caucasus under the name of *metushke uz*—literally, the disease of Russian women" (Tekuyeva 2006, 68).
8. D. Northrop gives an example of such discourse in the early Soviet period when Oriental backwardness began to be opposed to Soviet modernity. He quotes an Uzbek communist who in 1927 proclaimed at a local party meeting in Andizhan: "Together with the growth of Socialist elements in the economy, there will be a decline in the debauchery of women... Almost everyone knows that various forms of dissipation thrive among those who wear a paranjee. For example, the love of one woman for

another: this unhealthy phenomenon is very widespread among Uzbek women, from this fact you can see that the paranjee does not at all ward off debauchery" (Northrop 2004, 65).

9. Mainly it refers to timber, before most of the forests were destroyed by the Russian colonization.

10. Later it resulted in a higher racial and human status of Circassian diasporas in the Middle East, than that of their compatriots who stayed in Russia.

11. In fact the term is still around in some of the U.S. questionnaires.

Four   Quasi-scientific Racism and Gender in Russian and Soviet Discourses

1. Some Western specialists in Eurasian studies today tend to question the formula "divide and rule" and justify the Soviet imperial policies claiming that the Bolsheviks attempted to build a new and more progressive kind of colonialism (Hirsch 2000). Such an approach is based on erasing of race as a fundamental basis of coloniality in all variants of modernity, including the Soviet one.

2. This logic is also at work in the construction of Western museum starting from the eighteenth century onward. As is known, museums divided almost immediately into the reservoirs of art which constructed, preserved, and transmitted to future generations the memory of Western culture, and the museums of natural history representing the non-Western world including the natural and the provisionally human.

3. As a result of this anthropological mythology, particularly in the Soviet period, which was the most radical in its nation-building colonial discourses, the previously existing Central Asian category of *Sarts* completely vanished, as it did not correspond to ethnic-racial hierarchy invented and imposed onto this transcultural space. Scholars still argue on the origins of the word *Sart* (Abashin and Bushkov 2004, 40–43). However what is important is that *Sarts* (that is, the Central Asian creoles) represented the idea of mixed blood, of hybrid ethnicity which was inconvenient for the imperial taxonomies. As a rule, they had both Uzbeks and Tadzhiks, in the present ethnic understanding, among their ancestors. Being urban dwellers they often stood closer to Tadzhiks but spoke a Turkic (New Uzbek) language. The erasing of *Sart* identity was accelerated by the forceful imposition of linguistic hierarchies and the binary principle used in censuses, which in Czarist, Soviet times, or today are instrumental in constructing the national identities.

4. The Jadids (from the Arabic "new") were the Muslim reformers of the Russian Empire in the late nineteenth and early twentieth century (Khalid 1999).

5. In his insightful *Ghazali and the Poetics of Imagination* Ebrahim Moosa reflects on the meaning of *dihliz*—"an interspace, negotiating and struggling with the hegemonic and colonial knowledge traditions as well as the subalternized Islamicate knowledge systems to gain a modicum of emancipation and ultimately liberation from totalizing ways of existence" (Moosa 2005, 34).
6. A peculiar partial revival of the *Otin* institute is taking place today as I will demonstrate in part III.
7. It resembled the miseries of neoliberal multiculturalism that also strives to confine difference to safe and predictable packageable museum forms.
8. Trofim Lysenko was in charge of Soviet biology under Stalin. He rejected Mendelian genetics in favor of inheritability of acquired characteristics. The 1930s–1940s were marked by his powerful influence in the area of biology in the USSR, when Lysenkoism led to political repressions and the deaths of most Mendelian biologists, as well as a serious lag in the development of Soviet genetics.
9. Thus, instead of "harmful" feminism, a Soviet egalitarian gender discourse and a quite moderate women's ideal were launched, instead of comparative studies a historical-comparative method was invented, instead of race a theory of nationality and ethnos was produced.

Five   Dirt Fetish and Commodity Racism Soviet Way

1. The glass of water theory was the basis of the early Soviet sexual revolution according to which the satisfaction of one's sexual desires was as simple as drinking a glass of water. This theory is (wrongly) attributed to Alexandra Kollontai.
2. An example of commodity racism in McClintock's interpretation is the *Pears* soap commercial that was sanctified by the domestic sanctum of the White man's bathroom as a quintessence of progress and civilization exported to other spaces. There were no women in *Pears* commercials. It was always advertised by the burdened White men or the male representatives of the colonized. Here imperialism existed in a domestic form but this imperial domesticity lacked a female element. What had no place in male rational discourse—the economic value of female domestic labor in Victorian England—was disqualified and put into the realm of the primitive, the barbarian, in the colonies, whereas the economic value of the colonized cultures was domesticated and projected onto the space before modernity (McClintock 1995, 34–35).
3. Translation of excerpts from Mayakovsky's advertisements is mine—M.T.
4. A quotation from 1925 Lyubimova's pamphlet speaks for itself: "They are ill with syphilis, with rashes, with gynecological and skin diseases…All of this sicknesses are connected by the fact that there is much filth in the

kibitki and yurts, by the fact that both the sick and the healthy drink and eat from the same dishes, sit on common cushions and blankets; for years at a time they do not wash their children, or wash themselves, or wash their clothes" (Lyubimova 1925, 3).

Six Colonial Gender Tricksterism in Central Asia and Caucasus

1. Figures 6.1 and 6.2 show a woman-intellectual from the Soviet colony visiting India with the delegation of educational workers in the late 1950s. She is putting on different identities—first wearing a modernized variant of the Uzbek dress, and in figure 6.2, being dressed as a Soviet university professor of Urdu from Uzbekistan with the completely visually erased colonial status. This image is pointedly opposed to the visual representations of the educated women in the "developing" India. This picture is a clear example of the second world using the colonial difference to juxtapose itself to the third world, once again, to demonstrate its closeness to the First world, not in concrete ideological terms, but in the wider modernization and civilizing discourses, masked behind the proletarian internationalism.
2. I interviewed R.K. in person in May 2009. The complete interview was published in Tlostanova 2009, 280–297. Excerpts from this interview are given here in my translation— M.T.
3. All photographs in this section come from my personal archive.
4. These were the Central Asian intellectuals, poets, and writers who opposed colonization in different ways and were subsequently erased from the official canon.
5. Her father was a driver of the first secretary of the local committee of the communist party.
6. *Kurban Hait* is a Turkic name of the Muslim holiday *Eid al-Adha* (Arabic)—a festival of sacrifice; *Uraza Bairam* is a Turkic name of the Muslim holiday *Eid al-Fitr* (Arabic) that marks the end of *Ramadan* (the month of fasting).
7. *Namaz* is a Turkic name of the Muslim prayer *Salat* (Arabic).
8. Figure 6.6 is particularly graphic as it illustrates a complex and self-contradictory hierarchy of ideological constructs concerning the Orient in the Soviet official discourse of the mid-1950s. The local girl symbolizing the new Uzbek woman teaches Hindi to local Uzbek children in the Old Town. It is obviously a sign of desirable intimacy between the two Orients—the Soviet Central Asia and the postcolonial India which the Soviet Union was attempting to actively push toward the Socialist future at the time. The actors in this scene are the local people learning (and teaching) one Oriental language as (to) native speakers of another Oriental language (while the languages are historically indirectly connected). But these actors are not free because they express the will of empire. This will

is represented by a poster on the wall that depicts two males and reads: Russian and Indian are brothers forever. This signalizes the erasing of Uzbek identity in the official discourse and imagery, while the Soviet identity equals Russian. The local Uzbeks whose subjectivity is used by the empire in order to make the desirable connection and interaction with India easier, find themselves in a complex situation of a trickster play and a self-negation. They are chosen for the role of the negotiators precisely because they are Uzbek, yet they are not allowed to be seen as such or to keep their identity officially because the mission of the empire requires them to become Russians.

9. *Beshagoch* is a central Tashkent square where before the 1890s there was an old entrance through the city wall to a district of the same name meaning "five willows."

10. Semyon Budyeny was a Soviet military commander whose name was given to many streets all over the Soviet Union.

Seven   Eurasian Borderlands in Dialogue with Mesoamerica

1. Such a model of other knowledge and other university is already being implemented in the Intercultural University "Amawtay Wasy" of the Indigenous Nationalities and peoples of Ecuador where teaching is not focused on Western system but on an active use of an Indigenous epistemic model, where European legacy is included in the program but is not prevalent, and where the most important element is not to supply the students with a sum of facts, but to allow them to be themselves. The latter is connected not only with their acquiring of positive knowledge, but also with the necessity of its constant critical analysis and a correlation with the immediate individual and social experience of the learner. Hence the principle of this university: learning to unlearn in order to relearn.

2. Even leaving Caucasus en mass, as a result of the Russian colonization in the mid-nineteenth century and crossing the Black Sea in the direction of the Ottoman Sultanate, many Cherkess people hastily adopted Islam only on board of the ships.

3. The interview with L.K. was by e-mail in February 2010. The translation of its excerpts is mine—M.T.

4. *Tabib* (f. *tabiba*) means a doctor, a healer in Turkic cultures.

Eight   Two Dialogues

1. The interview with F. Zh. was by e-mail in February 2010. The translation is mine—M.T.

2. Idries Shah (Sayed Idries el-Hashimi) was an influential twentieth-century Sufi teacher, a paradigmatic example of transcultural and

trans-epistemic border individual, who made Sufism understandable to the West.

3. Helena Blavatsky's *The Secret Doctrine* (1888) is a classic in Theosophy. Jual Khul was a Tibetan "Master of the Wisdom" who is said to telepathically dictate his ideas to Alice Bailey—a very controversial figure in modern Occult and Esoteric movements which influenced the evolvement of New Age and neo-paganism.

4. The interview with Svetlana Shakirova was by e-mail in June 2009. Translation is mine—M.T.

5. *Akimat* is a Turkic name of the municipal council in modern Kazakhstan.

Conclusion: Why Cut the Feet in Order to Fit the Western Shoes?

1. This refers, for instance, to the women's part of the international peasant movement *La Via Campesina*.

2. *Adat* is a set of local pre-Islamic customary laws, regulating social, political, economic, and other spheres in Turkic and Caucasus as well as other societies in the world, often in contradiction with Muslim law.

Bibliography

Abashin, Sergei. 2007. *Natsionalizmi v Srednei Azii. V poiskakh Identichnosti* (Nationalisms in Central Asia. In Quest of Identity). Saint-Petersburg: Aleteya.

Abashin, Sergei, and Vladimir Bushkov, eds. 2004. *Ferganskaya Dolina. Etnichnost. Etnicheskie Protsessy. Etnicheskie Konflikty* (Fergana Valley. Ethnicity. Ethnic Processes. Ethnic Conflicts). Moscow: Nauka.

Abasov, Ali. 2006. Genderny analiz sotsialno-poiliticheskoi zhizni Azerbaidzjana (Gender analysis of the social and political Life of Azerbaijan). *Gender Studies. Central Asian Network.* http://www.genderstudies.info/magazin/magazin_02_01.php (August 25, 2006).

Adams, Laura L. 2005. Modernity, Postcolonialism and Theatrical Form in Uzbekistan. *Slavic Review*, Vol. 64, No. 2: 333–354.

Ahmed, Leila. 1992. *Women and Gender in Islam: Historical Roots of a Modern Debate*. New Haven: Yale University Press.

Alban Achinte, Adolfo. 2006. *Conocimiento y lugar: más allá de la razón hay un mundo de colores. En Texiendo textos y saberes. Cinco hijos para pensar los estudios culturales, la colonialidad y la interculturalidad.* Popayán, Editorial Universidad del Cauca, Colección Estiodios (Inter)culturales.

Alexander, Jacqui. M. 2005. *Pedagogies of Crossing*. Durham and London: Duke University Press.

Alexander, Jacqui M. and Chandra Talpade Mohanty. 1997. Genealogies, Legacies, Movements. In *Feminist Genealogies, Colonial Legacies, Democratic Futures*, eds. Jacqui M. Alexander and Chandra Talpade Mohanty, xiii–xlii. New York and London: Routledge.

Ali, Kecia. 2003. Progressive Muslims and Islamic Jurisprudence: The Necessity for Critical Engagement with Marriage and Divorce Law. In *Progressive Muslims: On Justice, Gender, and Pluralism.* ed. Omid Safi, 163–189. Oxford: Oneworld Publications.

Allen, Paula Gunn 1992. *The Sacred Hoop: Recovering the Feminine in American Indian Traditions*. Boston: Beacon Press.

Allione, Constanzo. 1997. *Habiba: a Sufi Saint from Uzbekistan*. A documentary. New York: Mystic Fire Video.

Amina Mama. 2001. Sheroes and Villains: Conceptualizing Colonial and Contemporary Violence against Women in Africa. In *Postcolonial Discourses. An Anthology.* ed. Gregory Castle, 252–268. London: Blackwell.

Antelava, Natalia. 2008. Crossing Continents: Uzbekistan. BBC News. BBC Radio 4's Crossing Continents, broadcast on Thursday, April 3, 2008 at 1102 BST. http://news.bbc.co.uk/2/hi/programmes/crossing_continents/7325384.stm

Anzaldúa, Gloria. 1999. *Borderlands/La Frontera: The New Mestiza*. San Francisco: Aunt Lute Books.

Arrighi, Giovanni. 1994. *The Long Twentieth Century*. London: Verso.

Ashwin, Sarah. 2000. *Gender, State, and Society in Soviet and post-Soviet Russia*. London and New York: Routledge.

Badran, Margot. 1995. *Feminists, Islam, and Nation: Gender and the Making of Modern Egypt*. Princeton: Princeton University Press.

Balibar, Étienne. 1991. Is There a Neo-racism? In *Race, Nation, Class: Ambiguous Identities*, eds. Étienne Balibar and Immanuel Wallerstein, 17–28. London and New York: Verso.

Barthes, Roland. 1977. *Image/Music/Text*. Trans, Stephen Heath. New York: Hill and Wang.

Behbudi, Mahmud Khoja. 1914. Hifz-i sihat-i oila. *Oina*, No 48, 49.

Beknazarova, Gulnora. 2005. Transformatsija normi—osobennosti perekhodnogo perioda (The transformation of the norm—features of transition period). In *Gender Studies. Central Asian Network*, http://www.gender-studies.info/telo/telo_sexs16.php (August 20, 2009).

Bestuzhev-Marlinsky, Alexander. 1958. Mulla-Nur. Byl (Mulla-Nur. A true story). In *Complete Works in 2 volumes*. Vol. 2, 314–462. Moscow: Khudozhestvennaya Literatura.

Blumenbach, Johann Friedrich. 1865. *The Anthropological Treatises of Johann Friedrich Blumenbach: De Generis Humani Varietate Nativa* [1795]. Ed. and trans. Thomas Bendyshe. New York: Bergman Publishers.

Bogues, Anthony. 2003. *Black Heretics, Black Prophets. Radical Political Intellectuals*. Oxford: Oxford University Press.

———. 2006. The Human, Knowledge and the World: Reflecting on Sylvia Wynter. In *After Man towards the Human. Critical Essays on Sylvia Wynter*, ed. Anthony Bogues, 315–338. Kingston, Miami: Ian Randle Publishers.

Brower, Daniel R. 1993. *Images of the Orients: Vasily Vereschagin and Russian Turkistan*. Berkeley: Center for German and European Studies. University of California.

Broxup, Marie Benningsen, ed. 1992. *The North Caucasus Barrier: The Russian Advance towards the Muslim World*. London: Hurst & Co.

Caroe, Olaf. 1967. *Soviet Empire. The Turks of Central Asia and Stalinism*. New York: Macmillan.

Castro-Gómez, Santiago. 2007. The Missing Chapter of Empire: Postmodern reorganization of Coloniality and Post-Fordist Capitalism. *Cultural Studies*, Vol. 21, No. 2–3: 428–448.

Castro-Gómez, Santiago and Eduardo Mendieta, eds. 1998. *Teorias sin disciplina (latinoamericanismo, postcolonialidad y globalizacion en debate)*. México: Miguel Ángel Porrúa.

CaucAsia. International Information-Analytical Electronic Journal of the International Coalition of Gender Journalists. http://www.wcg.org.ge/gmc/Kavkazia2006–1.pdf (July 20, 2009).

Cavanaugh, Cathy. 2001. Backwardness and Biology: Medicine and Power in Russian and Soviet Central Asia, 1868–1934. PhD. Diss., Columbia University.

Chatterjee, Partha. 1988. *Nationalist Thought in the Colonial World. A Derivative Discourse?* Minneapolis: University of Minnesota Press.

———. 1993. *The Nation and its Fragments. Colonial and Postcolonial Histories.* Princeton, N.J.: Princeton University Press.

———. 1997. *Our Modernity. South-South exchange programme for research on the history of development and the Council for the development of social science research in Africa. Rotterdam/Dakar* http://www.sephis.org/pdf/partha1/pdf (January 10, 2010).

———. 2004. *The Politics of the Governed. Reflections on Popular Politics in Most of the World.* New York: Columbia University Press.

Chechuyeva, Angela. 2007. Torgovaya Politika Osmanskoy Imperii na Severo-Zapadnom Kavkaze v kontse vosemnadtsatogo—pervoi polovine devyatnadtsatogo veka (Trade Politics of the Ottoman Empire in the North-Western Caucasus in the late eighteenth—first part of the nineteenth century). *Vostok (Oriens)* 2, 111–117.

Chipchikov, Boris. 2006. *Nerestilis Ryby v Svete Lunnom* (The Fish were Spawning in the Moonlight). Nalchik: Elbrous.

Chukovsky, Korney. 1969. Futuristy. In: *Complete Works in 6 Volumes.* Moscow: Khudozhestvennaya Literatura, 202–259.

Cooke, Miriam. 2000. *Women Claim Islam: Creating Islamic Feminism through Literature.* London: Routledge.

Crenshaw, Kimberlé Williams. 1989. Demarginalizing the Intersection of Race and Sex: A Black Feminist Critique of Anti-discrimination Doctrine, Feminist Theory and Antiracist Politics. In *The University of Chicago Legal Forum*, 139–167.

Curzon, George Nathaniel. 1967. *Russia in Central Asia in 1889 and the Anglo-Russian Question.* London: Frank Kass.

Cusicanqui, Silvia Rivera. 1990. El potencial epistemológico y teórico de la historia oral: de la lógica instrumental a la descolonizacion de la historia. *Temas Sociales* 11, 49–75.

Danylevsky, Nikolay. 1895. *Rossiya i Yevropa. Vzglyad na Kulturniye i Politicheskie Otnosheniya Slavyanskogo Mira k Germano-Romanskomu* (Russia and Europe: a Glance at the Cultural and Political Relations of the Slavic and Germanic-Romance World). Saint-Petersburg: Tipografiya bratyev Panteleyevykh.

Davidoff, Leonore. 1983. Class and Gender in Victorian England. In *Sex and Class in Women's History,* eds. Judith L. Newton, Mary P. Ryan, and Judith R. Walkowitz, 17–71. London: Routledge.

Davydov, Alexander. 1999. Problema sredinnoy kulturi v rossiiskoi tsivilizatsii (The Problem of Mediating Culture in Russian Civilization). In *Rossiisky Tsivilizatsionny Kosmos* (Russian Civilizational Cosmos), 25–62. Moscow: Eydos.

Dostoyevsky, Fyodor. 2002. Dnevnik Pisatelya za 1877 (Writer's Diary for 1877). In *Russkaja Ideya* (Russian Idea), 154–162. Moscow: Iris Press.

Douglas, Mary. 1966. *Purity and Danger*. London: Routledge.

Dussel, Enrique. 1985. *Philosophy of Liberation*. Trans. Aquilina Martinez, Christine Morkovsky. Eugene: Wipf & Stock.

———. 1995. Eurocentrism and Modernity (Introduction to the Frankfurt Lectures). *Boundary 2*, Vol. 20, No 3: 65–76.

———. 1996. *The Underside of Modernity: Apel, Ricoeur, Rorty, Taylor, and the Philosophy of Liberation*. Atlantic Highlands: Humanity Books.

Erdem, Y. Hacan. 1993. Slavery in the Ottoman Empire and its demise, 1800–1909. Ph.D. Diss., Oxford University.

Escobar, Arturo. 2007. Worlds and Knowledges Otherwise: The Latin American Modernity/Coloniality Research Program. *Cultural Studies*, Vol. 21, Nos. 2–3: 179–210.

Espiritu, Yen Le. 1997. Race, Class, and Gender in Asian America. In *Making More Waves*, eds. Elaine H. Kim, Lilia V. Villanueva, and Asian Women United of California, 135–141. Boston: Beacon Press.

Euben, Roxanne L. 2006. *Journeys to the Other Shore: Muslim and Western Travelers in Search of Knowledge*. Princeton: Princeton University Press.

Fanon, Franz. 1967. *Black Skin, White Masks*. New York: Grove.

Faruqi, Maysam. 2000. Woman's Self-Identity in the Quran and Islamic Law. In *Windows of Faith: Muslim Women Scholar-Activists in North America*, eds. Gisela Webb, Syracuse, 72–101. New York: Syracuse University Press.

Fitrat (Abd al-Ra'ūf). 1919. *Sharq Siyosati* (Eastern Question). Tashkent.

Foucault, Michel. 1998. *The History of Sexuality. The Will to Know*. Vol. 1. London and New York: Penguin.

Gasparov, Boris. 1992. Moy do dyr. *NLO*, No 1. http://www.chukfamily.ru/Kornei/Biblio/gasparov.htm (February 20, 2010).

Glissant, Édouard. 1998. Le divers du monde est imprevisible. Keynote address at the conference Beyond Dichotomies. Stanford University, Stanford, May 8–10.

Goldstein, Joshua S. 2001. *War and Gender: How Gender Shapes the War System and Vice Versa*. Cambridge: Cambridge University Press.

Göle, Nilufer. 1996. *The Forbidden Modern. Civilization and Veiling*. Ann Arbor: University of Michigan Press.

Gordon, Lewis. 2006. *Disciplinary Decadence: Living Through in Trying Times*. Boulder: University of Colorado Press.

Gorky, Maksim. 2008. *Nesvoyervremmenye Mysly: Zametki o Revolyutsii I Kulture* (Ill-timed Thoughts: Notes on Revolution and Culture). Moscow: Azbuka.

Haraway, Donna. 1991. *Simians, Cyborgs, and Women: The Reinvention of Nature*. New York: Routledge.

———. 1998. Situated Knowledges: The Science Question in Feminism and the Privilege of Partial Perspectives. *Feminist Studies*, Vol. 14, No. 3: 575–599.

Harris, Colette. 2004. *Control and Subversion. Gender and Socialism in Tajikistan*. London: Pluto Press.

Harris, Wilson. 1995. The Limbo Gateway. In *Postcolonial Studies Reader*, eds. Bill Ashcroft, Gareth Griffiths, Helen Tiffin, 370–374. New York and London: Routledge.

Headley, Clevis. 2006. Otherness and the Impossible in the Wake of Wynter's Notion of the "After-Man. In *After Man towards the Human. Critical Essays on Sylvia Wynter*. Ed. Anthony Bogues, 57–75. Kingston, Miami: Ian Randle Publishers.

Herbst, Tara. 2006. Interview with Beatriz Preciado. Queertheorist. Paris/ Princeton. http://www.google.com/search?q=cache:f0aARXpKm88J:www. assembly-international.net/interviewz/Interview-Beatriz%2520Preciado.ht m+interview+with+B%C3%A9atriz+Preciado&hl=ru&gl=ru&ct=clnk&c d=1 (August 25, 2006).

Hinkelammert, Franz J. 2004. The Hidden Logic of Modernity: Locke and the Inversion of Human Rights. In *Worlds and Knowledges Otherwise*. A Web Dossier. Volume 1, Dossier 1. http://www.jhfc.duke.edu/wko/ dossiers/ (January 1, 2007).

Hirsch, Francine. 1998. Empire of Nations: Colonial Technologies and the Making of the Soviet Union, 1917–1939. PhD. Diss., Princeton University.

———. 2000. Toward an Empire of Nations: Border Making and the Formation of Soviet National Identities. *Russian Review*, Vol. 59: 201–226.

———. 2002. Race without the Practice of Racial Politics. *Slavic Review*, Vol. 61, No 1: 30–43.

Holmes, Rachel. 2006. *The Hottentot Venus*. Bloomsbury: Random House.

Horrible Traffic in Circassian Women-Infanticide in Turkey. *New York Daily Times*, August 6, 1856, 6. In *The Circassian Beauty Archive. The Lost Museum*. http://chnm.gmu.edu/lostmuseum/lm/311/ (February 10, 2010).

Iasevich, Vassily. 1928. K voprosu o konstitutsionalnom i antropolog- icheskom tipe uzbechki Khorezma (On the Question of Constitutional and Anthropological Type of Uzbek Women from Khorezm). *Meditsinskaya Mysl Uzbekistana*, No. 5: 32–50.

Jayawardena, Kumari. 1986. *Feminism and Nationalism in the Third World*. London: Zed Books.

———. 1995. *The White Woman's Other Burden. Western Women and South Asia During British Rule*. New York and London: Routledge.

———. 2000. *Nobodies to Somebodies. The Rise of the Colonial Bourgeoisie in Sri Lanka*. New York and London: Zed Books.

Jersild, Austin. 2002. *Orientalism and Empire*. Montreal and Kingston: McGill-Queen's University Press.

Jiménez-Lucena, Isabel. 2008. Gender and Coloniality: The "Moroccan Woman" and the "Spanish Woman" in Spain's Sanitary Policies in Morocco. *Worlds and Knowledges Otherwise*, a Web Dossier, Spring, http://www. jhfc.duke.edu/wko/dossiers/1.3/documents/JimenezWKO2.2_002.pdf (January 10, 2010).

Kamp, Marianne. 2006. *The New Woman in Uzbekistan. Islam, Modernity and Unveiling under Communism*. Seattle and London: University of Washington Press.

Kandiyoti, Deniz. 2002. Post-Colonialism Compared: Potentials and Limitations in the Middle East and Central Asia. *International Journal of Middle Eastern Studies*, Vol. 34, No. 2: 279–297.

Karam, Azza. 1998. *Women, Islamists, and the State.* New York: St. Martin's Press.

Kasymova, Sofya. 2005. Genderny poryadok v postsovetskom Tadzhikistane (Gender order in Post-Soviet Tadzhikistan). In *Gender: Traditsii i Sovremennost* (Gender: Traditions and Modernity). ed. Sofya Kasymova, 177–197. Dushanbe: Shkola Gendernogo Obrazovanija.

Katz, Katarina. 2001. *Gender, Work and Wages in the Soviet Union: A Legacy of Discrimination.* London: Palgrave Macmillan.

Khalid, Adeeb. 1999. *The Politics of Muslim Cultural Reform: Jadidism in Central Asia.* Berkeley: University of California Press.

———. 2007. *Islam after Communism: Religion and Politics in Central Asia.* Berkeley: University of California Press.

Khatibi, Abdelkebir. 1990. *Love in Two Languages.* Trans. Richard Howard. Minneapolis: University of Minnesota Press.

King, Deborah. 1988. Multiple Jeopardy, Multiple Consciousness: The Context of Black Feminist Ideology. *Signs* 14, 42–72.

Kotkin, Stephen. 1995. *Magnetic Mountain: Stalinism as a Civilization.* Berkeley: University of California Press.

Kotsonis, Yanni. 2000. Introduction: A Modern Paradox—Subject and Citizen in Nineteenth and Twentieth-Century Russia. In *Russian Modernity: Politics, Knowledge, Practices,* eds. David L. Hoffman and Yanni Kotsonis, 1–18. New York and London: Macmillan Press, St. Martin's Press.

Kristeva, Julia. 1981. Women's Time. Trans. Alice Jardine and Harry Blake. *Signs* 7.1, 13–15.

Lebedev, Andrey and Alexander Solodovnikov. 1987. *Vassily Vereschagyn.* Leningrad: Khudozhnik RSFSR.

Lenkersdorf, Carlos. 1996. *Los Hombres Verdadero: Voces y Testimonios Tojolabales.* Mexico: Fondo de Cultura Economica.

Lermontov, Mikhail. 2001. *A Hero of our Time.* New York and London: Penguin Classics.

Li, Xiaojiang. 1993. Zouxiang nuren—Zhongguo (dalu) funu yenjiu jishi (Heading Towards Women—A True Account of Women's Studies in Mainland China). Hong Kong: Qingwen Shuwu.

———. 1994. Economic Reform and the Awakening of Chinese Women's Collective Consciousness. In *Engendering China: Women, Culture and the State.* Eds. Christina Gilmartin at al., 360–382. Cambridge: Harvard University Press.

———. 1996. *Challenge and Response: Lectures on Women's Studies in the New Period.* Zhengzhou: Henan People's Press.

———. 1998. *Questions and Answers about Women.* Nanjing: Jiangsu ren-min chubanshe.

———. 1999. With what discourse do we reflect on Chinese Women? Thoughts on Transnational Feminism in China. In *Spaces of their*

Own: Women's Public Sphere in Transnational China, ed. Mayfair Mei-hui Yang, 261–277. Minneapolis: University of Minnesota Press.

———. 2003. Interview with Shu-mei Shih. Beijin, China, January 30, 2001. Qtd. in Shu-mei Shih. 2005. Towards an Ethics of Transnational Encounters, or "When" Does a "Chinese" Woman Become a "feminist"? In *Dialogue and Difference. Feminisms Challenge Globalization*, eds. Margueritte Waller and Sylvia Marcos, 22. New York and London: Palgrave Macmillan.

Logofet, Dmitry. 1913. *V gorakh i na ravninakh Bukhary. Ocherki Srednei Azii* (In the Mountains and Valleys of Bukhara. Sketches of Central Asia). Saint-Petersburg: Izdatel V. Berezovsky.

Lugones, María. 2003. Playfulness, "World"-Traveling and Loving Perception. In *Pilgrimages/Peregrinajes. Theorizing Coalition against Multiple Oppression*, 77–100. Lanham, Boulder, New York, Oxford: Rowman and Littlefield Publishers Inc.

———. 2007. Heterosexualism and the Colonial/Modern Gender System. *Hypatia*. Vol. 22, No.1: 186–209.

———. 2008. The Colonial Difference and the Coloniality of Gender. A talk presented at Drew Transdisciplinary Theological Colloquium VIII Decolonizing Epistemology New Knowing in Latina/o Theology, November 20–23, in Madison, NJ. http://depts.drew.edu/tsfac/colloquium/2008/presenters2.html.

Lykoshyn, Nyl. 1916. Doloy Bachei (Away with Bachas). In *Polzhizni v Turkestane. Ocherky Byta Tuzemnogo Naseleniya* (Half of Life in Turkistan. Sketches of the Life Mode of Aboriginal Population). Petrograd, 358–359.

Lyubimova, Serafima. 1925. Communist! Yesli ne khochesh, chtoby narod vymiral... esli ty ne bai, ne mulla... ty dolzhen rabotat po raskreposcheniju zhenschin (Communist! If You Do Not Want the People to Die... If You Are Not a Bai or a Mullah... You Must Work for Liberation of Women). Tashkent.

Macaulay, Thomas Babington. 1957. Minute of February 2, 1835 on Indian Education. In *Prose and Poetry*, selected by G.M. Young, 721–729. Cambridge, MA: Harvard University Press.

Mahmood, Saba. 2005. *Politics of Piety. The Islamic Revival and the Feminist Subject*. Princeton and Oxford: Princeton University Press.

Maldonado-Torres, Nelson. 2007. On the Coloniality of Being. *Cultural Studies*, Vol. 21, No. 2–3: 240–269.

———. 2008. *Against War. Views from the Underside of Modernity*. Durham & London: Duke University Press.

Marcos, Subcomandante. 1997. *El Sueño Zapatista. Realizadas por Yvon le Bot*. Barcelona: Plaza y Janés.

Marcos, Sylvia. 2005. The Borders within: The Indigenous Women's Movement and Feminism in Mexico. In *Dialogue and Difference. Feminisms Challenge Globalization*, eds. Marguerite Waller and Sylvia Marcos, 81–112. New York: Palgrave Macmillan.

Marcos, Sylvia. 2006. *Taken from the Lips: Gender and Eros in Mesoamerican Religions*. Leiden & Boston: Brill.

Martin, Terry. 2001. *The Affirmative Action Empire. Nations and Nationalism in the Soviet Union, 1923–1939*. Ithaca and London: Cornell University Press.

Massel, Gregory J. 1974. *The Surrogate Proletariat: Moslem Women and Revolutionary Strategies in Soviet Central Asia, 1919–1929*. Princeton: Princeton University Press.

Mayakovsky, Vladimir. Internet Resource "Vse-Vsyem" (Industrial Commercials). http://vlmayakovsky.narod.ru/reklama/reklama_index.html (July 20, 2009).

McClintock, Anne. 1995. *Imperial Leather. Race, Gender and Sexuality in the Colonial Contest*. New York: Routledge.

Mekhti, Niyazi. 2005. Virtualny Hijab (Virtual Hijab). In *Gender: Traditsii i Sovremennost*. ed. Sofya Kasymova, 136–145. Dushanbe: Shkola Gendernogo Obrazovanija.

Memmi, Albert. 1991. *The Colonizer and the Colonized*. Boston: Beacon Press.

Mernissi, Fatima. 1993. *The Forgotten Queens of Islam*. Trans. M.J. Lakeland. Minneapolis: University of Minnesota Press.

Mignolo, Walter D. 1995. *The Darker Side of the Renaissance*. Ann Arbor: University of Michigan Press.

———. 2000. Coloniality at Large: Time and the Colonial Difference. In *Time in the Making and Possible Futures,* ed. Enrique Rodríguez Larreta, 237–272. Rio de Janeiro: Unesco-ISSC-Educam.

———. 2000a. *Local Histories/Global Designs. Coloniality, Subaltern Knowledges, and Border Thinking*. Princeton: Princeton University Press.

———. 2002a. The Zapatistas Theoretical Revolution. *Review.* Fernand Braudel Center, Vol. 25, No. 3, 245–275.

———. 2002b. The Enduring Enchantment: (or the Epistemic Privilege of Modernity and Where to Go from Here). *The South Atlantic Quarterly*, Vol. 101, No. 4: 927–954.

———. 2007. Delinking. The Rhetoric of Modernity, the Logic of Coloniality and the Grammar of Decoloniality. *Cultural Studies*, Vol. 21, Nos. 2–3: 449–514.

Mignolo, Walter. D. and Freya Schiwy. 2003. Double Translation: Transculturation and the Colonial Difference. In *Translation and Ethnography. The Anthropological Challenge of Intercultural Understanding,* eds. Tullio Maranhao and Bernhard Streck, 3–28. Tuscon: The University of Arizona Press.

Mignolo, Walter D. and Madina Tlostanova. 2006. Theorizing from the Borders: Shifting to Geo- and Body-Politics of Knowledge. *European Journal of Social Theory*, Vol. 9, No. 1: 205–221.

———. 2007. The Logic of Coloniality and the Limits of Postcoloniality. In *The Postcolonial and the Global,* eds. Revathy Krishnaswamy and John

C. Hawley, 109–123. Minneapolis and London: University of Minnesota Press.

———. 2009. Global Coloniality and the Decolonial Option. *Kult 6—Special Issue. Epistemologies of Transformation: the Latin American Decolonial Option and its Ramifications.* Fall 2009, Department of Culture and identity, Roskilde University, 130–147.

———. 2011a. *Geopolitics of Knowing: Imperial and Colonial Epistemic Differences.* Forthcoming.

———. 2011b. *Learning to Unlearn.* Forthcoming.

Mohanty, Chandra Talpade. 1984. Under Western Eyes: Feminist Scholarship and Colonial Discourses. *Boundary 2,* Vol. 12, No. 3: 333–358.

Moosa, Ebrahim. 2005. *Ghazali. The Poetics of Imagination.* Chapel Hill & London: The University of North Carolina Press.

Murray Ballou, Maturin. 2006. *The Circassian Slave, or, the Sultan's Favorite.* Gloucester: Dodo Press.

Nalivkin, Vladimir, Nalivkina Maria. 1886. *Ocherk Byta Osedlogo Tuzemnogo naseleniya Fergany* (A Sketch of the Way of Life of the Indigenous Sedentary Population of Ferghana). Kazan: Typografiya Imperatorskogo Universiteta.

Navailh, Françoise. 1996. The Soviet Model. In *A History of Women in the West. Towards a Cultural Identity in the Twentieth Century,* ed. Françoise Thébaud, 226–254. Cambridge, MA and London: Belknap Press of Harvard University Press.

Northrop, Douglas. 2004. *Veiled Empire. Gender and Power in Stalinist Central Asia.* Ithaca and London: Cornell University Press.

Ostroumov, Nikolay. 1880. Kharakteristika religiozno-nravstvennoy zhizni musulman preimuschestvenno Srednei Azii (An Analysis of the Religious-Ethical Life of Mostly Central Asian Muslims). *Pravoslavnoye Obozrenie.* June–July 1880.

Ovilo y Canales, Felipe. 1886. *La Mujer Marroqui. Estudio Social.* Madrid: Imprenta de Manuel G. Hernandez.

Oyěwùmi, Oyèrónke. 1997. *The Invention of Women: Making an African Sense of Western Gender Discourses.* Minneapolis: University of Minnesota Press.

Paksoy, Hasan B. 1995. Dastan Genre in Central Asia. In *Modern Encyclopedia of Religions in Russia and the Soviet Union.* Academic International Press, Vol. V, http://vlib.iue.it/carrie/texts/carrie_books/paksoy-6/cae05.html (September 10, 2007).

Polovtsoff, Alexander. 1932. *The Land of Timur: Recollection of Russian Turkistan.* London, Methuen.

Posadskaya, Anastasia. 1994. *Women in Russia. A New Era in Russian Feminism.* Trans. Kate Clark. London and New York: Verso.

Pratt, Mary Louise. 1992. *Imperial Eyes: Travel Writing and Trans-culturation.* London: Routledge.

Preciado, Beatriz. 2000. *El Manifesto Contra-Sexual.* Paris: Balland.

Pushkin, Alexander. 1934. Puteshestviye v Arzrum (A Journey to Erzurum). In *Polnoye Sobraniye Sochinenii v 6 tomakh* (Complete Works in 6

Volumes), Volume 4, 737–788. Moskva, Leningrad: Khudozhestvennaya Literatura.

Quijano, Aníbal. 2000. Coloniality of Power, Knowledge, and Latin America. *Nepantla: Views from South*, No. 1, 533–580.

Rabasa, Jose. 1993. *Inventing America*. Norman: Oklahoma University Press.

Robles Mendo, Caridad. 1953. *Antropologia de la Mujer Marroqui Musulmana*. Tetuan: Ed. Marroqui.

Rorlich, Azade-Ayse. 2004. The Challenge of Belonging: The Muslims of the Late Imperial Russia and the Contested Terrain of Identity and Gender. In *Democracy and Pluralism in Muslim Eurasia*, ed. Yaacov Ro'i, 39–52. New York and London: Frank Cass.

Saadawi, Nawal el. 1998. *The Nawal el Saadawi Reader*. New York and London: Zed Books.

Sahadeo, Jeff and Russell Zanca, eds. 2007. *Everyday Life in Central Asia. Past and Present*. Bloomington and Indianapolis: Indiana University Press.

Sahni, Kalpana. 1997. *Crucifying the Orient. Russian Orientalism and the Colonization of Caucasus and Central Asia*. Oslo: White Orchid Press.

Sandoval, Chela. 2000. *Methodology of the Oppressed*. Minneapolis and London: University of Minnesota Press.

Savelyeva, Olga. 2006. Sovetskaja reklama 20-ikx godov kak sredstvo agitatsii i propagandy (Soviet Advertisement of the 1920s as a Means of Agitation and Propaganda). *Chelovek* 2–3, http://vivovoco.rsl.ru/VV/PAPERS/MEN/SOVIET_20/SOVIET_20.HTM (February 10, 2010).

Shaikh, Sa'diyya. 2003. Transforming Feminism: Islam, Women and Gender Justice. In *Progressive Muslims on Justice, Gender, and Pluralism*, ed. Omid Safi, 147–162. Oxford: Oneworld.

Shakirova, Svetlana. 2005. Zhenschini.SU-Zhenschini.KZ: osobennosti perekhoda (Women.SU-women.KZ—Features of Transition). In *Gender: Traditsii i Sovremennost* (Gender: Traditions and Modernity), ed. Sofya Kasymova, 92–135. Dushanbe: Shkola Gendernogo Obrazovanija.

———. 2006. Zhenskoye Dvizheniye: ot neuteshitelnogo diagnoza k effektivnym strategiyam (Women's Movement: From the Unconsoling Diagnosis to Effective Strategies). In *Central-Asian Gender Net* www.genderstudies.info (November 27, 2006).

Shami, Seteney. 2000. Prehistories of Globalization: Circassian Identity in Motion. *Public Culture*, Vol. 12, No. 1: 177–204.

Shami, Seteney, Lucine Taminian, Soheir A. Morcy et al., eds. 1990. *Women in Arab Society: Work Patterns and Gender Relations in Egypt, Jordan, and Sudan*. Providence, R.I., Paris: Unesco.

Shih, Shu-mei. 2005. Towards an Ethics of Transnational Encounters, or "When" Does a "Chinese" Woman Become a "Feminist?" In *Dialogue and Difference. Feminisms Challenge Globalization*, eds. Margueritte Waller and Sylvia Marcos, 3–28. New York: Palgrave Macmillan.

Shyshov, A. P. 1928. Malchiki-uzbeki: antropometricheskoye issledovaniye (Uzbek Boys: An Anthropometric Study). *Medistiskaya Mysl Uzbekistana*, Vol. 1: 16–41.

Simanovsky, Nikolay. 1999. Dnevnik, 2 aprelya—3 oktyabrja 1837 goda. Kavkaz (Diary April 2–October 2, 1837. Caucasus). *Zvezda*, Vol. 9: 184–216.

Smith, Andrea. 2005. *Conquest. Sexual Violence and American Indian Genocide.* New York: South End Press.

Solovyeva, Greta. 2006. Gender i dekonstruktsija territorialnoi politiki (Gender and Deconstruction of Territorial Politics). In *Gender Studies. Central Asian Network.* http://www.genderstudies.info/politol/6.php (August 25, 2006).

Suny, Ronald Grigor. 2001. The Empire Strikes Out: Imperial Russia, "National" Identity, and Theories of Empire. In *A State of Nations. Empire and Nation-Making in the Age of Lenin and Stalin,* eds. Ronald Grigor Suny and Terry Martin, 23–66. Oxford, and New York: Oxford University Press.

Tapia, Ruby C. 2001. What's Love Got to Do with It? Consciousness, Politics and Knowledge Production in Chela Sandoval's *Methodology of the Oppressed. American Quarterly,* Vol. 53, No. 4: 733–743.

Tekuyeva, Madina. 2006. *Muzhchina i Zhenschina v Adygskoi Kulture: Traditsii i Sovremennost* (Man and woman in the Adyghean culture: traditions and modernity). Nalchik: El-Fa.

———. 2006a. Praktiki zhenskoy povsednevnosti (Everyday Women's Practices). In *Text: Humanities Discourse Yesterday and Today. A Collection of Essays,* 105–112. Nalchik: Poligrafservis i T.

Thomas, Greg. 2006. *Proud Flesh* Inter/Views: Sylvia Wynter. *Proudflesh: A New Afrikan Journal of Culture, Politics & Consciousness.* Issue 4. http://www.proudfleshjournal.com/issue4/toc4.htm (May 22, 2010).

Tishkov, Valery. 2004. *Chechnya. Life in a War-Torn Society.* Berkeley: University of California Press.

Tlostanova, Madina. 2000. *Problema Multikulturalizma i literatura SSHA Kontsa Dvadtsatogo Veka* (Multiculturalism and the U.S. Literature of the Late Twentieth Century). Moscow: Naslediye.

———. 2003. *A Janus-Faced Empire.* Moscow: Blok.

———. 2004. *Postsovetskaya Literatura i Estetika Transkulturatsii: Zhit Nikogda, Pisat Niotkuda* (Post-Soviet Literature and the Aesthetics of Transculturation: Living Never, Writing from Nowhere). Moscow: URSS.

———. 2008. Dekolonialny Proyekt (Decolonial Project). *Lichnost. Kultura. Obschestvo.* Issues. 5–6: 170–183.

———. 2009. *Dekolonialnie gendernie epistemologii* (Decolonial Gender Epistemologies). Moscow: OOO IPTS Maska.

Tokhtakhodzhayeva, Marfua. 1996. *Docheri Amazonok: Golosa iz Tsentralnoi Azii* (Amazons's Daughters. Voices from Central Asia). Tashkent: Women's Resource Center.

———. 1999. *Mezhdu Lozungami Kommunizma i Zakonami Islama* (Between the Communist Slogans and the Islamic Laws). Tashkent: Women's Resource Center.

Tokhtakhodzhayeva, Marfua. 2001. *Utomlennye Proshlym. Reislamizatsiya Obschestva i Polozheniye Zhenschin v Uzbekistane* (Weary of the Past: Reislamization of Society and the Condition of Women in Uzbekistan). Tashkent: Women's Resource Center.

Tokhtakhodzhayeva, Marfua, Dono Abdurazzakova, and Almaz Kadyrova. 1995. *Sudbi i Vremya* (Destinies and Time). Tashkent: Women's Resource Center.

Toledano, Ehud. R. 1993. Shemsigul: A Circassian Slave in Mid-Nineteenth Century Cairo. In *Struggle and Survival in the Modern Middle East*, eds. Edmund Burke, III and David N. Yaghoubian, 59–74. Berkeley: University of California Press.

Tyomkina, Anna. 2005. Genderny Poryadok: Postsovetskiye transformatsii (Severny Tadzhikistan) (Gender Order: Post-Soviet Transformations [Northern Tadzhikistan]). In *Gender: Traditsii i Sovremennost*, ed. Sofya Kasimova, 6–91. Dushanbe: Shkola Gendernogo Obrazovanija.

Vigmann, Gunda. 2005. Tadzhikskie Zhenschini i Sotsialnie Izmenenija—vzgljad s Zapadnoi Storoni (Tadzhik Women and Social Change—A View from the West). In *Gender: Traditsii i Sovremennost*, ed. Sofya Kasimova, 162–176. Dushanbe: Shkola Gendernogo Obrazovanija.

Vyshnevsky, Anatoly. 1998. *Serp i Rubl* (Sickle and Ruble). Moscow: OGI.

Walsh, Catherine, Freya Schiwy, and Santyago Castro-Gómez, eds. 2002. *Interdisciplinar las ciencias sociales*. Quito: Universidad Andina/Abya Yala.

Wang, Zheng. 1999. *Women in the Chinese Enlightenment: Oral and Textual Histories*. Berkeley: University of California Press.

Weindling, Paul. 1992. German-Soviet Medical Cooperation and the Institute for Racial Research. *German History*, Vol. 10, No 2: 177–206.

Weiner, Amir. 2002. Nothing but Certainty. *Slavic Review*, Vol. 61, No. 1: 44–53.

Weitz, Eric. 2002. Racial Politics without the Concept of Race: Reevaluating Soviet Ethnic and National Purges. *Slavic Review*, Vol. 61, No. 1: 1–29.

Wiegman, Robyn. 1995. *American Anatomies. Theorizing Race and Gender*. Durham & London: Duke University Press.

Wood, Elizabeth A. 2000. *The Baba and the Comrade. Gender and Politics in Revolutionary Russia*. Bloomington: Indiana University Press.

Wu, Yenna. 2005. Making Sense in Chinese "Feminism"/Women's Studies. In *Dialogue and Difference. Feminisms Challenge Globalization*, eds. Marguerite Waller and Sylvia Marcos, 29–52. New York: Palgrave Macmillan.

Wynter, Sylvia. 2000. Africa, the West and the Analogy of Culture: The Cinematic Text after Man. In *Symbolic Narratives/African Cinema: Audience, Theory and the Moving Image*, ed. June Givanni, 25–76. London: BFI Publishing.

Yan, Haiping. 2006. *Chinese Women Writers and the Feminist Imagination 1905–1948*. New York and London: Routledge.

Zalkind, Aron. 1924. Dvenadtsat polovykh zapovedei revolyutsionnogo pro-letariata (The Twelve Sexual Commandments of the Revolutionary

Proletariat). In *Revolyutsiya i Molodyezh* (Revolution and the Youth), 76–91. Moscow: Izdatelstvo Kommunisticheskogo Universiteta imeni Y.M. Sverdlova.

Zezenkova, Vera. 1953. Materialy po antropologii zhenschin razlichnykh plemyon i narodov Srednei Azii (Materials on the Anthropology of Women of Various Tribes and Ethnicities of Central Asia). In *Voprosy entogeneza narodov Tsentralnoy Azii v svete dannykh antropologii* (Questions of Ethnogenesis of Central Asian Peoples in the Light of Anthropological Data), eds. L. Oshanyn and V. Zezenkova, 57–60. Tashkent: Akademia Nauk Uzbekskoi SSR. Institut istorii i arkheologii.

Zubkovskaya, Olga. 2007. Postkolonialnaya teoriya v analize postsovetskogo feminizma: dilemmy primenenija" (Postcolonial Theory in the Analysis of Post-Soviet Feminism: The Dilemmas of Application). *Ab Imperio*, No. 1: 395–420.